Praise for *Crisis Leadership Now* and Laurence Barton

"Larry Barton addresses topics that are typically swept under the rug in most corporations. His vast knowledge and expertise in the area of crisis management is evidenced throughout this book. Dr. Barton gives concrete advice on the means to avoid, mitigate, and respond to crises that occur somewhere in the world's workforce every day. This should be mandatory reading for every security and human resources professional, as well as company CEOs."

Alicia C. Parker
Senior Director of Security
ESPN

"Larry Barton has done it again with a work that is a must-read for every organizational leader. He has taken his vast experience of working with CEOs, boards, lawyers, human resources, and communicators during critical incidents and shares his roadmap to prevention, response, and recovery. Wherever you are located and whatever your enterprise, this definitive work will help you with specific insights, checklists, and case studies that demystify crisis management."

Bill Turner
Director of Retail Operations
Nike, Inc.

"Leaders, like companies, often live in a state of denial. Many lack a radar screen that alerts them to angry employees, customers, or strangers who may wish to do them harm. By planning for the inevitable "worst-case" scenario, Larry Barton shares hundreds of solutions that he has embedded in many of the world's best-run companies. From psychology to the law, human resources to communications, his interdisciplinary thinking shines in *Crisis Leadership Now.*"

Alan Friedman, Ph.D.
Associate Professor of Psychiatry and Behavioral Sciences
Northwestern University

"*Crisis Leadership Now* is a powerful reminder to corporate leaders that American businesses remain prime targets for terrorist acts. Preparation for the impact of a terrorist event is critical for the welfare of employees and customers, and Larry Barton provides the definitive roadmap to organizational readiness. This is the valuable resource for business executives and law enforcement officials—the ultimate guide to crisis management planning."

Kathleen McChesney
Former Executive Assistant Director
FBI

"Larry Barton provides a powerful wake-up call for many companies, many of which are vulnerable because their leaders repeatedly ignore warning signs and are poorly prepared to manage a variety of threats. He redefined the architecture for protecting our people and brand when disaster strikes, whether training our engineers at the Arctic Circle or helping our executives in board room simulations."

Joseph Liska
Retired Director of Crisis Management
British Petroleum

"Larry Barton is well regarded throughout Asia as one of the world's thought leaders on crisis prevention. He has lived here, worked here, understands our cultures, and holds extraordinary insight on how breaking news can shape your reputation and stock price, let alone the confidence of your customers, on a global scale. This book will transform your company."

Ken Yamazaki
President, Koukusai Security
Shiuzoka, Japan

"*Crisis Leadership Now* is more than simply the title of the book—it is a salutary warning about the potential for crisis that lurks the corridors of organizations. Organizations worldwide are craving for solutions on what to do, how to manage, and, most importantly, how to prevent scandal, product disasters, and the resulting negative impact to flow across borders. In a wired world, Larry Barton outlines how fast bad news can spread and what steps should be taken to mitigate the impact now—when it matters most. The book should be required reading in boardrooms . . . You have been warned!"

Denis Smith
Professor of Management
University of Glasgow

crisis leadership now

Also by Laurence Barton

Crisis in Organizations
Ethics: The Enemy in the Workplace
Crisis in Organizations II

crisis leadership now

A REAL-WORLD GUIDE TO PREPARING FOR THREATS, DISASTER, SABOTAGE, AND SCANDAL

laurence barton

New York   Chicago   San Francisco   Lisbon   London   Madrid   Mexico City
Milan   New Delhi   San Juan   Seoul   Singapore   Sydney   Toronto

1 2 3 4 5 6 7 8 9 0   DOC/DOC   0 9 8 7

ISBN 978-0-07-149882-1
MHID 0-07-149882-6

McGraw-Hill books are available at special quantity discounts to use as premiums and sales promotions, or for use in corporate training programs. For more information, please write to the Director of Special Sales, Professional Publishing, McGraw-Hill, Two Penn Plaza, New York, NY 10121-2298. Or contact your local bookstore.

This book is printed on acid-free paper.

Library of Congress Cataloging-in-Publication Data

Barton, Laurence.
  Crisis leadership now / by Laurence Barton.
      p. cm.
  Includes bibliographical references and index.
  ISBN-13: 978-0-07-149882-1 (hardcover)
  ISBN-10: 0-07-149882-6 (hardcover)
 1. Leadership.   2. Crisis management.   I. Title.
HD57.7.B369 2008
658.4'092—dc22   2007040363

Disclaimer

This book shares observations and facts related to risk, threat assessment, violence, terrorism, accidents, natural disasters, and other critical incidents that can dramatically change the lives of people and institutions. As such, the omission or inclusion of any company or institution does not imply any judgment whatsoever on the people, products, or capabilities of that organization. You should not make any decision regarding the health, safety, and security of your business or people based on information in this book. Rather, you should rely on your own independent assessment and consult with trusted advisors who specialize in your area of interest. The author and publisher accept no liability for any decision or action you may or may not make based on this work.

For Eliza

CONTENTS

ACKNOWLEDGMENTS

It has been a joy to collaborate with a number of gifted colleagues in preparing this work. I have learned much from my clients and contemporaries over the past two decades and appreciate all of them. In preparing this book, several professionals were especially helpful with specific insight and suggestions.

I am appreciative of Dr. Steven Krotzner of the Mayo Clinic; Dr. Denis Smith of the Crisis Management Program at the University of Glasgow; Dr. Ed Goodin, professor emeritus at the University of Nevada, Las Vegas; Jason Zimmermann of the Centers for Disease Control; Rena Langley of Disney Cruise Line; Dr. Alan F. Friedman of Northwestern University; Phil Rothstein of Rothstein Associates; risk consultant Geary Sikich; Bill Turner of Nike; Joseph A. Liska, retired director of crisis management for British Petroleum; Dr. Stephen Sloan of the University of Central Florida; forensic accountant Frederick H. Graessle, CPA; Alicia Parker of ESPN; former FBI executive assistant director Kathleen McChesney, Charles Chamberlin of Management Consulting Services; Bill Warren and Jeff Villella of The Walt Disney Company; Tony Vermillion of Emerson; Dr. Mary Ellen O'Toole, supervisory special agent in the Behavioral Analysis Unit at the Federal Bureau of Investigation; and Ken Yamazaki of Kokusai Security Company of Japan. My executive assistant at The American College, Mary Varner, is an extraordinary resource whom I treasure.

Leah Spiro, senior editor at McGraw-Hill, provided encouragement and meaningful insight from the moment we discussed the concept for *Crisis Leadership Now*. In addition, I am grateful to editorial assistant Morgan Ertel, account representative Colin Kelley, and the entire team at McGraw-Hill for their collaboration in this effort. Many thanks as well to Westchester Book Group.

INTRODUCTION

Frantic parents and siblings were calling from Florida, the Philippines, St. Louis, and Los Angeles. They had heard on CNN about a massacre and had to get word to their loved ones to stay inside, to bolt the door. Don't go outside: There's a perpetrator with a gun somewhere on *your* campus.

When emergency responders raced to Virginia Tech University's campus on April 16, 2007, in the wake of the worst mass murder in American history, they hadn't expected this.

They were trained in triage and had practiced responding to the needs of seriously wounded people on highways and in backyards many times. In this case, radio dispatchers had warned the first responders to expect injuries and possibly several fatalities.

But they didn't expect *this*.

As the wounded were separated from the deceased and the coroner began making decisions about how 32 bodies could be moved after being photographed, the victims' cell phones started ringing. Not one . . . or two . . . but dozens. Ringing . . . unanswered . . . ringing again.

Now, first responders are a pretty hardened group. Whether they are police, firefighters, or EMTs, these professionals are accustomed to curbing their emotions in the face of an injured victim who has been struck and seriously injured by a car or motorcycle. But this—to see the enormity of the loss of life in classrooms and hallways and to hear all of these phones that would never be answered again—in the midst of agony, of lives that couldn't be saved—many responders broke down emotionally because no one wanted to tell the victims' loved ones the grim news.

While we often think that first responders only work in contexts similar to that of the Virginia Tech shootings, first responders exist in companies as well. You may not be as familiar with them, but I assure you that they reside within just about every major company you can think of. At Procter & Gamble (P&G), America's largest maker of consumer goods, they're embedded in the company's public relations department. P&G generates about $68 billion in sales a year by selling everything from Crest toothpaste to pet food. As such, they have to worry about product recalls, extortion, embezzlement, kidnapping of executives, and the impact of a disabling fire at one of their major suppliers. At the financial services firm Morgan Stanley, first responders are concentrated in the company's corporate communications department. First responders in your company may be located in the legal, human resources, or public relations departments, but regardless of their specific job titles, they must be capable of grasping the enormity of a critical event as it unfolds. Before first responders arrive to assess a crisis, your internal leaders need to be prepared for—and trained in—the science of crisis response.

Crisis managers understand that what at first appears to be a minor problem could rapidly escalate into being a genuine crisis. At Intel, one of the world's semiconductor giants, those responsible for identifying potential crises can be found in the public affairs division, where they are called "issues managers." One of Intel's worst fears is that the sophisticated chips it manufactures—there are a couple of hundred of them in the dashboard of your automobile—could fail, leading to system malfunction and potential injury. A massive product recall by Intel could blossom into a crisis that requires costly notifications to customers, regulators, and many others. And that's just what happened at Intel's competitor, Sony Semiconductor, in October 2006, when six million of the company's semiconductors were recalled after some batteries containing Sony chips exploded in a number of name-brand laptop computers, including those distributed by Dell. Liability is not pretty; in fact, it's downright ugly.

Companies worldwide have found themselves awash in unexpected catastrophe. In Europe, you'll find that companies who understand just how ugly corporate liability can be often place crisis managers and first responders in their office of environmental and occupational health. But even taking many precautionary steps does not necessarily mean that a company will not be visited by catastrophe. At British Petroleum (BP), for instance, company leaders are worried about a refinery fire or explosion—and there are sufficient grounds for that concern. In 2005 in Texas City, Texas, 15 people died and some 170 were injured following a horrific explosion that was later attributed to a massive vapor cloud ignited by a spark from an idling truck. BP has an enviable record of safety worldwide, but even the best crisis prevention cannot always prevent human error, nor can it head off an industrial accident before it wreaks havoc.

Regardless of who owns your crisis radar screen, it's pretty clear that someone needs to.

According to a major survey by PricewaterhouseCoopers in 2007, 49 percent of all U.S.-based multinationals have experienced a high-level crisis in the last three years—some event that had a catastrophic impact on one or more of their business units. About 53 percent of these companies said they had experienced a true crisis due to a natural disaster, while 31 percent experienced a complete shutdown of a major business unit. Some 20 percent reported a crisis related to a U.S. Securities and Exchange Commission or Sarbanes-Oxley compliance investigation, and 20 percent reported significant problems due to management upheaval. That should make you worry whether you're a director, shareholder, or employee.

A crisis, as you will see, *is any event that can seriously harm the people, reputation, or financial condition of an organization.* In this book, I'll take you through my journey of many years of advising corporations and governments about crisis events. We'll look at how they are defined, how early warning signs can help you better recognize a potential crisis, how some threatening situations can be mitigated, and, when "it" hits the fan, how to manage events as skillfully as possible.

What's the Worst That Could Happen?

You may be surprised.

You and I wear seatbelts not just because the law requires us to, but because we're rational enough to know they save lives. Companies, unfortunately, don't wear seatbelts. They just cruise on the highway they know. Sure, they are familiar with the road—their customers, suppliers, and employees. But companies can get broadsided, just like a passenger in a sedan. I want you to be in a Volvo.

Some company leaders act like they're on perpetual cruise control. Instead, I suggest they think about an ex-employee returning with a gun with the intention of committing an act of vengeance. But most companies forget the seatbelt analogy and hope the disgruntled ex-worker will go away, unaffected by his dismissal. They know they should think about an earthquake that could cause a roof to collapse and cause considerable damage, but it's just easier to buy insurance and deal with the ramifications of such a freak occurrence later. They know they should think about one of their top executives being arrested for a DUI, or what would happen if their vice president of sales were arrested in a pedophile sting operation, but those things happen to *other* companies. In this book, we'll tell real stories and name real names to demonstrate that these things happen to real companies—and to real people—every single day. We can learn from organizations that have confronted crises.

Regardless of where you work—whether it is a small company, large enterprise, government agency, or nonprofit—I'd really like you to think about those events that could cause significant disruption to your enterprise. When I'm offering a seminar, I'll often ask the audience to fill in the blanks to this simple question: "What are the five worst things that could happen to your organization?" They face these five blank lines . . . and have two minutes to identify worst-case scenarios. So go ahead . . . try it:

_____

_____

_____

_____

_____

My audiences are often composed of senior executives, so their lists usually fill up fairly quickly; virtually any leader who has several years of experience will have experienced one or more workplace threats or tragedies. Inevitably, I have found that the crises that fill many executives' notepads are some of the major issues that can— and will—emerge in most companies. You'll find that their answers are often the same, regardless of the industry group or company to which I have been invited:

- Workplace violence
- Product recall
- Violent weather/damage to facility
- Ethics violation and prosecution
- Fire or flood
- Pandemic/E. coli contamination
- Terrorism
- Industrial accident
- Chemical spill on-site or nearby

What's interesting about this exercise is that managers tend to gravitate toward citing major, headline-busting topics. Based on statistics, however, there are few major industrial fires anymore because of the prevalence of sophisticated sprinkler and warning systems. Similarly, catastrophic industrial accidents are increasingly rare because safety training and site visits by regulators are now widely embedded in the manufacturing process. We tend to think about prominent incidents we remember from news events rather than considering the *specific* typologies of risk that are inherent to *our* company and *our* marketplace. After you read this book, I'll ask that you step back and complete this list again. I have high confidence that the topics you list *will* be different.

For instance, here's a sampling of how executives responded at two of my recent seminars. See if you can figure out what industries they represent and where each is physically located:

Company A
Prostitution ring arrested on-site
Food poisoning impacts hundreds of guests
Accident on stage during performance

Robbery

Rape

Company B
Counterfeit product uncovered
Geopolitical unrest leads to potential revolution in key market
Current devaluation causes massive financial loss
Extended loss of electricity
Alleged ethics violation

Company A is a major casino located in the U.S. Midwest. Just because it isn't located in Las Vegas or Macau doesn't mean it isn't subject to the same types of exposures as those generally associated with the Las Vegas Strip; in fact, all five situations *have* happened to *them*. That's why this particular casino's security team is well trained and why it takes risk management seriously. It has learned to embrace crisis prevention as an *enterprise strength* after having faced several close calls.

Company B is a multinational electronics manufacturer located in China. Its leaders have been lucky. Although they have been forced to close facilities and send employees home in several plant locations due to massive power outages that lasted three to five days, they learned from those events that a crisis can cause considerable disarray for customers (and employees, who are left without work—and, more importantly, pay—during that period), as well as trigger questions from the financial analysts that continually evaluate their stock.

Throughout this book, you'll read stories of companies that *anticipated* some of the crises they faced. Typically, when a company makes a meaningful investment of time and energy in crisis prevention, that decision will pay rich dividends when disaster strikes. Their spokespeople in risk management will generally be more eloquent and reassuring in front of television cameras. Their employees will feel that they are a genuine part of the company's solutions. Their customers will be informed promptly as to when shipments will be resumed. Their stockholders won't panic and sell their shares. In essence, prevention *pays*.

Those companies that live in denial will devise some clever excuses as to why they don't need a crisis plan or why they can't find the time to stage a half-day simulation that will prepare their employees for a flood or an act of terrorism. They'll find some creative reason why they wouldn't dare interrupt their annual strategy meeting at a golf resort to discuss contingency planning. Their CEO will say, "I'm sure our security folks have their hands around that." When I hear these executives tell me how confident they are about the caliber of their crack security team, I bounce back with: "Have you looked at your security guards lately?"

For some, of course, it's too late: Litigation is underway, their market share has eroded, and the news media has maligned their brand.

So, let's dig deeper. Think for a minute about this. You are the spokesperson for US Airways, you get a phone call, and the person on the other end of the phone line begins the conversation in the following way:

> Ah . . . we thought we should call you right away. I wanted you to know that our CEO, Doug Parker, was arrested last night in Phoenix for a DUI. His blood alchohol level was 0.096. We're getting pounded by media calls; you may recall that he had two prior DUIs, including one when he worked for American Airlines in the 1990s.

Or, let's say you work for World Wrestling Entertainment:

> This is hard, but one of our top wrestling stars, Chris Benoit, was found dead this morning . . . a murder-suicide at his home in Fayetteville, Georgia. It looks like he murdered his wife and smothered his special-needs son with a pillow; investigators suspect he may have been seriously impaired by steroids.

Now let's go to Natural Selection Foods, a division of Earthbound Farm:

> Jane, we're getting calls, about one an hour, that our spinach may be the cause of some serious cases of E. coli. Yesterday it

was reported in three states, but now we are getting calls from nine states!

Or, let's shift to Coca-Cola:

We just learned from the Federal Aviation Administration that a private plane crashed, and four of our executives were on board. They're all dead.

Each case is real. Each involves fine companies and good people. But when tragedy strikes, management is tested on its ability to understand the enormity of the crisis at hand, to differentiate rumor from fact, and to respond to victims and other stakeholders sincerely and quickly. And, as you'll see, some managers shine in a crisis, while others stumble. The difference between the two is often defined by preparedness, candor, rehearsal, and anticipation of the needs of stakeholders. While good luck may help, having a crisis plan is likely to increase both the quality of your responsiveness and your stakeholders' perception of you.

> While good luck may help, having a crisis plan is likely to increase both the quality of your responsiveness and your stakeholders' perception of you.

Most managers are savvy enough to realize that horrible things happen to good companies, and that even the most stellar business leaders in the world can stumble in a crisis. We can learn from them. In fact, we're crazy not to.

As you read the following chapters, you'll meet a cast of characters that practices just about every style of management. You'll meet highly intuitive leaders who have helped their companies navigate some seriously disruptive events. The people of Marsh, a major insurance broker, responded to the tragedies of September 11, 2001, with an almost unparalleled degree of abiding care for employees and their families. One of Marsh's senior vice presidents, Al Hyman, personally called over a hundred families the evening of the World Trade Center attacks in an emotionally tormenting attempt to reach out and determine which Marsh employees had survived and which needed help. But when Marsh faced a different crisis involving ethics and compliance problems two years later, the same company stumbled horribly. Some of their leaders engaged in what was seemingly a case of common sense malpractice.

Consider the wide spectrum of threats that can impact you. When Hurricane Katrina virtually destroyed New Orleans and much of the U.S. Gulf Coast in 2005, Wal-Mart not only promptly redirected hundreds of its trucks in order to continue moving vital products to its customers; it also deployed a SWAT team to distribute paychecks to employees who were living in the impacted region. Yet when Wal-Mart was faced with a volatile unionization attempt in Jonquiere, Canada, in 2005, it responded not with compassion and negotiation, but by promptly closing the door of that store forever out of defiance. In doing so, many Canadians pledged never to shop at Wal-Mart again. How can there be such a bipolar approach to decision making in one company? Answer: A company's reaction to catastrophe depends on what *kind* of catastrophe the company is facing.

Some crises occur without warning. The impact of these incidents—industrial accidents, airline crashes, or random acts of violence, for instance—will cause disruption and enormous pain. They are usually unpredictable, unless, of course, we later learn that there were warning signals on the organizational radar screen.

Other crises emerge slowly, over time. In these cases, the radar screen is on, but organizational leaders either ignore the signals of dysfunction or are in denial that a genuine crisis is emerging. A case in point: The Catholic Church had decades—not months—to see a radar screen filled with documented cases of pedophilic priests who were molesting young children. Instead of confronting the issue and addressing the problem candidly, some bishops and cardinals engaged in a web of conspiracy in an attempt to hide an already very public truth; in the end, the very important social and educational work done by many parishes was undermined by leaders who should have gone to jail for their corrupt behavior. Many wonderful parishes had to sell their assets to pay for the malfeasance of these "leaders."

Not into church politics? Ok, let's shift to something else—fast food.

When at least 39 people became seriously ill at Taco Bell restaurants in December 2006, it took days for the restaurant chain to get its hands around a brewing crisis as salmonella spread throughout its restaurants in New Jersey, New York, Pennsylvania, and Delaware. The company responded, but the public felt it did so too slowly. More about that later in Chapter 11.

Who owns *your* radar screen? As you read about these and hundreds of other cases that are analyzed in this book, keep in mind that most crises are defined by four basic questions. These are the ones that haunt executives after a crisis has rocked their organization:

1. What did you know?
2. When did you know it?
3. What did you do about it?

The fourth question is particularly important:

4. What are you going to do to ensure that it never happens again?

What Could Happen?

There are well over 30 books in the marketplace written by various "experts" in crisis management. All are well intentioned, but the vast majority was written by academics who have never managed an organization, let alone a crisis. Some were hastily written by former law enforcement officers who tried to cash in on the hysteria that followed the attacks of September 11, 2001. Many are filled with hypothetical models of who should grab the bullhorn and sound the alarm. So, having said that, I've tried to avoid theory and paradigms as much as possible in the following chapters. If you want theoretical models, read a textbook. If you want solutions, you've come to the right place.

I have personally managed crises that range from workplace murders to embezzlement, from the terminations of CEOs (my favorite was a CEO who routinely slept with prostitutes and whose board chairperson acted only when he became concerned that these indiscretions were about to go public) to nasty industrial accidents. I've either managed or helped to manage well over a thousand cases as a consultant to some of the world's greatest companies. Over the years, I've written crisis management plans, designed war rooms, and staged over 300 corporate simulations. I've had the opportunity to serve as a 24/7 consultant during some turbulent events, numerous close calls, and several monumental news-making events. I've learned so much, and I'll try to transfer much of that knowledge to you in the pages that follow.

Let's look at just a few of the crises that have impacted entire communities of employees, shareholders, neighbors, and the media:

- An earthquake measuring 9.2 on the Richter scale causes much of Anchorage, Alaska to collapse, and 131 die (1964)
- The atrium collapses at the new Hyatt Regency Hotel in Kansas City, Missouri, resulting in 114 dead and more than 200 injured (1981)
- Employee sabotage at Union Carbide triggers poisoning by a leak of methyl isocyanate, killing over 3,000 (1984)
- Bacteria in Jalisco cheese kills 62 in California (1985)
- Thirty-eight die and hundreds are injured after being stampeded by fellow fans at Brussels' Heysel Stadium during a soccer match (1985)
- Massive leak occurs inside a Chernobyl nuclear plant; an estimated 100,000 die during the following two years from immediate and lingering illnesses (1986)
- NASA astronauts die in-flight due to engineering/systems defects (1986 and 2003)
- Widespread damages devastate wildlife and fishing reserves in Prince William Sound, Alaska, after *Exxon Valdez* runs aground (1989)
- As part of a sadistic geopolitical plot, the Aum Shinrikyo domestic terror group releases sarin nerve gas on Tokyo subways, killing 12 and injuring hundreds of others (1995)
- Some 499 are killed when the Sampoong superstore in Seoul collapses after employees warn managers that the building is structurally deficient (1995)

- An earthquake in northwest Turkey claims 17,118 victims (1999)
- Coca-Cola recalls 11 million cases of soda after an alleged product contamination in Belgium (1999)
- A 20,000-ton Kursk submarine explodes in the Barents Sea, killing 118 Russian sailors (2000)
- Unprecedented terrorist attacks by al-Qaeda members on the World Trade Center and the Pentagon, using civilian aircrafts, cause the deaths of 2,997 in New York, Pennsylvania, and Washington, D.C. (2001)
- al-Qaeda members trigger a bomb in an Indonesian nightclub; 202 victims (2002)
- Motorcycle gangs clash at an annual festival in Laughlin, Nevada; the fight spills onto Harrah's Casino floor, killing three (2002)
- Canadian health officials close national borders after an outbreak of SARS (severe acute respiratory syndrome) (2002, 2003)
- Fourteen employees are shot and six killed at the Lockheed Martin Aeronautics subassembly plant in Meridian, Mississippi, by a disgruntled worker with a known history of racial slurs and provocative comments to coworkers (2003)
- One hundred die in a West Warwick, Rhode Island, nightclub after a rock band illegally uses pyrotechnics on stage, resulting in the ignition of a fireball (2003)
- Putnam Investments pays a $40 million fine after acknowledging management complicity in an after-hours trading scandal (2003)
- Famed magician Roy Horn almost bleeds to death onstage after being mauled by a tiger during a Las Vegas Mirage Hotel performance (2003)
- An astounding 14,802 victims die in France due to a massive heat wave; most were elderly or unable to reach air conditioned shelters; president Jacques Chirac is widely criticized for doing too little, too late (2003)
- Maine State Police report that Gustaf Adolf Lutheran Church parishioner Daniel Bondeson committed suicide after allegedly

poisoning coffee served at the church social hour in New Sweden, Maine; 1 dies, 14 are hospitalized (2003)

- Eleven are killed, 34 are injured after a famed Staten Island ferry slams into a pier; captain Richard Smith returns home and attempts suicide; he later pleads guilty to seaman's manslaughter and is sentenced to 18 months in jail; New York City later agrees to initial settlements of $27.6 million for failing to monitor the speed of incoming ferries (2003)
- Massive tsunami strikes Indonesia, Sri Lanka, India, and Thailand; estimated 225,000 deaths and 229,000 missing (2004)
- Hours before a major sales meeting, McDonald's chairman and CEO Jim Cantalupo unexpectedly dies of a heart attack in an Orlando, Florida, hotel at age 60. The company races to announce his successor within hours to demonstrate its managerial stability (2004)
- An Atlanta judge, court reporter, and police officer are killed in the courtroom the day after the judge warns the bailiff that the suspect could be violent (2005)
- al-Qaeda members detonate three bombs on the London subway system, killing 52 and injuring 700 (2005)
- Aruba tourism market collapses after the investigation into missing teenager Natalee Holloway is botched (2005)
- Wendy's sales plummet after false allegations are made that a human finger was found in the chain's chili; the perpetrator is later convicted (2005)
- Newlywed George Allen Smith IV mysteriously disappears on the Royal Caribbean cruise ship *Brilliance of the Sea;* the cruise line settles with Smith's wife months later; his family criticizes the cruise line and declares a conspiracy during CNN interviews (2005)
- Thirteen trapped West Virginia coal miners are reported safe by a mining representative, then 12 are found dead (2006)
- Mentally ill gunman assaults an Amish schoolhouse in Nickel Mines, Pennsylvania, torturing and killing five girls (2006)
- Denice Denton, chancellor of the University of California, Santa Cruz, leaps to her death (2006)

- A psychotic and depressed former postal worker returns to a Goleta, California, mail processing center years after being terminated; she kills six former colleagues (2006)
- Klaus Kleinfeld, CEO of Siemens Worldwide, resigns amid massive scandal involving an alleged bribe to government officials (2007)
- T.J. Maxx is widely criticized for its painfully slow reaction to the massive theft of the consumer credit card data of 45.7 million of its customers in New England (2007)
- Hilton Hotel at the Washington, D.C. Dulles Airport is closed after a major outbreak of the Norwalk virus (2007)
- Mattel recalls over 22 million toys manufactured in China due to the presence of potentially lethal levels of lead and other toxins in the products (2007)
- Four student athletes from Bluffton University die in a horrific bus crash on I-75 in Atlanta, Georgia; 29 injured in all (2007)
- The cruise ship *Sea Diamond,* which was carrying 1,547 passengers and crew members, sinks off the coast of Greece due to alleged error by the ship's captain (2007)
- Mayor Iccho Ito of Nagasaki, Japan, is murdered by yakuza gang members after he attempts to rid the city of their influence (2007)
- Five people are murdered at Trolley Square Mall in Salt Lake City, Utah, after a gunman who had cased the mall earlier that afternoon returns wearing a trench coat covering his rifle (2007)
- After 67 years in business as a leading provider of beef patties, Topps Meat of Elizabeth, New Jersey, permanently closes its doors six days after a massive recall of 21.7 million hamburgers that are feared to be tainted with E. coli bacteria (2007)

We rarely take the time to learn about what worked to mitigate or contain these incidents from expanding.

As you can see, these are representative crises. No doubt you have already thought about many others as you reviewed this list. In each of these disasters, lessons were learned about what *not* to do in a similar situation, yet we rarely take the time to learn about what worked to mitigate or contain these incidents from expanding. We seldom look back and conduct a diagnostic review of where otherwise talented managers simply failed. I want to prevent similar incidents from happening to *you*.

By now you have some sense that in order for an organization to manage a crisis, it must be able to recognize and interpret the various signals that appear on its radar screen. Organizations must share and collaborate with their stakeholders in a timely manner. They must quickly and honestly communicate vital information. And they must be candid about the four basic questions we addressed previously.

Let's go back to where we began—Virginia Tech. By the end of this book, you'll have a deeper, keener insight into what happened there. It was, in the end, a case about a highly troubled young man who cowardly murdered innocent people, seemingly without warning or provocation. But some people working in leadership positions at Virginia Tech knew about the perpetrator well before he pulled a trigger. The organization had a crisis management plan, but it lacked a radar screen (*What did you know?*), an air traffic controller (*When did you know it?*), and a pilot (*What are you doing about it?*).

Let's learn together.

1

SECURE THY WORKPLACE!

Corporate security is a bizarre field. I've found that there are several diamond security leaders out there who truly "get" how to protect the various human and physical assets of their companies. But for the most part, security leaders are underpaid, undervalued, and under-resourced.

Not to be harsh, but you can often judge how much a company values corporate security by looking at where it places the physical offices of its security managers. Sometimes you'll find them in the basement, right next to the soft drink machine that's been inoperative for a few years. Yes, they'll have a bullhorn handy, maybe even a few two-way radios that link them to the front gate, but don't expect much. Their budgets are puny. In these types of companies, the primary function of the security director typically is to ensure that the CEO gets to and from the airport in the company Escalade on time.

I'll tell you about exceptions to this reality in a minute, but I assure you that the summary I just provided is very close to the norm in many of the major corporations around the world. Yes, the security director may be involved in a blood collection drive to support the Red Cross, and yes, the security managers may coordinate annual fire drills and ensure that company identification cards are retrieved from exiting employees, but those are the fun aspects of the job. For the most part, you're likely to find that your well-being at work is the responsibility of some ex-cop who butted heads one too many times with the local chief of police, or an ex-Marine who convinced some vice president that he was "cutting edge." You get the point. While most of these security directors assumed their posts with good intentions and open minds, the manner in which they are treated is often so demoralizing that they essentially (and sometimes physically) fall asleep on the job.

Let me now take you to Tokyo, or Hong Kong, or Toronto. Most foreign-based companies are much better than their American counterparts at appreciating the strategic value—versus the need—for security at work. In non-U.S. companies, the head of security will often be a member of senior management, a director, or a vice president. Security directors at these companies are routinely asked their opinion on the areas in which the company may be vulnerable to safety breaches. They lead the company in thought-provoking simulations that prepare the organization for a wide spectrum of crises. These security strategists push their operational colleagues to ponder the ramifications of many types of disasters.

Now, as I said, there are exceptions—Disney (entertainment), Emerson (technology), and Coca-Cola (beverages) are all uniquely committed to corporate security in all its dimensions, including the physical detection of threats to the company's intellectual property. These and other smart companies give credence to their security leaders and listen to them when it comes to crisis planning. They get it: *The best crisis is the one that has been prevented.* That's why a smart security director understands that his or her company must be counterintuitive. The intelligent security manager will often push for higher standards in the hiring process to screen out potential problem employees, and he or she will usually succeed in securing budget approval for new surveillance and monitoring equipment.

> The best crisis is the one that has been prevented.

When a law firm that's planning to sue an employer calls me, almost regardless of the basis of the suit, I'll initially dig for information on the security team. Why? My experience is that diagnostic review of a company's security processes can be a goldmine of information on how seriously the organization cares about its vulnerabilities. Just test my system: If you call the director of security at most companies and you are told that he or she's at the golf course, or, better yet, at his or her third conference of the month, you've got a ringer! (These people are notorious for attending meetings of organizations that typically convene in convention cities, such as San Diego or Las Vegas. I'm still waiting for them to convene in Buffalo.)

But back to how to benchmark your security team and what to look for when it comes to a serious investment in protecting people and facilities. Here are 10 questions that I ask almost every time I audit a firm from a security point of view, and why I ask them:

1. **What's the average number of hours that your security guards are trained by you or your company before they put on their badges?**
A few years ago, I was asked to help a litigation team that was suing a hotel in Hawaii after a guest suffered a loss of brain capacity as the result of a tragic incident at the resort. After poring over hundreds of pages of documents, I explained to the lead attorney that the biggest potential exposure to threat that the resort faced wasn't its lack of a working public address system that would have enabled employees to ask if there was a physician on the beach. It was this: I told the attorney to send me the records of how many hours of bona fide training in CPR and first-aid medical protocol their guards had actually received. I wanted to know who offered that training, where the records on medical training were kept, and if these guards were receiving any continuing education.

   A few weeks later, the attorney called me. He was floored (but I wasn't) by what the records from the opposing counsel showed: The hotel had trained the guards for an average of about four hours before these "deputies" assumed their posts, and medical issues were barely addressed in that training program. It's an alarmingly real problem, and it's not exclusive to the hospitality industry. As in the case we just discussed, it is not enough to simply hand these men and women a badge and two-way radio; we need to properly train them in what to look for, what to do, and how to do it when crisis strikes.

2. **What's your annual turnover in security personnel?**
I'm well aware of what you're going to say about this: "Hey, we pay these people so little. Do you really expect us to retain

them beyond six months?" Here's my reply: Well, what's the cost, both financially and in terms of lost time and productivity, of a revolving door of security personnel? Do you actually have a career track for guards that encourages them to take courses at a community college; to broaden their knowledge of law enforcement; and possibly even to transition over time into IT security or other areas? Such an initiative can enhance the retention of skilled people in sensitive safety positions.

3. **How many of the leaders in your security organization have a bachelor's degree from an accredited college? What about a master's degree?**

   This sounds pretty snooty, but again, I'm sharing what I've observed in my almost 30 years of working with great (and sometimes not-so-great) companies around the world. The diamond leaders in security have a college degree, at a minimum. What's more, they attend a few high-end strategic seminars at leading universities annually. They take the time to achieve credentials in strategy, leadership, and organizational behavior. An increasing number of them achieve an MBA.

   If you find that your security director graduated from high school and has been in the same role for at least 10 years, I suggest that you ask yourself this question and then call a search firm (I don't want your blood pressure to be too high when you call the headhunter): If a former employee returned with a revolver and killed four people, could you defend your security "leader" and his or her credentials on the witness stand? You may now call the headhunter. While you're at it, have a Jack Daniels.

4. **Has your director of security ever worked at another company in your industry?**

   I love it when the vice president of a company answers this with some rehearsed response, like: "What? No way! We groom our people from the inside! Why, Jim was an intern here after high school, and he's our poster child of what can happen when you find great talent!"

Are you nuts? Find a security leader who has worked at a company you admire (preferably your competition) and encourage that person to stretch his or her mind and career by coming to work for you. Encourage that person to benchmark others in your industry. Empower the individual to allow security to become a center of excellence at your organization, not just an afterthought.

5. **Has your company ever conducted an audit of your top talent to determine if they leave confidential memos and reports out that others can read or copy after hours?**
   When I was the vice president of crisis management at Motorola, my team and I would literally walk the floors of corporate headquarters late on a random night, gain access to everyone's office—even that of the CEO—and look on their desks for any information that might be of strategic value to our competitors. We knew that some unethical companies were notorious for hiring rogue contractors or employees and placing them inside Motorola to steal valuable information on sales leads, production numbers, pending patents, or cash flow. We even tried to access the computers of these executives using common-guess passwords. If we found someone in violation of our safety guidelines, that executive would come in the next morning to find a letter from Motorola's senior vice president of human resources that stated that he or she had violated the "Protect Our Proprietary Information," or POPI, rule. Most managers were given one free pass for their first violation, but if they were found again in violation of POPI, they were fired, regardless of rank. Motorola's director of security led the project like a titan in the hundreds of plants and offices where the company occupies space worldwide. In my time at Motorola, we said adios to about 20 people a year worldwide who didn't "get" it until it was too late.

6. **What is the relationship between your director of security and your leadership in IT? Do they even know each other?**
   Common response: "Oh, they get along great!" Dig deep, and you'll uncover a far more realistic answer. They might get

along just fine on the ball field at the company picnic, but we're talking about whether they perceive their counterpart to be a strategic partner or a nuisance. Do they meet once a month to discuss organizational safety objectives? Does the director of security understand the nuances of encryption and data mining utilized by competitors? Do these two leaders regularly brief organizational leadership on what your company can do to protect the enterprise from hackers or a discontented employee? If there are any two departments that should share a common agenda, it's IT and security. Make it happen.

7. **How many times in the last year has the security director spent a day at each major site in the company—either at your various sales offices or key facilities?**
I'm blown away at the zealot-like fervor of some security leaders. They are the ones I admire and publicly praise because they secure the budget needed to meet with teams throughout their companies. They routinely brief leaders on threats, issues, and opportunities to improve. They help organize simulations or tabletop exercises to illustrate how local teams may better respond to a natural disaster. They don't cry wolf—they are true thought-leaders who persuade their organizations to simply be *better*.

   Conversely, you should ask to see the schedule of your director of security for the past six months—and give him or her no notice when you make this request. If you find that your security director spent 90 percent of his or her time at the office (or worst yet, his or her schedule was "lost" or "stolen"), you need to call that headhunter I mentioned earlier.

8. **Has the security director ever invited the regional office of the FBI, Postal Service, or others to provide an annual briefing on potential corporate threats?**
The best leaders in corporate security typically develop a strong working relationship with the leadership of their local or regional law enforcement organizations. They meet with

them from time to time to discuss issues of mutual interest, and they will periodically invite them to speak to corporate leadership about trends relative to threat management. I can assure you that if the day you meet the FBI is the day of a shooting at your property, it will be too late to engage them in an informal chat.

9. **Does human resources routinely call upon security when a problem employee is about to be exited?**

While it's true that human resources and security cooperate in the same sandbox at many companies, this is not a universal standard. In some companies, the two departments openly detest each other. Human resources often considers security to be second-rate, and security thinks the people in human resources have no idea how to recruit promising talent. If they did, turnover wouldn't be so high!

Regardless of who is right, here's the truth: The very best companies understand that both human resources and security are two core competencies of smart, learning organizations. Security can enhance

> The very best companies understand that both human resources and security are two core competencies of smart, learning organizations.

human resources' performance and drive higher standards for comprehensive preemployment background screening. It can help the woman who reports to human resources that her ex-boyfriend is stalking her. It can offer workshops on proper self-protection techniques in cities with high crime rates to employees who routinely travel. Similarly, human resources can work with security leaders to increase its understanding of how assessment instruments, such as Fitness for Duty (FFD) evaluations, can periodically assist in identifying high-risk employees. I can assure you that if your security and human resources teams are not working as strategic partners, your company's worst day won't just be rough—it will be a nightmare.

10. **Is there any book on the security director's shelf that's been published in the last five years?**
    It sounds simple, but trust me on this. When I visit a director of security, I do two things: First, I count the number of coffee mugs that he or she has collected ("This one is from our vendor who installed our new fence—is that awesome or what?"), and second, I look at which books, if any, are on his or her shelf. Smart security leaders are reading current books and technical literature that's pertinent to their industry. They are reading thought-provoking books on threats to corporations, or terrorism, or how the avian flu would be managed from a security perspective, or related issues. The bottom line is that they're out there, searching, exploring, and trying to adapt to the new dynamics of the workplace.

If you're getting nervous reading this chapter because you suspect there's a deficit of talent in your security organization, take comfort in this: My informal guess is that about 70 percent of security leaders that are responsible for "protecting" their organizations are completely in over their heads, uninformed, and/or poorly resourced. About 20 percent of them are superstars who would ace my informal test and whom I'd recommend to their competitors in a heartbeat; they are smart, driven, and strategic. The other 10 percent should be fired tomorrow. They don't even know why the questions that I have been posing are even asked—or that books like this exist.

I'm serious!

Your Privacy at Work

Civil libertarians despise the effort, but surveillance of human behavior, both at work and on the streets, via videos and computers is one of the most effective ways to prevent disruptive events in the workplace, whether the disruption is a computer worm or a series of concurrent bombings in a major city. Britain monitors more than four million closed-circuit security cameras, with locations ranging from London streets and central rail stations, to rural shopping centers and at the port of Dover. The Associated Press reports that the average British citizen is now captured on video about 300 times a day; New York City, Paris, Miami, and São Paulo all are racing to fund comparable projects.

The purpose of surveillance is clearly to reduce the possibility of a crisis, and when it is conducted in a legal manner, there is strong anecdotal evidence to suggest that it is a deterrent to premeditated acts of violence. But smart security at work does not consist solely of cameras. Iris-scanning devices are now being implemented at a number of tech companies in Silicon Valley, and numerous other public venues have smartly invested in employee thumbprint access devices to help ensure public safety. The United States and Canada are developing national identification cards in the hopes that they will eventually replace driver's licenses as the one-source, use-everywhere form of identification.

Screening Your Talent

I always find it interesting that company leaders talk a good game about recruiting and screening for new talent but then rely heavily on a single interview as the foundation for their hiring decisions. While interviews are important, it is not difficult for people to mask a variety of issues and behaviors during these one- to two-hour conversations. Thus, smart hiring is preventative crisis management. What matters is that you screen out potential problems *before* they end up on your payroll.

A secure workplace is achieved when a company considers the hiring process to be the professional equivalent of dating. To achieve a proper level of comfort, you ask scores of questions and benefit from multiple opportunities to become more acquainted with the person you're courting. You verify, both formally and informally, that the person is who he or she represents him- or herself to be. In all likelihood, you wouldn't marry someone you didn't know well, so why would you make a different kind of proposition—one that could last 20 or 30 years—to someone without doing the same kind of background check?

A case in point: Marilee Jones, dean of admissions at The Massachusetts Institute of Technology (MIT), was a unique voice among college admissions administrators. While most colleges demand that applicants demonstrate achievement in many personal and academic arenas, Jones presented a contrary view: Worry less about credentials and look at life as a mosaic. Well, she was some contrarian. It turned out that she had falsified her credentials to get a job at MIT, and over the course of her career, Jones claimed to have earned degrees from three schools. When she resigned amid scandal in 2007, MIT officials revealed that they had no evidence to suggest that Jones ever graduated from any college at all. Wasn't this the person responsible for validating the qualifications of all your applicants? Wasn't she supposed to be the vanguard of your institutional quality?

Jones reportedly had declined multiple opportunities to correct claims about her credentials over the years. Ironically, she was quoted as having said that colleges should "lower the flame" of their admissions policies. But wait: MIT has booted out accepted students who were later found to have lied on *their* applications. Given their strict standard, how could MIT retain a leader who had falsified her credentials? A week after her dismissal, a letter to the editor in *Time* magazine summed up the feelings of many:

> We live in a time when people and animals die from poisons substituted for food and medicine, when buildings collapse because of shoddy construction, and when American soldiers are being killed in a conflict initiated because of faulty intelligence. It is more important than ever that we restore honesty and honor to all facets of our lives. I do not want to see what happens to a world in which the graduates of MIT or any other college can build a career on fabrications.
>
> —Barbara Davis of Syracuse, New York

Bravo!

Warning Signs Include Grievances

Although most employees will depart the workplace without incident after their company-mandated separation, this is not always the case.

Prior to firing an employee, you should be especially careful to read and review any claims that he or she has made that suggest a deep and long-standing grudge or grievance against the company. In many cases, the e-mails, com-

> E-mails, comments, or behavior of a person will all serve as very important indicators of his or her intentions.

ments, or behavior of a person will all serve as very important indicators of his or her intentions. When an employee airs a grievance against the company, he or she might simply be blowing off steam, but because we do not know that person's mental state or level of anger, only trained specialists and your threat assessment team may be able to avert disaster.

In 1998, a tragic situation turned into a classic case of "who processed the warning signals?" when a disgruntled accountant for the Connecticut state lottery, who had recently returned from medical leave, came back to the workplace and killed four of the senior officers of the Lottery Commission before killing himself. The president of the state lottery was actually chased into the parking lot before the accountant gunned him down with a semiautomatic handgun.

The employee, 35-year-old Matthew Beck of Cromwell, Connecticut, had complained that he had been given responsibilities that were outside of the realm of his stated job profile and was not being properly compensated for his work. Several months earlier he had been placed on leave for unspecified medical reasons, and his father Donald told the news media, "Yes, he has been troubled."

Sometimes family members observe warning signs of depression, anger, and hostility, but the correct interpretation of that behavior is best left to clinically trained specialists. One of my colleagues, supervisory special agent Mary Ellen O'Toole of the FBI, writes in a personal communication:

> Therefore, in training on this topic, we encourage people to observe, and let the TATs (threat assessment teams) interpret. In my experience, I find that untrained but well intentioned family members, classmates, and work colleagues will rationalize and minimize the troubling behavior they observe.

Whether they have a responsibility to inform people who may be in harm's way, however, is largely for lawyers to determine. In this case, the perpetrator clearly sought out the leadership of the lottery to express his displeasure with how his claims had been managed; in addition to murdering the Lottery Commission president, he also killed the organization's chief financial officer, its vice president of operations, and its director of information systems. Even now, a decade later, employees at the lottery acknowledge that although physical access to buildings improved and counseling services increased after the killings, the lingering and profound sense of anxiety caused by Beck's murders remains. The memory of these events does not simply float away.

The Threat Within

As illustrated by the Lottery Commission case, perpetrators of violence in the workplace usually are not strangers or terrorists from a foreign land; more often than not they are former employees, vendors, or, in one disturbing case, customers.

On August 27, 1980, the FBI was forced to detonate a 960-pound bomb in Harvey's Hotel and Casino in Lake Tahoe, Nevada. The blast left a three-story-high hole in the building. The good news was that, prior to detonation, the hotel was warned by an anonymous caller that a bomb had been placed in its human resources office. The bad news was that a search by hotel security found that the device was so advanced in its design that it could not be removed from the hotel's premises safely; it had to be detonated. The hotel was evacuated, and as hundreds of bystanders watched from the street, a major part of the hotel literally blew up.

The perpetrator was a VIP player at the casino, John Birges, a Hungarian-born landscaper who stole nearly 1,000 pounds of dynamite from a Fresno, California, construction site. He reportedly lost about $750,000 at Harvey's throughout the course of the prior year. To recover his losses, Birges and two co-conspirators had concocted a plan to extort some $3 million as ransom for not detonating the bomb. Birges was convicted and died while serving his sentence in 1996.

I've interviewed a number of people involved with the Harvey's case and found that the most fascinating aspect of the event is that the perpetrators entered the hotel wearing uniforms from a computer company—surveillance tapes showed the perps carrying large boxes with the IBM logo emblazoned on the side—and employees just assumed that the hotel was receiving a new shipment of computers. Instead of being stopped or even questioned, the three men involved in the plot rolled the boxes onto the second floor with ease, confidently acted as though they had been in the human resources office many times before, and left the boxes behind a closet door that few employees ever used.

If the perpetrator had not called in the extortion threat and the bomb had been detonated without warning, experts believe that hundreds would have likely died in the blast. A key lesson was learned in the Harvey's case: Take every bomb threat and extortion claim seriously; document every word the perpetrator utters; and involve law enforcement experts quickly.

Motivations differ in each case, and we are increasingly seeing changes in the demography of perpetrators. On February 5, 2001, for example, 66-year-old former Navistar engine factory employee Willie Dan Baker returned to his workplace outside Chicago, killing four people and wounding four others before committing suicide.

What is interesting about this case is that he was not a new employee with an untested record. In fact, Baker was a Navistar veteran who had nearly 40 *years* of employment under his belt—that is, before he was terminated in 1995 for stealing engine parts.

A month before the killings, Baker was convicted on counts of conspiracy to commit interstate theft, a crime for which he was given jail time and fined $195,000. Just days before he was to start his five-month jail sentence, he sought revenge on those he felt had ruined his life—his former colleagues.

An alert security guard relied on her intuition and refused Baker entry when she saw the former Navistar employee trying to gain entrance to Navistar's offices with a golf bag in tow. But Baker overpowered her, forcing his way into the facility with the shotgun, AK-47 rifle, hunting rifle, and revolver that he carried inside his bag. To this day, police believe that the killings were random. Baker sought revenge but had not personalized his anger, potentially because it was his theft—and not another employee—that ended what had been a noneventful career with the company.

As in many cases of workplace violence, colleagues said that this perpetrator seemed like an "average guy." Navistar fuel systems engineer Robert Jones, who had worked with Baker for 15 years, told reporters, "All I know is that Bill was an easygoing guy."

But remember that one of the reasons your human resources and security teams need to have a radar screen is because employees who are under review for one infraction may have other serious issues underway in their lives. The same year that Baker was fired from Navistar for theft, he also was charged with criminal sexual assault involving a family member who was under the age of 18, according to police in Carol Stream, Illinois. Baker was convicted of the crime in 1998 and sentenced to home confinement, which leads me to the following observation: Baker was already registered as a convicted sex offender with the Carol Stream Police Department. Did Navistar know this? Did it periodically crosscheck the names of current employees with those lists? Unfortunately, the answers to these questions are unclear due to the limited amount of information Navistar could provide as a result of confidentiality and legal restraints.

There is one fact that provides some solace in the Baker case: Many more people might have died that tragic day in October had Baker utilized his full arsenal of weapons and traversed more of the almost two million square feet of the Navistar plant. The security guard who was overpowered by Baker at the plant's gates reportedly acted like she was shot and pretended to be dead, which likely saved her life. But the guard's use of survival tactics led to allegations that the company did not fulfill its Duty to Warn and alert the plant that a gunman was on the loose.

In response, Navistar claimed that the guard followed procedures by trying to prevent Baker entry to the plant, but it was also her first day at that gate following a two-week orientation program. She had nine years experience working security. What would you do in a similar circumstance? Who is to blame for the company's exposure to threat here, given the fact that Baker's personal life was complicated and troubled? Can and should employers monitor employee behavior off-site if they suspect that the person may be agitated?

Navistar responded quickly and appropriately after the crisis by bringing in counselors to help witnesses and others deal with the impact of violence and loss. The company also distributed flyers regarding the incident and the availability of its Employee Assistance Program (EAP), but this was of little solace to those who lost loved ones.

The Navistar case serves as a glimpse of issues that I often raise with corporations. The American population is currently in the midst of a tidal wave of 76 million baby boomers, people who were born between the years of 1946 and 1964, the majority of whom will work well into their mid-70s, as gerontology guru Ken Dychtwald notes in his wonderful book, *Age Wave*.

The good news is that the overwhelming majority of boomers are physically fit, mentally alert, and highly adaptive to the changing dynamics of work. There is a secondary issue, however, which I am researching in considerable depth with various case studies. Parallel to the tens of millions of boomers remaining on the job after their prime years is a preponderance of cases of older people committing violent crimes at work. Reliable statistics from the FBI and state authorities on this trend will take years to compile, but in the meantime, it is important that we remember that some older workers will harbor illnesses—not just aches and pains, but more chronic illnesses—that can trigger abnormal reactions in them as they grapple with work. Very few will ever be violent. But at Navistar, no one thought a 40-year veteran would become a murderer. I assure you that we will see similar cases in the years to come.

Preventing Crisis: Background Checks

After you have interviewed a candidate and have a sense of how well their personality will mesh with your company's culture, one of the most prudent next steps is

If you really want to gain a more complete picture of an individual, hire a qualified employment verification firm.

ensuring that they are who they say they are—simple identity verification is not sufficient. If you really want to gain a more complete picture of an individual, hire a qualified employment verification firm and insist that it completes the following checks on the potential employee:

- Validate that the candidate is using his or her true name
- Check for a history of credit fraud
- Verify that the social security number the candidate provided is that of a living person (and don't kid yourself—a surprising amount of applicants will use the number of a deceased relative with a similar or the same name to hide a checkered financial past)

If one or more of the previous checks turns up some questionable information, pause and continue researching the candidate:

- Does the person have a genuine physical address or is he or she using a mail receiving/forwarding service?
- Is the candidate living in a hotel/motel/temporary residence?
- Does he or she frequently use a check-cashing service, or does the person have a legitimate checking account? (A colleague of mine who is a former FBI agent estimates that about a quarter of all crimes at work are committed by those who receive a paper paycheck as opposed to those who have their pay direct-deposited into their checking accounts; the former often can escape the reporting and identification requirements of the U.S. Patriot Act by cashing their checks at for-fee check-cashing locations and avoiding the banking system completely.)
- Does the background check show any time lapses in employment? The lapse could indicate that the person was caring for an aging parent, but it could also correlate to time spent in a correctional institution.

Your security team will want to look at applicants' criminal records and keep a specific eye on financial—or "white collar"—crimes. For the most part, criminal background checks are retained by research firms for only seven years or less, which means that you could be hiring someone with a checkered past who has evaded detection for some time. Nevertheless, many of the more accomplished research firms will look for incidents such as:

- Arson
- Weapons violations
- Stalking
- Menacing
- Simple assault
- Resisting or evading arrest
- Domestic violence
- Obstructing an officer
- Child abuse or neglect
- Sex-related offenses, including soliciting, lewd acts, prostitution, and public indecency
- Possession of controlled substances
- Possession of drug paraphernalia
- Substance abuse
- DUI

Looking into these issues could prevent a crisis. Do it.

Lessons from Virginia Tech

Although most murders in the workplace target a single individual, we have begun to witness a profound change in incidents in that their dynamics are now involving increasingly greater numbers of individuals. Think back to the killing of seven engineers at a Xerox office building in Nimitz Highway, Hawaii, in 1999, or the murder of seven software and office personnel at an office park in Wakefield, Massachusetts, in 2000. The sadistic killings of 13 high school students and teachers in Columbine, Colorado, on April 20, 1999, and the murders of five Amish schoolchildren in Nickel Mines, Pennsylvania, on October 2, 2006, are all vivid reminders of the need for ongoing security.

The most notorious case in recent history, of course, was the killing of 32 innocent students and faculty members at Virginia Tech University on April 16, 2007. Any independent analyst looking at the facts surrounding the perpetrator would find him- or herself pondering whether monumental errors in professional judgment were made. The questions raised in this book's Introduction ("What did you know? When did you know it? What did you do about it?") are thus more relevant than ever.

University administrators, like corporate leaders, are not trained experts in the signals of personality disorders. But leaders who hold positions of responsibility in any organization in which a large number of people congregate—like hospitals, colleges, and corporations— similarly cannot say that they have *no* culpability when stakeholders have tried to *warn them* about disturbed people in their midst. In the case of Virginia Tech, the university's leadership appears especially vulnerable to criticism. Here is what we know about perpetrator Cho Seung-Hui based on a variety of crime scene, media, and witness reports:

1. Prior to shooting 32 people over a two-hour period, Cho was a known loner on campus who refused virtually all live conversation with other students or faculty members. When asked his name, he would often vacantly look at the person or refuse to answer. His living space was likewise completely absent of expression. As *Newsweek* reported, "His dorm room was as affectless as he was— no posters or photos, just cinder block."

2. At least two faculty members relied on their intuition that Cho had a disturbing obsession with violence. When two plays he submitted for his creative writing course were found to contain overt expressions of his desire to perform acts of violence, faculty members spoke up. Professor Nikki Giovanni requested that Cho rewrite two papers that blatantly discussed pedophilic acts and murders, but Cho refused. At many universities, such a stand-off would have been arbitrated under the school's guidelines. In addition, Lucinda Roy, codirector of the school's creative writing program, told *Newsweek* that she went to *five* different entities on campus, including the division of student affairs, Cook Counseling Center, Schiffert Health Center, Virginia Tech police, and College of Liberal Arts and Human Sciences, regarding her concerns about Cho. *Who connected those dots?* Did a threat assessment team representing leaders from these different organizations ever meet to discuss how Cho might benefit from clinical intervention?

3. University police admitted days after the massacre that Cho was no stranger to them. Of course, they did not tell the news media that they recognized Cho even after they saw his body at the crime scene and realized that he had perpetrated a mass murder-suicide. What they could have told the campus community and public that awful day is that they were aware that at least two female students had sought police intervention when Cho reportedly engaged in stalking behavior. Although the women chose not to pursue charges against Cho, the fact that they—among others, including Cho's classmates and professors—had *warned* the university about Cho raises profound questions of accountability. *Just who owned the "radar screen" at Virginia Tech?*

4. The university's president, Charles Steger, was familiar with dealing with crisis. Several months prior to the massacre, a prison convict had escaped near campus and killed a hospital guard and a sheriff's deputy. In that situation, Steger reportedly ordered students to evacuate the campus grounds. But during the first minutes of the April 16, 2007, massacre, there was understandable confusion. In an effort to counter the crisis with appropriate action, Steger met with his crisis management team from 7:15 a.m. to 9:45 a.m., after the first 911 emergency calls regarding the murder of two students inside West Ambler Johnston Residence Hall had been made. Then a second round of shootings was reported at Norris Hall. But evacuations were apparently not ordered out of concern that the gunman would shoot down those fleeing campus. Both then and now, there remain significant questions regarding what type of warning should have been shared, beyond all-campus e-mails, that would have enabled individuals to make their own decisions about whether to evacuate or lock themselves in place. Steger, however, acted to protect the safety of administrators. When he heard gunshots near his emergency operations boardroom at Burress Hall, he asked that the doors to his office be locked, saying, "I thought it could be a target."

Benchmark Away

Every organizational leader needs to be periodically updated on his or her company's security practices, from closed-circuit television and other surveillance systems, to the prescreening protocols that are used when hiring new employees. This is a minimum expectation that is widely accepted by the American Society for Industrial Security, the Business Continuity Institute, and other similar organizations. This review should result in a brief report that outlines goals and objectives for keeping customers and employees safe—and the report should end up in the hands of the company's chief executive. Among other things, the report should include what security issues will require extraordinary budgeting in the year ahead, such as perimeter security, IT safeguards, and related needs.

In higher education, every college and university is required to abide by the Clery Act, a benchmark federal law passed in 1990 that requires school administrators to disclose to the proper authorities any information regarding potential harm or acts of violence perpetrated by or against members of the university community. In recent years, parents and relatives have sued administrators for gross negligence, arguing that teachers, deans, and senior leaders had failed to exercise the Duty to Care and Duty to Warn standards that were discussed earlier.

Example: In March 2007, Eastern Michigan University placed its vice president of student affairs on forced leave after freshman Laura Dickinson, 22, was found murdered in her dorm room. According to *The Chronicle of Higher Education*, "Staff members told students there was no need to worry," even though foul play was suspected from the moment her body was found naked from the waist down with a pillow over her head. No need to worry? Get this: The day after Dickinson's body was found, the "leadership" of the college issued a written statement that said, in part, "At this point, there is no reason to suspect foul play. We are fully confident in the safety and security of our campus environment."

Nice try. A fellow student, Orange Amir Taylor III, was eventually charged with the murder. On July 15, 2007, Eastern Michigan

University fired its president, its
vice president of student affairs,
and its campus police director
amid widespread criticism for the
university's handling of the case.

With Virginia Tech, Eastern
Michigan, and numerous other
university cases, administrators
faced a principal test of crisis
management: When in doubt, act quickly, tell your public what you
know and don't know, and over-communicate at every step of
your decision-making process. It sounds pretty basic, but somehow
even very seasoned and talented professionals can find a way to mess
it up.

> When in doubt, act quickly, tell
> your public what you know and
> don't know, and over-
> communicate at every step of your
> decision-making process.

Workplace Violence Policy

If your organization doesn't have a formal workplace violence policy,
you may want to remember that U.S. employers are required by the
Occupational Safety and Health Administration (OSHA) to have
both a policy and training program that informs employees of the
proper methods of sharing and reporting concerns about intimidating
and threatening workplace behavior.

Here is a model policy that nicely captures many of the elements
of a best practices plan, one in which your organization is seen to
model exemplary practices; we will use a fictitious company name
for illustrative purposes.

Pacific Ventures Model Policy

Pacific Ventures believes that all employees and visitors deserve dig-
nity and respect and should be able to conduct business in a safe environment. Any threat, whether verbal, written, or physical, that is
committed at work or impacting your work, or other acts of violence, intimidation, or harassment, is prohibited.

Although this list is not exhaustive, please know that we will take seriously any report of behavior that could be considered threat-based. You may face disciplinary action, up to and including termination, for any act that:

- Causes others to fear for their physical safety
- Contains statements, whether verbal or written, that appear to threaten individuals or groups, or physical acts of aggression, such as yelling, swearing, shoving, hitting, or kicking
- Includes inappropriate remarks, comments, or gestures; a good rule to remember is, if you would not say or do something at an airport, don't say or do it at work
- Includes stalking of any person, including harassment by cellular or other device, in person or by any other means, that causes him or her to fear for his or her safety or for the property of another employee, visitor, or customer
- Includes possession of any weapon on company property, even if it is in your vehicle
- Results in damage to company property or that of our customers, coworkers, or vendors

Reporting Concerns

In the event that you are aware of a threat or incident that requires immediate attention, you are encouraged to call 911 immediately. In the event that you are aware of a situation that is not imminent but nevertheless serious, please contact our security team or a member of human resources immediately. Our company has a threat assessment team that will confidentially collect information from you and possibly others, and we will review that situation and ascertain the most prudent manner to reduce the likelihood of escalation.

Within the boundaries of confidentiality, we will try to keep you updated on the progress of our investigation as best as possible. Please be aware that even though we might not inform you of each milestone in our management of the case, we are managing the incident or threat that you brought to our attention.

If you have any questions about this policy, please contact our security team at X5050.

A Case Study: Exiting the Problem Employee

Recently a client called me with an all-too-common question. Here are my notes of what the members of my client's threat assessment team told me during our initial phone call, followed by an abridged memo I developed for them that evening. As you read this, think about all of the ramifications of case management. Although you may have a different and possibly better solution than the one I propose, focus on the policy questions that emerge from this kind of threat situation.

Note Summary

We have a long-standing employee that we just learned about at headquarters. Although Carlos has an excellent work performance history with us, we were never told by our plant management that he has a record of intimidating coworkers and that his behavior has been spiraling out of control since last fall. Local management appears to want to refrain from firing him because he's a bully—they really fear he will retaliate. They have been retaining this person because he openly admits he has committed acts of violence—we know he has a gun. What should we do?

These are just some of the many details that were shared during that initial call.

Here are excerpts from my memo to that team.

Summary of Facts

The company has employed the individual for 14 years and his employment record indicates that his service has been generally strong in his role as manager, from a performance point of view. It was reported that he has a domineering personality that is disruptive to some, creates a sense of high anxiety and fear among others, and that he is a loner in general; you noted in our telecommunications that he has poor social skills and has been specifically hostile to female coworkers throughout his years at your company. The individual reportedly has said that he has access to and uses weapons—he is licensed to carry a firearm for hunting purposes.

Recent Incidents

You reported several increasingly hostile incidents that appear to have emerged in the employee's behavior over the past several months. Carlos reportedly brought a long-blade knife to the plant while in costume for your Valentine's Day party, and that knife was determined to be an actual weapon, not a toy. In addition, Carlos told two coworkers that he took a photograph of his female supervisor, superimposed her face on the body of another person, and used the image as a target poster. It was brought to your attention just yesterday that this same individual brought onto your property a DVD player, on which he played a sadistic amateur video featuring overt sexual content, and showed this to a coworker.

Considerations

The proper ownership of a licensed weapon by a responsible user is not yet of immediate concern. The other allegations are of considerable interest for several reasons:

1. The company has a code of conduct and a clear policy regarding appropriate behavior at work; this individual has violated these policies, not once, but on numerous occasions.

2. Because the factory has a history of high personnel turnover, it is fair to conclude that the events you shared with me are only those about which you currently know and likely do not constitute a full repertoire of inappropriate acts by this individual.

3. It appears that leadership at the site is afraid to act against the employee because of his threats and bullying. This is of considerable

interest because it underscores a culture of *tolerating* abusive behavior; as such, this type of behavior may be permeating your workplace. You will want to consider whether the lack of reprimands, progressive discipline, or separating this person earlier in his employment constitutes negligent retention.

4. We may have a case that merits legal review if, in fact, the company is aware that a video showing an intoxicated or drugged female, who may have committed acts against her will, was shown to others on company property. This video is now known to the company and you need to consider how it should be disclosed to law enforcement. Only your legal counsel can advise you on whether it is your duty to disclose this information under the law, but the company should consider the *nonlegal* ramifications of this case: If a local newspaper were to print a story about this employee and ask what information the company knew, when it knew the information, and what it did in response, I would not want to be your spokesperson for obvious reasons. The issues and implications here are not just legal; they raise profound questions about the integrity of a fine company. Women's groups and others would likely be justifiably outraged, not just at the company, but also at management's reluctance to exit an individual with this kind of employment history.

5. Human resources should review several issues. As I mentioned during our conference call, this is not, at first glance, a case of negligent hiring, since the employee has been with the factory for 14 years. There are questions, however, regarding the possibility of negligent retention and negligent supervision. It is fair to say that your company would not condone the retention of any employee who has a known history of bullying, even if his or her work record is otherwise satisfactory. Again, legal and human resources issues aside, could you defend his retention with the news media? In addition, if you were to defend him, how could you possibly justify your decision to retain him after you were aware that he had both made statements that were threatening to his manager and brought a provocative video, which may or may not show an illegal act, into your workplace?

The Memo Continues

This is not a time to be moralists. You told me that this manufacturing location is scheduled for permanent closing next March and that Carlos's job is slated for elimination at that time. An early elimination is thus an easier route of action than confronting him about his varied infractions. My role is to recommend specific policy questions for your threat assessment team to ponder. Again, with the very limited information we have on hand, I recommend that the company separate Carlos from the company now, as your investigation uncovered provocative findings. There are clear violations of the company code of conduct. There are potential violations of law.

Recommendations

Because the employee has an interest in weapons and a capacity to use them, and because he has a history as a bully, we have a complicated case at hand. Raising issues with Carlos that extend back several months and that were not documented by human resources would be a complicated affair. I am concerned that raising them post facto could trigger the individual to personalize his rage against a specific manager. The fact that Carlos has over a dozen years of positive performance reviews, despite these and other issues, could lead him to question: "Why me? Why now? What's different?" You have logical answers, but articulating them may enrage Carlos; only a licensed clinical psychologist can ascertain how he might respond.

My suggestion is that you separate the employee after legal counsel reviews the case. Security leadership and his supervisor could conduct an unscheduled meeting that is limited to five to seven minutes in length. We know that separation discussions that generally last more than five minutes can be potentially volatile. Here are several talking points for you to consider as you rehearse for the conversation:

1. Carlos, you have served the company for over a dozen years. I want you to know that we value your service to us. You have made a difference for us, and we know that.

2. We are separating you from the company today. We want you to know that you are not eligible to transfer to another company location. Thus, we wanted to approach you now, at the earliest possibility, so you can think about your alternatives.

3. We are very aware that you have invested time and energy in us. Thus, we worked very hard to get you the best separation package possible. We are eliminating your position immediately, and we will give you one week's pay. We will also continue your benefits for the next three months. After that, you have the option of continuing with COBRA. All of these details will be spelled out in a letter we have prepared for you. However, the good news is that we want to give you a modest bridge to your next employment opportunity.

4. Unfortunately, we have to *separate* you today, and that means that we will be asking that you pack up your belongings and turn in your badge. There is no room for negotiation. (I recommend that you do not use the word termination, as it is harsh and is easily equated with terminal, which effectively means no chance for recovery!)

5. We want you to be successful in your new career and we want good things for you in the future. If you have a few questions, we'll be glad to try to answer them, but this decision is irreversible.

Nine Questions the Employee May Ask

1. Why am I the only employee being fired?
Carlos, your position is being eliminated. (Remember to use the terms *separation* or *elimination*. Do not discuss specific reasons for the action.)

2. Did the store manager order this?
This is a decision made by a management team and not by any one person. We want to focus on helping you get to your next employment opportunity.

3. Are you telling me that I am getting only one week's severance?
Yes.

4. I have tons to do here. You have no idea how much I am responsible for here. No one understands my job but me. Are you crazy?

Thanks for the head's up on your role, and we will have someone look into how we can continue your work. But you need to start packing up, and the two of us are here with boxes to help you with that.

5. Is this because of that video that I brought in? That was a joke.

Carlos, we are here to discuss your separation. Let's focus on helping you get to your next place of employment.

6. You know that [I am a veteran, received a special commendation for service, am vested in our pension plan]—what you are doing today is just illegal.

Carlos, we are not lawyers. But we are confident that our decision is the right one for you and for us. If you want to confer with an attorney, that is your prerogative. However, we *are* separating you today.

7. Can I relocate to one of our other sites? I know that you are hiring at other plants. You can keep the severance. I just want to relocate. Let's make that happen. I need this job!

We do not want to raise any false hopes for you. The bottom line is that relocation just isn't possible.

8. Will you give me a positive reference? I have never worked anywhere else.

We will be glad to confirm your dates of employment and job title, but we do not provide references to any employee.

9. If you do this, you have my promise that you have not heard the last from me. I know where you are vulnerable. You people have no idea what I am capable of.

That's a direct threat. If you mean what you just said, we have an obligation to go to law enforcement officials, now—not later, but right now. We have zero tolerance for threats. I would urge you to focus on your future, not on making threats. (If he repeats his threat, do not delay and do contact 911 immediately, given his history. It will demonstrate that you take his threat seriously.)

Disclaimer: This is not a source of legal or clinical advice.

Questions to Ponder

Notice that my advice to the client does not focus on the infractions of company policy by Carlos, nor does it center on his history of bullying; rather, my suggestions pertain to the immediate issue of separating him from the organization. Why aren't specific references to the sexually explicit video, his access to weapons, and alleged abuse of his colleagues mentioned in Carlos's separation meeting? In this case, there is a high possibility that referencing these issues could escalate his level of hostility. What's more, Carlos's infractions raise profound questions about the progressive discipline policy of the company.

I wanted you to read this case and these representative talking points so that you might be better able to realize that each element of a threat at work must be considered unique. Other professionals might have offered similar or different recommendations. Similarly, each perpetrator has different "hot" points. It is important to remember that no professional can predict violence, so when your company encounters a problem employee, your threat assessment team will need to review that specific employee's history, as well as how you can best protect those who worked with him or her.

> Realize that each element of a threat at work must be considered unique.

In the case of Carlos, our objective was not to focus on infractions that would likely embarrass or infuriate him, but rather to concentrate on offering Carlos a modest, short-term financial bridge. The conversation with Carlos could well have been conducted in a different manner, and for a number of reasons, such as if the company's lawyers determined that the video he brought to work showed potentially illegal acts. That's why companies must carefully ponder all facets of negligent retention before they race to end the career of a potentially violent person.

Suicide and Work

Psychologists report that for years, even decades, after someone close to you takes his or her own life, questions linger—dark, probing questions. You might ask yourself, "What could I have done? What signals did I miss? Why didn't he or she leave a note?" Even after hundreds of clinical studies on suicidal trends and behavioral signals, we really don't understand how at-risk people evaluate their options before they decide to commit such an act. Being neither a psychologist nor a doctor, I rely on my experience in helping leadership teams grapple with the aftermath of such a tragedy. Here is a quick summary of what I've learned:

- When a well-publicized scandal strikes a company, some managers and executives cannot comprehend the enormity of the negative publicity that has been thrust upon them.
- Although nonexecutives, especially teenagers, are likely to exhibit warning signs that they are experiencing a serious bout with depression and anxiety and are contemplating suicide, such behaviors are less common at work. When the 43-year-old former vice chairman of Enron, J. Clifford Baxter, was found dead in his car on January 25, 2002, from a self-inflicted gunshot wound, his former coworkers expressed surprise that a past superstar chose not to confront the widely anticipated litigation stemming from his company's financial problems. CNN suggested that in the weeks before his death, Baxter had been subpoenaed for documents and that he was increasingly concerned that the investigation had moved from being an Enron scandal to a personal one.
- Never forget the role that recent rejection can play in the case of an individual who is undergoing severe mental stress; how we process loss is quite different from how we process rejection,

which is a far more personal and direct hit on our ego and sense of self-worth. When you encounter someone who has recently been told that he or she has been fired, or that his or her spouse wants a divorce, or that his or her last legal appeal has failed, a sense of rejection can transition into rage—and thus it is prudent to thoughtfully, discreetly, and carefully monitor those who are undergoing such issues.

Does Evil Exist?

There are criminals, and then there are seriously *disturbed* criminals who have no sense of remorse. These perpetrators are seemingly emotionally vacant; they appear to have no sense of guilt. They are, some experts argue, purely evil. In 2005, for example, Dr. Michael Stone, an eminent psychiatrist at Columbia University, released a landmark study based on a detailed analysis of some 500 violent criminals. His research concluded that there are 22 hierarchical levels of what can only be described as evil behavior.

The dark and twisted acts of these perpetrators are difficult for us to comprehend. While there are dozens of personality disorders that may contribute to violent behavior, a small percentage of perpetrators appear to be psychopathically "evil" and hold a predisposition to orchestrating calculated attacks upon strangers. These criminals sometimes co-opt and then victimize their targets as part of a sadistic, self-serving ritual of evil.

You may recall that John Wayne Gacy murdered 33 boys and young men over the course of six years on the northwest side of Chicago. Law student Ted Bundy confessed to charming and then sadistically murdering 30 women, whom he referred to as "cargo." Unemployed factory worker and drifter Jeffrey Dahmer sexually abused at least 17 victims before killing them; he ate the body parts of at least one victim. In these and numerous other widely studied cases, before these perpetrators were even caught, they were regarded by others as strange or hostile people. We will never know if early clinical or police intervention can prevent the heinous crimes perpetrated by such seemingly evil individuals, but we can say with certainty that sharing your concerns with others may prevent potential sadists from becoming experienced ones. You can read more about personality disorders at apa.org.

We Have Security Guards, but . . .

Having a guard at the front door of your business may be reassuring, but it won't always serve as an effective deterrent to a perpetrator who is seeking to rob your business or who is intent on gaining entry to your workplace to harm his or her ex-spouse. Increasingly, companies are instituting comprehensive programs to deter attacks at their workplaces. In lawsuits against employers, litigators investigate whom you hire as guards, how much training they receive on signal detection and response, and what kinds of safeguards you have invested in to protect your people and other assets. Professional security consultants recommend that you evaluate how you would be ranked, as compared to your competitors, in categories such as fencing and barricades, exterior lighting, and closed-circuit television for key access and egress areas. It is also recommended that you incorporate into your security processes bomb detection screening in the mailroom and public address systems that can rapidly issue alerts to your employees in case of emergency.

In a private communication to me, supervisory special agent Mary Ellen O'Toole of the FBI notes:

We have a phrase that we use here: "mission-oriented" . . . If an offender is mission-oriented to commit violence, and their mindset is backed up by planning, and strategic thinking—they do not want to be deterred in their mission, and that makes this type of individual more dangerous. They could care less about metal detectors or other physical deterrents.

2

MANAGING THREATS
AND WORKPLACE VIOLENCE

*Some companies quite innocently recruit individuals with psychopathic
tendencies because some hiring managers may mistakenly attribute
"leadership" labels to what are, in actuality, psychopathic behaviors.
For example, taking charge, making decisions, and getting others to do
what you want are classic forms of leadership and management, yet
they can also be well-packaged forms of coercion, domination, and
manipulation. Failing to look closely beneath the outer trappings of ste-
reotypical leadership to the inner working of the personality can
sometimes lead to a regrettable hiring decision.*

— SNAKES IN SUITS, BY PAUL BABIAK AND ROBERT D. HARE

Although there are many kinds of incidents that could cripple your
business, none are perhaps more serious than when a threat or
act of violence impacts your employees. Although statistically speaking your chance of experiencing such a serious incident is small, the
facts can be misleading; in reality, thousands of incidents occur in the
workplace every day, but few people are aware of them because they
usually do not make the nightly news. In a survey I conducted in
2007, one in three of over 1,600 responding managers reported that
he or she had to confront "an openly hostile and/or potentially violent" associate in the past year. That is numbing. And if you think that
workplace violence only happens to others, here is a reality check:

> On average, three individuals are murdered at work *each day* in the United States.
> —NIOSH Annual Report, 2006

- On average, three individuals are murdered at work *each day* in the United States. The most dangerous occupations are those in the retail (especially convenience stores), manufacturing, service, and hospitality sectors.
- When murders occur in the workplace, the most common motive is robbery, but the second most common motive—and this is growing—is *retribution*.
- There are over 8,000 incidents *per day* involving some kind of assault at work in the United States. The most commonly used weapon is a fist, not a gun.
- Although there are many reasons why people become agitated at work, primary motivators include terminated romances, jealousy, and mental illness.

We must reflect on how and why some people transition from experiencing feelings of anger to desiring to commit violence. Not surprisingly, substance abuse plays an extraordinary role in these people's emotional shifts. According to the FBI, well over half of all Americans incarcerated on convictions of felony assault were intoxicated or on drugs at the time of committing the crime. Although we are repeatedly reminded that employees are entitled to their privacy, this policy sometimes conflicts with the employer's right to provide a safe workplace for its employees. If you become aware that someone is threatening a coworker and suspect that the aggressor has a history of substance abuse, what should you consider more important—his or her *privacy* needs or the need to *protect others* from harm?

"It Won't Happen Here"

When I was vice president of crisis management at Motorola, several murders and assaults unfortunately occurred on my watch. In the aftermath of these events, I met with families of victims, interviewed supervisors and coworkers of those killed, and asked a series of difficult questions: Why did this person become violent? Were there any pre-incident behavioral signals? Did anyone ever share concerns that the perpetrator's behavior was becoming increasingly hostile or desperate?

Over the years I have reflected on those tragic events, one of which included a Seguin, Texas, plant employee, who shot his estranged wife and her girlfriend in the back late one night during their shift and then, that same night, committed suicide after barricading himself outside Motorola's credit union. Through this and similar incidents, I learned much about the signals that can emerge before violence occurs.

In the vast majority of workplace violence cases, the perpetrator is acting on a real or perceived grievance. The person may have been denied a worker's compensation claim and is now experiencing physical pain while at work, or he or she may have been reprimanded in front of peers and is now embarrassed. Maybe the employee was dismissed or reassigned, which has caused him or her to feel so angry, frustrated, or impassioned that he or she seeks revenge on a supervisor in an effort to regain control of life. No matter what the employee's motivation, the real question is: Are we *listening?* Consider the range of potential threats:

- Stalking of an employee by a former spouse, partner, or coworker
- Threats to bring a weapon to work, possibly preceded by a sarcastic comment; or the employee "accidentally" leaves a hunting rifle in the back seat of an automobile for others to see
- Comments made by a former employee that are intentionally provocative in nature (e.g., "She has no idea how much I want to see her dead.")
- E-mails or posted blog messages that threaten the life of a coworker
- Behavior that is intended to cause concern, such as mimicking the gesture of firing a weapon at a coworker

A smart way to begin is to differentiate between *a problem employee* (a person who has a constant temper, or whose bullying behavior causes others to worry about their safety) and an *employee with a problem* (a person who may be experiencing a temporary dysfunction in his or her personal life, but who is mentally healthy and not prone to violence). When a manager understands the difference between these two types of employees, he or she is better equipped to know what questions to ask and what roadmap to follow.

Nearly four decades of detailed research by criminologists and forensic scientists has revealed that workplace violence is becoming more understandable and, to a certain degree, more preventable. Dr. Alan Friedman, associate professor of psychiatry at Northwestern University Feinberg School of Medicine, notes:

- About 20 percent of your employees are, on any given day, experiencing a personal but temporary issue that is negatively impacting their work. That does not mean they will be violent. It means that whatever the issues they are facing, they are likely to decrease their productivity at work. If they operate machinery or have a fiduciary role in your company, the impact of that stress could impair their judgment and resultantly cause harm. But the good news is that these individuals usually rebound and return to normalcy. For any number of reasons, most of us face life's challenges with resiliency and "come through the clouds."

- The next group, however, creates cause for concern. Based on data from the various studies that are cited at the end of this book, researchers have learned that about 10 percent of your employees or customers have an *ongoing clinical disorder* that could be diagnosed as chronic by a clinician. These individuals are grappling with an issue that could cause them to become angry, moody, or, in very rare cases, violent. Mental health providers generally agree that these people should be receiving some type of periodic or routine treatment. In most cases, they are. Many individuals in this category routinely control their anger, anxiety, insecurities, or outbursts. But if they unilaterally reject their medication, or if their ordeal of mental illness turns to depression, anger, or worse, they may cause their coworkers to fear for their well-being.

- The most serious category of persons is composed of those people—somewhere between 1 percent and 3 percent of your employees or customers—who have a serious, *chronic* mental health condition that merits treatment or intervention, yet who either do not pursue treatment or cannot afford it. A single altercation at work—such as an innocent payroll mistake—could trigger an outburst. You may think that 1 to 3 percent is a small percentage, but for a company with tens of thousands of employees, that's a pretty disturbing number. Just ask any human resources manager.

Although we are focusing on threats and violence, remember that employers tend to gloss over issues of mental illness among their employees out of privacy concerns. The bigger question to ponder is: What matters more—the privacy of an employee whose behavior is disturbing, or his or her potential to wound or kill someone you are supervising? And just in case you think that the media oversensationalizes the impact of stress on society, get this: About 10 million Americans are in psychotherapy in any given year. According to the April 9, 2007, issue of *Forbes*, these individuals make nearly 84 million office visits to their psychotherapists and spend about $9 billion for their treatment, plus another $13.5 billion for antidepressants. The majority of these people are in their working years.

Assessing a Threat

Many industries, such as retail, health care, and hospitality, are dependent on a high degree of interaction with clients that are total strangers. Companies in these industry sectors sometimes offer their security supervisors and customer service managers a basic primer in managing hostile persons. Although there is no single model that can predict whether someone will become violent in the workplace, we have learned much in recent years regarding specific behavioral and clinical signs of those who pose *a potential risk* to themselves and to you.

Many companies have a threat assessment team whose members represent their human resources, security, IT, EAP, and legal departments. The team is typically deployed when an employee surfaces that is making or posing a threat. In many cases, this team will be supplemented by the supervisor of the problem employee. Companies such as Intel, IBM, and British Airways have threat assessment teams that receive and evaluate concerns from various segments of the organization, and these professionals often confer with mental health counselors on case management procedures. Threat assessment teams sometimes turn to external threat assessors to gauge whether an employee outburst could escalate into violence and, most importantly, whether the person has the *capacity* to act on his or her threats.

It's not enough to say that you will consult a psychologist when a challenging situation emerges. You need to remember that employers can be charged with tort liability for failing to prevent someone from hurting him- or herself or someone else. When offering seminars on this subject, I always advise managers to remember that virtually every employer, from hotels to financial service companies, has three paramount duties when threats arise: Duty to Care, Duty to Warn, and Duty to Act. Let's review them.

Duty to Care

Of course you care—you're a manager. But in today's litigious society, *saying* that you care is not enough. What if someone were to bring a gun into your workplace and harm your customers and the news media later reported that you were *previously aware* that this person had made threats? Consider the ramifications that stem from those essential questions mentioned earlier: What did you know? When did you know it? What did you do about it?

These probing questions are the foundation of every employer's general legal obligation to *demonstrate* that he or she cares. You can fulfill this duty by taking and evaluating every threat or act of violence seriously. If your supervisor informs you, for example, that she has just intercepted an e-mail from a former employee suggesting that he has a disturbing obsession with a former colleague, your Duty to Care obligates you to ponder how to inform potential victims that may be in harm's way. You may also need to commission an off-duty officer to inform the perpetrator that if he or she makes an overt threat, legal proceedings will commence. Although these and other Duty to Care tasks are not particularly pleasant, they could help defend you against later allegations that you negligently managed *potential* threats.

Duty to Warn

Sometimes a perpetrator acts without warning. When a gunman murdered five New York City Wendy's employees in 2000 during a robbery, it was clear that no one could have predicted the heinous act. It is even possible that the perpetrator was not aware of the final outcome. Remember, however, that there are often *pre-incident indicators* before an assault at work.

Sometimes a customer or employee will make a threatening phone call or repeatedly harass a colleague in a manner that meets the legal definition of stalking. From the moment you are made aware of such threats, it's smart to assume that you have a Duty to Warn others. One way to minimize your exposure is to confer with legal counsel, security, and human resources as soon as a threat surfaces.

Many threat assessment teams will meet to discuss the advantages and drawbacks of placing a restraining order against a disturbed individual. You may need to inform coworkers that an ex-boyfriend or wife is threatening to come to your location to seek revenge on one of their colleagues. Regardless of the nature of the threat, reflective thinking is essential. Remember that notifying coworkers of threats of violence could cause undue anxiety. If not properly worded, the perpetrator could later claim that you libeled or slandered him or her with your "concern." For all of these reasons, you need to think about *how* to warn others. This is called risk communications. It requires a collaborative discussion regarding the advantages and drawbacks of a small group meeting, a memo, individual sessions with potentially impacted persons, or other options. The involvement of law enforcement officials during these deliberations is strongly encouraged.

Duty to Act

Let's say that an employee walks into your office and informs you that her ex-husband is stalking her; in fact, she saw him drive by a few minutes ago in the parking lot while brandishing a knife. Unfortunately you don't have a security team, and the local police are overwhelmed by other matters. You don't have a large human resources department, and you certainly don't have private investigators on your payroll.

This scenario is all too real, and variations of this incident happen tens of thousands of times *each month* in the United States. In fact, the U.S. Secret Service says that over three million Americans are stalked at work or in their personal lives each year. About 87

> Over three million Americans are stalked at work or in their personal lives each year.

percent of stalking victims are female, and when a person has been sexually intimate with the stalker, his or her chances of being killed are 400 percent greater than those who are targeted by a stranger. These issues are real, and it's not just celebrities that are stalked, although the press frequently reminds us just how complicated stalking cases can be. If a stalking case emerges in your organization, remember that its length could be measured in years, not in days or weeks.

You may have an obligation to act when an employee informs you that he or she is being harassed or threatened. Among the more common steps taken by management are: offering a cell phone to the employee so that he or she can phone police when coming to and from work if he or she is physically pursued; encouraging the employee to contact the police; hiring an external security firm to patrol the parking lot until a restraining order is achieved; and documenting any and all suggestions you make to the employee that he or she work from an alternate location, if possible.

Astoundingly, I've seen some executives make a complicated situation even worse by admonishing an employee for bringing his or her personal issues to work ("Hey, we don't get involved in domestic disputes—that's your problem!"). Acting in this manner is not a solution, and no one would want to defend such arrogance before a jury. We are surrounded in our personal and professional lives by a small but disturbing percentage of people who are pathological in their narcissism and behavior. So here's your bottom line: If an employee or contractor expresses a serious concern about anyone, be it a coworker or a customer, confer with law enforcement officials immediately and then inform human resources and your legal department of the problem. Remember that ignoring the issue—or hoping it will go away—could gravely cost you and your company. Abide by the same great phrase that many soldiers learn at boot camp: When in doubt, *do something*.

Specific triggering events, such as losing a custody battle for children, participating in a contentious bankruptcy or court hearing, or receiving a reprimand or termination notice, may cause a nonviolent person to become violent. Case study upon case study on workplace crime is filled with documentations of poorly managed terminations, even when the reasons for the firing were legitimate. A classic case study is that of Wanda Rodgers, a California child social worker who was terminated by the State Department of Child Welfare for her bizarre behavior and "proper lack of respect for authority." In 1995, a full year after her termination, she returned to her former workplace and, using a 38mm revolver, shot her former boss between the eyes at point-blank range. Among the many factors that a threat assessment team might have considered is that Rodgers was terminated on Valentine's Day, in the midst of a divorce and a losing custody battle for her two children. In addition, when she was fired, Rodgers was just about as old as her mother had been when she committed suicide years prior. Wanda openly told coworkers of her paranoia, complaining, "Management is out to get me." Dates, family history, and family dynamics are all important considerations when assessing a potential threat. The need to be sensitive to the specific dynamics of an individual at risk cannot be overstated.

Assessing Violent Factors

Most people don't simply become violent overnight. Their path to violence and harming those they work with is usually evolutionary. Their tendency toward destructiveness can take months, even years, to advance to such a point that it becomes identifiable, but we have begun to understand that violent behavior is categorizable. In a landmark study, "The School Shooter: A Threat Assessment Perspective," one of the FBI's premiere profilers, Mary Ellen O'Toole, outlined four district categories of threats that are pertinent to all work sites:

1. A *direct threat* identifies a specific act against a specific target and is delivered in a straightforward, clear, and explicit manner: "I am going to place a bomb in your convention center."
2. An *indirect threat* tends to be vague. The plan, the intended victim, the motivation, and other aspects of the threat could be masked: "If I wanted to, I could kill everyone at this school!" While violence is implied, the threat is phrased tentatively and suggests that a violent act *could* occur, not that it *will* occur.
3. A *veiled threat* is one that strongly implies but does not explicitly threaten violence. "We would be better off without you around anymore" clearly hints at a possible violent act, but leaves it to the potential victim to interpret what the threat means.
4. A *conditional threat* is the type of threat often seen in extortion cases. It warns that a violent act will happen unless certain demands or terms are met: "If you don't give me two more months of severance, I will place a bomb inside one of your delivery trucks."

What follows are some of the major contributing factors to violence, as cited by investigators who evaluated cases in which perpetrators shared signals with others prior to their destructive acts. This list, based on the O'Toole study, should serve as a starting point if ever you encounter a belligerent or hostile person at your place of work:

1. Low tolerance for frustration
2. Poor coping skills
3. Lack of resiliency
4. Failed relationships
5. Signs of depression
6. Pathological narcissism
7. Unusually quiet and isolated
8. Habitually blames others
9. Lack of empathy
10. Exaggerated sense of entitlement
11. Attitude of superiority
12. Pathological craving for attention
13. Masks low self-esteem
14. Anger management problems
15. Intolerance
16. Inappropriate humor
17. Seeks to manipulate others
18. Lack of trust/paranoia
19. Progressive and negative change of behavior
20. Unusual interest in sensational violence
21. Turbulent parent/child relationship
22. Access to weapons
23. Abuse of drugs and alcohol

Source: O'Toole, Mary Ellen, "The School Shooter: A Threat Assessment Perspective," by the Critical Incident Response Group (CIRG), the National Center for the Analysis of Violent Crime (NCAVC), and the FBI Academy.

Now It's Your Problem

The public expects you—whether you employ three or three hundred thousand people—to understand the basics of threat assessment when your company is faced with possible workplace violence.

You're saying to yourself: What? I have no training in criminology or forensics, and I'm certainly not a licensed psychologist! How can I possibly know if someone could pose a threat to my workplace? The good news is that you can learn from case studies about how to evaluate the *probability* of violence. Here are some basic facts to consider:

A violent past is the single best predictor of future violence—period.

- A violent past is the single best predictor of future violence—period. "When an individual has a past conviction for a robbery, or if they were a victim of abuse as a child, they may be more prone to violence in their adult years, because evidence suggests that being abused can have a lifelong, negative impact," notes Alan Jaffee, Psy.D., a Chicago-based clinical psychologist who evaluates threatening behavior. "That's why all job applicants should be prescreened by an outside agency that will investigate their background to determine if they have ever been arrested or convicted of a crime. It's not fail-proof, but it's better than having no screening," he adds.

- An employee's interest in and access to weapons are certainly critical factors. "If an employee mentions that they want to see a knife in someone's back, or you hear that they were arrested at a local pub after a brawl last Friday night, it may be time for human resources to interview the subject and decide what to do. In some cases, you may be charged with negligent retention," notes Dr. Friedman of Northwestern University. "Managers need to listen, document, and follow up—if you know or suspect there may be a threat, you may have a burden to act on that knowledge," he adds.

- Even physical appearance should be considered as you view the mosaic of the perpetrator. For instance, many persons who are contemplating suicide provide physical warning signs to those around them in the days immediately preceding their act. They may give some prized personal items away to friends or mention that "it's over" to a family member. In many cases, these at-risk persons stop caring about personal hygiene and will not shower or shave in the days immediately preceding a suicide attempt. Prominent persons who previously enjoyed

positive public relations and who face humiliation or
embarrassment are at a higher level for depressive moods that
can lead to suicide. James Forrestal, secretary of defense to
president Franklin D. Roosevelt, jumped 16 stories to his death
at Bethesda Naval Hospital in Maryland on May 22, 1949. He
had been observed by the U.S. Secret Service in the period
leading up to his suicide to be in depressive and lethargic states;
president Roosevelt's successor, Harry S. Truman, had forced
Forrestal to resign two months before his death. Another case
in point: After Japan's agriculture minister killed himself on
May 28, 2007, amidst accusations that he defrauded the
government of over $236,600, friends stepped forward and
spoke to the news media. Several said that Toshikatsu
Matsuoka, who was 62 when he committed suicide, had not
returned phone calls in the days preceding his death, had
looked depressed, and was almost catatonic to most friends in
private.

"Over the past 30 years I've evaluated thousands of
individuals, and those who committed suicide inevitably shared
signs with family members and coworkers, but most of the time
their family or boss would turn to me and say, 'We missed those
signals,'" notes Dr. Friedman. Research also suggests that we
should consider the role that heat and humidity play in violent
behavior, especially in self-inflicted violence. The hotter the day,
the higher the humidity level, the more intense the anxiety level
of those who may be contemplating violence against themselves
or someone else. There's good reason to factor the weather into
the threat assessment process—just ask any police officer. Law
enforcement officials will tell you that domestic crime, violence
at work, and even self-mutilation can increase exponentially in
direct correlation to extreme heat.

These are just a few factors for you to consider when assessing an
individual's potential for violence. Although there's no single best
model for proper assessment, there are empirical findings that can
help you understand the dynamics of threats at work—and you
should know them. According to the U.S. Occupational Safety and

Health Administration (OSHA), employers are expected to offer awareness programs regarding the four primary types of workplace crimes:

1. Those crimes committed by an individual who has *no connection* to the workplace, such as a homicide during a robbery
2. Aggression *targeting employees* perpetrated by customers, clients, patients, students, inmates, or any others for whom you provide a service or product
3. *Worker-against-worker* violence, such as between a manager and his or her subordinate, or between a former employee who returns with the intention to injure a former supervisor
4. Aggression stemming from a *personal relationship*, such as a former business partner who returns to the work site to seek revenge for a financial disagreement

Understanding Threats

Once a manager is aware that a problem employee is exhibiting disturbing behavior, a threat assessment team should review several key issues in a timely manner. You should begin by:

1. Evaluating specific content of the threat. Is it credible? Does it explicitly suggest intent to do harm?
2. Reviewing the capacity, skill set, and mental state of the person posing the threat. Who is this person? Where are they now? *How* are they?

Your human resources manager and security director may want to work with law enforcement officials to better understand the perpetrator's personality and character traits. Sometimes a coworker will share with you bits of information, such as, "My coworker Jeff is undergoing major stress. His divorce is going badly and he's losing the custody battle for his children." By itself, such a statement may not be a warning signal. But personal loss, the diminishment of self-esteem, and the erosion of work performance could make people say and do extremely uncharacteristic things. When you then hear, "Jeff told a coworker at lunch that he'll kill his wife if it means he loses his kids," your evaluation should move to code red. If Jeff has a serious mental illness or has chosen to go off his medication, only a trained team will be able to determine the most appropriate next steps.

Two leading researchers, R.A. Fien and B. Vossekuil of the U.S. Department of Justice, Protective Intelligence and Threat Assessment Investigation, tell us in their informative study, "A Guide for State and Local Law Enforcement Officials" (1998), that:

1. Some individuals who *make* threats ultimately *pose* threats
2. Many individuals who *make* threats *do not pose* threats
3. Some individuals who *pose* threats *never* make threats

Read these sentences a few times, and slowly, until you understand their nuances.

It should be noted that even when a person has no intention to do harm and merely verbally expresses a threat, others could still be psychologically harmed by the enormous fear that such a threat could elicit. When an employee tells you that he or she feels as though a coworker may do him or her harm, my recommendation is that you take their comments seriously and act on the warning. Document what this person has said and the responsive actions you are taking. Involve law enforcement officials when appropriate. Think about your Duty to Care, Warn, and Act. As stalking expert Gavin De-Becker notes in his book *The Gift of Fear*, listen and react to your intuition. If you see a customer or coworker in distress and his or her actions or statements suggest to you that that person may cause harm to him- or herself or others, seek the aid of an expert who can help.

I have been called by threat assessment teams in dozens of cases in which an employee or contractor began to seriously disturb the organization with threats or actions that were increasingly violent in tone. In many cases, someone on the team will say, "We should have called you earlier. We knew he was spiraling out of control. He's been increasingly agitated, he leers at people with eyes of steel, and he's been making threats that at first we didn't take seriously. Now we feel he's out of control." Listen to your intuition as these teams did, but do so earlier.

One of the most profound examples in which the bell of intuition was sounded but ignored occurred at the Fulton County Courthouse in Atlanta, Georgia, on March 11, 2005.

You may recall the case: Brian Nichols was on trial for rape when he overpowered a female deputy in his basement holding cell. Nichols had been in and out of two buildings—one was the jail, the other the adjacent courthouse—throughout his trial on at least 10 different occasions over the course of a 10-day period, allowing him ample opportunity to scout out the vulnerabilities of those overseeing his detainment. On the day that he executed his plan, Nichols seized the officer's weapon, went across the street to the courtroom where he had been on trial, and then killed the judge, the sheriff's deputy, and the court reporter that were working on his trial.

As the city panicked and grappled with an intensive search to find the perpetrator, Nichols took a woman hostage and eventually let her go, but only after she negotiated with him for hours in a smart, calm manner. The hostage, Ashley Smith, told Nichols that she was a widow with a five-year-old daughter; she politely submitted to his requests to talk about life and what he had just done. Rather than pass judgment or act scared, she offered empathy. She told police that the defining moment in her ordeal was when she asked Nichols for permission to read the Bible and a second book, *The Purpose-Driven Life*. He allowed her to do so. On CNN, Smith recounted her experience with Nichols:

> I said, "Do you believe in miracles? Because if you don't believe in miracles—you are here for a reason. You're here in my apartment for some reason. You got out of that courthouse with police everywhere, and you don't think that's a miracle? You don't think you're supposed to be sitting here right in front of me listening to me tell you, you know, your reason here?" I said, "You know, your miracle could be that you need to—you need to be caught for this. You need to go to prison and you need to share the word of God with them, with all the prisoners there."

What you may have missed if you just read the headlines was how an inmate could escape inside a secure jail, grab a weapon, enter a courthouse with a weapon, kill innocent people, and depart . . . undetected.

The day before the shooting, Nichols was in court. He was leering at the judge and court reporter, ranting about the system and spewing ugly remarks to everyone around him. The judge told the bailiff to remove the water pitcher that was in front of Nichols for fear that Nichols could pick it up and throw it at him. The judge's intuition was right—something told him that Nichols was going to assault him.

On the night of the shooting, CNN's Nancy Grace interviewed Nichols' attorney:

GRACE: You know, Barry Hazen, the judge actually spoke to you about your safety from this man.

HAZEN: Yes, he did . . . One of the last things we talked about before we went back on that Thursday into the courtroom, the judge said that he thought the people who were most at risk in the courtroom were defense attorneys, because angry defendants aren't expected to be angry at prosecutors and perhaps judges, because they were just doing their job, but if a case was being lost or you lost a case, then an angry defendant would conclude that the defense attorney did not do his or her job.

And the very last thing he said to me, he was—the prosecutors went out, and then I went out, and he was behind me. He was the last to leave. He put his hand on my shoulder, and he said to me as we walked in, he said, "Be careful."

The next day, Nichols shot that judge dead in the courtroom.

Resources

Many employers have Employee Assistance Programs (EAP) at their disposal. These companies employ counselors who claim that they are trained in evaluating at-risk employees. However, my work on numerous threat cases suggest that while many EAP counselors are excellent at managing issues involving substance abuse or

Companies need trained clinicians who are qualified risk assessors and who have some formal forensic training.

relationship dysfunction, few are clinically trained in psychology or psychiatry and thus cannot diagnose or manage cases of violent behavior or threats. They may be qualified counselors who hold a master's degree in social work, but companies need trained clinicians who are qualified risk assessors and who have some formal forensic training.

When a psychologist or psychiatrist interviews a potentially violent person, he or she can choose from a number of different models of interview techniques. But the National Center for the Analysis of Violent Crime at the FBI Academy in Quantico, Virginia, suggests the use of these questions:

- Why has the offender threatened or made comments that have been perceived by others as threatening, or why has he or she taken this action at this particular time? What is happening in his or her own life that has prompted this?
- What has been said to others (i.e., friends, colleagues, coworkers) regarding what is troubling him or her? Were the comments specific? General in tone? Were they directed to everyone, or only to certain individuals?
- Does the person feel that he or she has been wronged in some way? Has the employee filed any grievance or complaint? Has the tone of those complaints changed dramatically recently?
- Does the person feel that he or she is being treated fairly or unfairly by the organization? Is he or she beginning to focus on one department or a specific coworker or supervisor?
- Does the person accept responsibility for his or her own actions? Does he or she show any remorse for what was said or done?
- How does the offender cope with disappointment, loss, or failure? Does he or she have a genuine maturity of mind and understand that he or she causes others to be concerned for their safety?

- Is the individual concerned with job practices and responsibilities? Does he or she feel overwhelmed? Could he or she be experiencing financial or relationship stress that is making him or her feel that the world has turned against him or her?
- Has the individual received unfavorable performance reviews or been reprimanded by management?
- Is the individual experiencing personal problems, such as divorce, death in the family, health problems, or other personal losses or issues?
- Is there evidence of substance abuse, alcoholism, or mental illness/depression?
- Is there a preoccupation with violent themes, interest in publicized violent events, or fascination with and/or recent acquisition of weapons?
- Is there evidence of obsession with others or any stalking or surveillance activity?
- Does the individual have a plan for what he or she would do? Has he or she shared this with others?
- Does the offender have the means, common knowledge, and capacity to carry out the plan?

NASA Needs a Microscope, Not a Periscope

Often we think that deranged ex-felons, who drive back to their former employers in a revenge-hungry rage, are the most common type of perpetrators. The case of NASA astronaut Lisa Nowak, just like the case of football giant O.J. Simpson (who was convicted in civil court of murdering his wife Nicole Brown and her friend Ronald Goldman), reminds us that even those who project a stable personality can mask potentially dangerous desires.

Nowak, a 43-year-old mother of three, was arrested in February 2007, on charges that she pepper-sprayed, planned to kidnap, and may have intended to murder a romantic rival. She drove nearly 900 miles from Texas to Miami and allegedly wore diapers throughout her journey to minimize the time required for bathroom breaks.

Police found a steel mallet, an air gun, a knife, and rubber tubing in her car.

At first, NASA was stunned by the news report (a classic case of denial—this *can't* be happening to us) and largely shunned the media for two weeks, until investigators concluded that Nowak had dated a fellow astronaut, commander William Oefelein, up until a month prior to her arrest. What set Nowak off, according to press reports, was her interception of steamy e-mails sent by Oefelein to his new girlfriend, fellow NASA captain Colleen Shipman, while he was in space. Nowak reportedly then embarked on a plan to seek revenge on Shipman.

Although NASA has documented advice in its operating manuals on coping with a crewmember that experiences a mental breakdown in space, it lacked any such protocol about crew behavior on the ground. This case raised serious questions about NASA's pre-employment screening. It also raised concerns that NASA does not adequately monitor employee behavior before, during, and after missions. Why are astronauts allowed to send provocative e-mails from space? Are these communications monitored, and by whom? Who administered and interpreted the results of the various psychological exams given to Nowak during her initial astronaut evaluations and promotions? Was NASA aware that police had been called to Nowak's home in Texas on several occasions prior to the kidnapping attempt due to reported domestic disputes with her husband?

NASA fired Nowak three weeks after her arrest, and Oefelein departed three months later. But serious damage was done to NASA's credibility as an employer of public trust. The space agency may own the largest radar screen in the world, but it missed important signals—not in space, but on the ground.

Cassius said it best: "The fault, dear Brutus, lies not in our stars, but in ourselves."

Even though NASA has some of the most comprehensive contingency planning tools and systems in place for any imaginable engineering or technical emergency, it is like most organizations in that it tends to concentrate on those threats it knows. The death of three astronauts inside an *Apollo I* capsule in a devastating fire on a launching pad in 1967 spawned a massive organizational overhaul. Similarly, when seven astronauts died aboard the *Challenger* in 1986 as a horrified world watched on live television, the agency once again revisited safety procedures. (An engineer with subcontractor Morton Thiokol blatantly told mission control in a prelaunch memo that launching in cold temperatures could compromise the spacecraft's vital "O" ring, which potentially could lead to catastrophe.) With the case of Nowak, NASA yet again acknowledged its need to revisit its recruitment, selection, and psychological testing procedures. It is unfortunate but true that it often is only *after* we learn of a new *kind* of case that we return to those haunting questions: What did we know? What did we learn? How can we avoid this from happening again? And, in this case, What if she had done this while in space?

The consequences can be astronomical!

Watching for Signals

The U.S. Secret Service concluded in a major study that in nearly 75 percent of incidents of serious violence at schools, other students were aware the attacks had been planned *before* they actually occurred. In more than half of all cases, more than one person had expressed concern to others prior to the attack. The agency also found that over half of all perpetrators developed their plan at least one week prior to the incident. As Dr. Friedman of Northwestern University has noted, because these same findings are often also seen in violent workplace incidents, it is important for threat evaluators to speak with coworkers and others who may have *heard* the individual expressing indirect—or even direct—threats.

> In nearly 75 percent of incidents of serious violence at schools, other students were aware the attacks had been planned *before* they actually occurred.

Ponder this: Most people who are likely to commit violence rarely act without signals. The person will tell someone, leave a note, make a sarcastic remark, or post a statement on a blog. These communications sometimes *specifically identify a target* before the act occurs. In fact, studies suggest that perpetrators of workplace violence communicate their intentions to friends or coworkers in advance over 80 percent of the time.

When five girls were systematically assaulted and murdered at an Amish schoolhouse in Nickel Mines, Pennsylvania, in 2006, we again learned that violence can happen at any location, no matter how remote it is. Violence is obviously not limited to the United States, and that merits some thoughts as well.

When I was interviewing leaders of several Japanese companies for a research project several years ago, they were quick to tell me that the Japanese loathe violence; they claimed that incidents of murder and retribution are virtually unheard of in Japan. That's great public relations, but it's also untrue. On a per capita basis, threats and violence at work and school occur at about a 15 percent higher rate in Japan than in the United States. Japanese executives also will often try to suggest that terrorism is an issue that is an exclusive menace to Europeans (such as in the case of the horrible deeds perpetrated by the Irish Republican Army) or Americans (like when Timothy McVeigh killed 168 adults and children in Oklahoma City, Oklahoma). But when you remind them that 12 people died and nearly 3,800 others became seriously ill on March 20, 1995, after the Aum Shinrikyo domestic terror group released lethal nerve gas on five trains throughout the Tokyo subway system, Japanese managers typically end the conversation abruptly. When you remind them that Japanese high school students are *six times* more likely to commit suicide than American teenagers, they end that conversation, too. And one more statistic that may interest you: The Kyodo News Agency reports that over 32,000 Japanese people commit suicide a year in a country with a population of 127 million. The American Association of Suicidology reports that about the same number—33,000 Americans—kill themselves annually in a country with a population nearly three times larger, at 301 million. Denial regarding risk exposure appears to transcend geographic borders. For many, it's simply easier to believe that while others may be forced to face these problems, *our* team, *our* community, and *our* culture is stable and safe.

Digging Deeper

There are several resources to pursue if you come across a potential threat, but there are three that may be of specific interest.

First, Robert D. Hare, professor emeritus at the University of British Columbia, has designed an effective instrument for identifying psychopaths—the *Psychopathy Checklist-Revised (PCL-R)* (2003). This instrument assesses a blend of clinical data derived from in-depth interviews and focuses on such personality traits as superficial charm, narcissism, and manipulativeness. You can read more about Hare's research in his books and on the Web.

A second evaluative instrument is the *Minnesota Multiphasic Personality Inventory (MMPI-2)*, a tool widely used by public and private employers alike. This inventory of 567 true/false questions is self-administered and can reveal to trained interpreters if the test taker harbors psychological problems. When I teach courses on violence awareness, I often show the MMPI-2 results from three individuals—mass murderer Jeffrey Dahmer, San Diego police officer Henry Hubbard (who sadistically tortured and raped women while forcing their boyfriends to watch), and a mentally stable fashion model—but I leave it to the audience to determine which profile belongs to which person. The differences are readily apparent, but only a licensed clinician could interpret the results. It's analogous to a brain cancer patient who sees his or her own MRI scan: He or she can easily identify the "problem" if his or her prior MRI shows the brain without the tumor, but only an oncologist can know the exact ramifications of the growth.

Third, you may want to read more about the landmark *MacArthur Violence Risk Assessment Study*, a decade-long journey in which numerous issues—gender, past violence, race, and other sociological factors—were studied in relation to violence. Over 1,000 adults were sampled in acute civil psychiatric inpatient facilities. Writing about this study in a 2006 issue of the *Virginia Law Review*, author John Monahan notes that if you really want to evaluate a person's propensity to violence, you should examine:

1. What the person *is* (e.g., age, gender, personality)
2. What the person *has* (e.g., job, steady partner, children)
3. What the person *has done* (activities, e.g., athletics, piloting planes, rock climbing, past robberies)
4. What has been *done to* the person (e.g., victim of bullying as a child)

An understanding of these four factors can help you determine the likelihood that a person may become violent.

Violence and Mental Health

The number of people with psychopathic personalities suggests that most of us will come across at least one psychopath during a typical day . . . they are motivated to, and have a talent for, reading people and sizing them up quickly. They identify a person's likes and dislikes, motives, needs, weak spots, and vulnerabilities. We all have buttons that can be pushed and psychopaths, more than most people, are always ready to push them. In the great card game of life, psychopaths know what cards you hold, and they cheat.

—*Snakes in Suits*, by Paul Babiak and Robert D. Hare

As Dr. Friedman of Northwestern University has written in a forthcoming book, there are many misconceptions about mental illness. He notes that research findings suggest that, out of the 7,870 people without mental disorders that were polled, only 2 percent self-reported being violent in the prior year. "But individuals with diagnoses such as panic disorders, major depression, or schizophrenia reported themselves as being violent in the previous year much more frequently—11.5 percent, 12 percent, and 13 percent, respectively."

What we can learn from this is that when employees decide to self-diagnose and abruptly end a regimen of treatment—which is a common practice among those with bipolar disorder—the results can be dangerous to those around them.

Remember, too, that substance abuse plays an extraordinary role in an individual's propensity to violence. Alcohol is a disinhibitor that can trigger aggressive impulses; cocaine and amphetamines can trigger even more intense effects. As Dr. Friedman notes, "This [information] is supported by the *MacArthur* study data, which showed that individuals carrying a diagnosis of alcohol or drug abuse or dependence were 2.7 times more probable than those without such a diagnosis to behave violently within months after release from the hospital."

When I assist threat assessment teams, one of the most complicated questions I will raise relates to what the employer knows about the perpetrator's past—and it is often remarkably little. The supervisor may be able to produce the person's application for employment, copies of his or her annual performance review, and maybe some other documentation, but consider for a moment what you *don't* know about your employees: What happened to them in the past? Do those events in any way influence their behavior today? While a licensed clinical expert may be able to provide meaningful insight into some of your employees' issues, even trained clinicians can be misled by those who are highly skilled at hiding parts of their pasts. These experts tell us, for example, that those with histories of childhood abuse are six times more likely to abuse others as an adult, but we have no way of knowing who among our coworkers is shouldering the psychological difficulties that come with such enormous suffering.

Fitness for Duty

In the case of a problem employee with truly complex issues, it may be appropriate for you to require the person to undergo an FFD evaluation. The only individual who should conduct these evaluations is a licensed clinical psychologist or psychiatrist who is experienced in workplace—as opposed to domestic—relationship disputes. The evaluator will need to interview the employee, who must voluntarily submit to the evaluation.

The subject will be interviewed in a protocol that is mindful of the Americans with Disabilities Act (ADA), the Family and Medical Leave Act (FMLA), and other similar laws. The fitness evaluator might want to consult with supervisors, human resources, and sometimes the employee's physician, if the employee provides written consent to this end.

Once the interview and evaluation are completed, the evaluator may be compelled to alert someone who is a potential target of harm, which is why having a trained expert in this arena is vital. You may be interested to know that you are required by law to place FFD reports in the employee's locked medical—not personnel—file and the reports should be reviewed only by those who have a legitimate need to know. Also, remember that if you ask an employee to undergo evaluation because you are concerned about his or her behavior or statements, he or she is entitled to review the findings of the interviewing clinician. Finally, remember that if the evaluator determines that the employee does *not* pose a threat and *is* fit to work, the employer is generally required to allow that person to return to the workplace.

> You are required by law to place FFD reports in the employee's locked medical—not personnel—file.

The FFD report needs to be carefully worded so as to avoid language that may humiliate the employee. Evaluators should be very aware of how detailed an FFD report should be, and they need to be careful to comment on direct observations and statements, not assumptions.

Whether you are looking into a threat on your own or turning to an expert, remember that the Equal Employment Opportunity Commission (EEOC) requires that someone evaluate the following issues if a credible threat at work surfaces:

1. The duration of the statements or behaviors that may constitute a risk
2. The nature and severity of the potential harm

3. The likelihood that potential harm may occur
4. The imminence of potential harm

You will want to assemble other information, too, including:

1. If there is an identifiable target and, if not, who the likely targets are—as well as whether and how to communicate concerns to potential targets
2. The nature of the relationship between the employee and those with whom he or she is upset
3. If the employee is familiar with the daily work and personal schedules of those he or she are harassing
4. The extent to which your employees are vulnerable to an attack; you may want to suggest that potential victims relocate to a different work site from the one in which they have been targeted by a problem employee to reduce the likelihood that they will be successfully harmed
5. Whether the target individual, family members, or coworkers expressed fear of the employee, as well as the factual bases for such fear

Case Studies

What management teams do—or fail to do—can differentiate both the individuals at the helm as well as the organizations they represent from their competition. Here are a few composite cases that highlight issues of Duty to Care, Warn, and Act that are reflective of the kinds of calls I frequently receive. The names of the individuals and organizations have been changed, but the events and sequencing are detailed precisely as they unfolded.

Case One: A State of Denial

Katherine Keebow is the director of the Burlington Housing Authority (BHA), a public agency that provides some 400 units of elderly housing and over 850 units of family-based subsidized housing to her community. The BHA employs over 60 full-time administrative and maintenance workers.

An anonymous letter crosses Keebow's desk indicating that her chief of engineering, Frank Williams, was convicted of murder more than 20 years ago and that he spent time in jail for his crime. In fact, the authority was his first employer post-jail, where Williams began as a maintenance assistant and worked his way up through the organization.

Keebow advises the BHA board members of the letter, and they ask her to hire an investigator to conduct a background search on Williams. What emerges from that report is startling, disturbing, and all too real. When he was 19, Williams was indeed convicted of killing a fellow student at the community college he attended. He then spent 11 years in prison. Upon his release, he applied for work and was employed by the BHA. Because his first position was as a part-time maintenance assistant, he was employed without a formal application (where questions about his criminal background could have been asked and documented) or background check.

Following the advice of her legal counsel, Keebow determines to meet with Williams to discuss the issue at hand. Although he served his time in jail for his crime, she is concerned that the company will be accused of negligently retaining Williams, now that she is aware of his murder conviction. This is particularly true, given the consideration that in his senior post of chief of engineering, Williams is often inside the homes of BHA tenants. She is concerned that if his temper were to flare up, he might become violent, even though his record with the BHA is unblemished.

"I'm not sure what options we have," she tells the board of the BHA.

"If we put him on leave because he didn't inform us of his crime, I'm sure he could have a case against us. If we terminate him for failure to disclose his crime, we probably would be unable to defend our decision, because we never explicitly asked if he had a criminal conviction. We could offer him a buy-out, but that seems to put us at high risk for a media exposé. We just need direction."

The board spends three weeks in confidential meetings pondering its best course of action. A second anonymous letter then appears on Keebow's desk; this one informs the BHA that Williams has a gambling problem and frequents Atlantic City casinos at least every other weekend. Because his salary is somewhere in the vicinity of $79,000, the writer questions whether he steals equipment from the storage garage at the BHA and sells it at flea markets on weekends to generate the requisite cash to fund his gaming habits. "You have poor controls and no security, Katherine," the writer notes. "We know it as employees. Why are you so ignorant, and why do you fail to act?"

Given the facts, anonymous claims, Williams's past criminal record, and the other facets of the case, what would you do?

CASE RESOLUTION

The board of the BHA engaged labor counsel, who suggested that the BHA most likely was culpable of negligent hiring, as formal applications for both full- and part-time employment have been a standard practice for virtually any entity, including even the smallest of enterprises, for decades.

Significant debate ensued regarding to the location that would be used for the dialog with Williams. Since he had served time for his sentence, the decision was made to ignore the issue of that crime, since it had no relevance to his current role with the company. Although he may have had a theoretical obligation to inform the BHA of his criminal record, the fact that he was not specifically *asked* about past criminal acts meant that he had not lied.

Complicating matters was Williams's stellar job performance, which varied, depending on the year, from good to excellent.

The board determined that the most prudent route was to investigate the allegations made in the second letter to determine if Williams was selling BHA property on eBay or at flea markets to generate extra income. The board members were deeply concerned that the violent tendencies Williams had exhibited in his past would emerge when and if accused of a breach in ethics. The board struggled for no less than six hours in an executive session to determine whether it had a Duty to Care and, if so, how to exercise that duty.

"We can decide to retain him, but if we do, I want it on the record that I was against this course of action and that we are placing the community at risk," noted one board member. Another board member had a different perspective: "We are acting on a phantom complaint and potentially ruining someone's life who already has paid his debt to society. We should focus on his work performance and *not* act on petty accusations." Yet the executive director of the BHA brought forward two important considerations:

1. Williams's violent history was not only a matter of public record, but it was now also a matter of record at this employer due to the anonymous letter. A Duty to Care was triggered once the employer verified that Williams had a violent past.

2. A negligent retention claim, followed by massive negative publicity, was likely to emerge if Williams ever became violent again. The board's judgment could easily be called into question.

In the end, a compromise was reached. The director approached Williams regarding early retirement, and he was offered a six-month severance package if he resigned. He was given 21 days to make his decision. He was candidly told that information had surfaced regarding his past *and* suggesting his possible theft of company equipment, but that, rather than hire a private investigator and subject a good employee to potentially undue embarrassment, it was in his best interest to retire. Williams accepted and signed a comprehensive release letter two days later.

Case Two: Behavior Escalation

Donald Heese is the president of the Portland Humanist League (PHL), a 501 3(c) nonprofit that specializes in raising money for families who have recently lost a child to suicide. Heese began the charity in 2001, after his son took his life. The PHL raises an excess of $870,000 per year, mostly from banquets, silent auctions, and sales from a book that Heese authored—titled *Cast in Stone*—which explains how his own failure to seek professional assistance for his son led to a terrible outcome.

Heese is somewhat of a community hero in the greater-Portland area. He frequently speaks on local talk shows about at-risk youth, and he also authors a column in the local alternative weekly newspaper about parents and teens. His health in recent years has been declining; at the age of 71, Heese has hinted that he will soon retire from his post as president, a position for which he receives a stipend of $38,000 per year and reports to an independent board.

In recent weeks the board has been concerned about Heese, including his appearance and demeanor. At a recent board meeting, he demanded that the board establish a 403(b) retirement program for him because, as he said, "I don't have a retirement program and have given many years to this place. I need to do better. You need to help me." When the board informed Heese that the PHL was created to serve the public need for suicide information, not for personal gain, and that it is not a traditional employer (he receives no medical or other benefits and has never asked for them), Heese exploded.

"Are you crazy? I started this organization! This is my baby. If my son hadn't taken his life, we'd have no PHL, nor would we have a board. I cultivated all of you! I want and expect this, and I expect it funded in the next two months. I plan to retire in five years, and a retirement package will at least give me something to show for all of this." At one point he was seen weeping at the meeting. His outburst generated genuine concern among board members that other issues—possibly psychological in nature—were adding to Heese's erratic behavior.

One of the board members suggested that the PHL seek an FFD evaluation of Heese. Other members of the board believed that the FFD could conclude that Heese was of very sound mind and should be retained, or that his recent behavior was merely due to financial unpreparedness for retirement. One board member in particular expressed his deep anxiety: "Heese told me on the phone that if we don't start his retirement program, he'll quit the PHL, start a competing nonprofit, and bad-mouth us to the United Way and other charities and donors that sponsor us. He is full of spite and anger. I'm truly at my wit's end trying to figure out what to do."

Now it's up to you: Determine an appropriate course of action for the PHL and for Heese.

CASE RESOLUTION

Board members have a difficult role, especially when the administrator that personally cultivated them to serve in their positions presents him- or herself as a company liability. And while nonprofits face many challenges that don't encumber most for-profit companies, they are dealt one further blow by the fact that they rarely incorporate threat awareness processes into their infrastructures.

In this case, the board had a strong chairperson who, despite her tremendous admiration for Heese, felt that there were important issues that the board needed to consider:

1. Heese was undergoing significant emotional stress. Although there were no clinicians on the board, it was clear that he was on the verge of a potential mental breakdown, if not a financial one. The board felt it was imperative that someone intervene in a timely manner. The chairperson was especially adamant, however, that the organization not "cave in" to any extortion attempts by Heese. "If we approve this package now, he will ask for more. This could become viral. Our duty is to our donors, not to any employee, regardless of his accomplishments."

2. Other board members weren't so sure. Heese was a public figure, even though he was known to be somewhat of a bully to volunteers and others over the years. "If he is sick, we should seek an FFD examination and then decide," commented a long-term board member whose daughter had committed suicide the same year as Heese's son. Although Heese was his friend, he felt that a medical evaluation was necessary to ensure that the PHL had acted in a comprehensive, rather than hasty, manner.

The chairperson of the board phoned Heese at home and informed him that he was being placed on suspension pending the outcome of a required FFD evaluation. He was encouraged to cooperate with the evaluation. During her conversation with Heese, however, he launched a variety of racial slurs at the chairperson and indicated that he would not participate in any evaluation by a clinical counselor. "He basically said that he would end the PHL and then sue each of the board members for failure to honor a series of verbal promises that he claimed had been made over the years regarding his retirement," she reported.

There were no files or evidence to support Heese's claim that he had been promised retirement benefits. To be sure Heese's allegations were untrue, the board commissioned an independent auditor to contact all past board members and inquire if any of them were aware of any such promises. Each person responded that no such promises were ever made to Heese.

A few days after the uneasy call between Heese and the board chairperson, the editor of the local newspaper called the chairperson, indicating that Heese was reporting to the paper that the board had fired him. The chairperson responded that this was not the case but that she could not discuss the circumstance further because this was a personnel matter. She went "off the record" with the editor—a process not recommended by press experts—and the editor said he would hold off on publishing the story as long as possible so as to refrain from exacerbating any amount of mental strain Heese was undergoing.

The chairperson of the board decided on a bold move. She contacted Heese's daughter, Sharon, and informed her that the board was concerned about Heese and that she felt he should be evaluated by the family physician. "He has a problem, but I'm not a physician. You need to get him seen immediately. He is saying and doing things that are irrational." The daughter, who lived out of state, was grateful and indicated that although her dad had been on lithium (a prescription mood stabilizer) for years, he had completely gone off his medication several weeks prior. She indicated that this was the third time he had experienced bouts of depression, anxiety, and potentially violent outbursts. All of this stemmed, she believed, from the death of her brother.

Heese refused treatment and intervention. Over the next three weeks, the board tried repeatedly through social service agencies, mental health agencies, the local police, and family members to get professional help for this individual who had previously been celebrated as a community champion. In the meantime, Heese began a bizarre letter-writing campaign to the governor, the commissioner of banking, each member of the board, the local newspaper, and, for unclear reasons, the Federal Deposit Insurance Corporation (FDIC) in Washington, D.C.

Heese took his own life about a month into this tragic saga. To this day, the case remains baffling and emotionally traumatic for virtually everyone who knew and worked with Heese.

When it sought a grant from a major foundation, the PHL decided to use this case as an example of why its mission should be expanded to include not only those managing grief after the loss of a child, but also to increase awareness about at-risk adults.

The grant request is now pending.

3

THREAT AND VIOLENCE RESPONSE MODEL

Many organizations informally assess threats and reports of violence through their human resources, legal, or security departments. Regardless of the person responsible for organizing the threat assessment team in your organization, the methodology shown in the attached model will help your crisis management team with milestone decisions and options. Remember that those involved in assessing threats or actual cases of criminal activity should document key decisions after speaking with legal counsel just in case situations warrant a change in case management.

This model can be used as a guide to ensure that you document milestone decisions made by your team. As I often tell teams that call me during an emerging threat, the most important component of this model appears in the first box: Always ask yourself whether the situation could deteriorate to a point of severity.

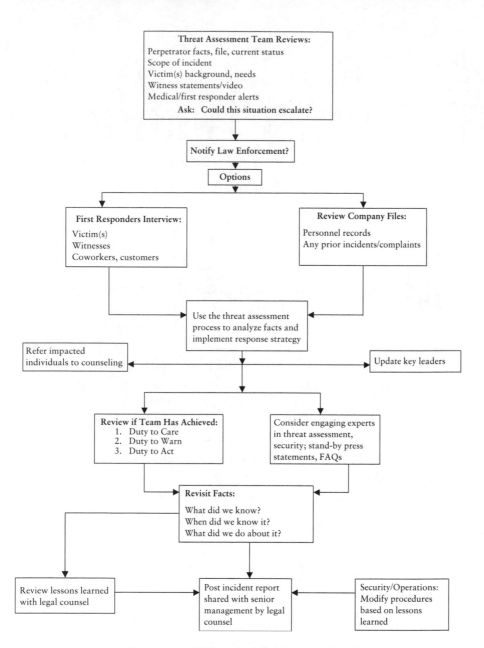

Threat and Violence Response Model

The flowchart contains the following elements:

Threat Assessment Team Reviews:
Perpetrator facts, file, current status
Scope of incident
Victim(s) background, needs
Witness statements/video
Medical/first responder alerts
Ask: Could this situation escalate?

↓

Notify Law Enforcement?

Options

First Responders Interview:
Victim(s)
Witnesses
Coworkers, customers

Review Company Files:
Personnel records
Any prior incidents/complaints

Use the threat assessment process to analyze facts and implement response strategy

Refer impacted individuals to counseling ← → Update key leaders

Review if Team Has Achieved:
1. Duty to Care
2. Duty to Warn
3. Duty to Act

Consider engaging experts in threat assessment, security; stand-by press statements, FAQs

Revisit Facts:
What did we know?
When did we know it?
What did we do about it?

Review lessons learned with legal counsel

Post incident report shared with senior management by legal counsel

Security/Operations: Modify procedures based on lessons learned

4

NEGLIGENT HIRING AND THE ROLE OF HUMAN RESOURCES

When I began my journey into corporate debacles, I never would have envisioned encountering so many companies experiencing negligent supervision or retention problems. After all, most of the companies I was working with were stable. Thirty years ago, few employers admitted publicly that they had problem colleagues in their ranks, and society was more focused on corporate environmental abuse than on employee malfeasance.

Even though people haven't fundamentally changed over the decades, technological advances, like the Internet and camera phones, certainly give us a better periscope through which to observe bad behavior, both on and off the job. Now we have definitive proof that actor Mel Gibson slurs Jews when under the influence of alcohol and that celebrity David Hasselhoff is a bad drunk. We also know that numerous scandals in recent years surfaced because information that employers thought was confidential became public.

That's what British Petroleum (BP) learned in May 2007, when CEO John Browne resigned just as he was about to be "outed" as gay. The BP board wasn't particularly upset about Browne's sexual orientation, as his preference for men was reportedly generally assumed in Britain's social and business hierarchy. What the board members were upset about, however, was that Browne refused to acknowledge his relationship with another man under oath after questions surfaced regarding his use of corporate funds for trips and other expenses related to that relationship. No one should care if

Browne is straight or gay; what matters is that he lied in a court of law, and that precipitated calls for him to accelerate his already-announced retirement. Once again, a stellar career as an executive was marred not by technical incompetence or embezzlement, but rather by one's false perception of immunity from organizational intervention. Just as an individual with a substance abuse problem needs a formal intervention to prevent him or her from destroying his or her life and the lives of others, many executives find themselves in situations in which they would benefit from organizational intervention. In the case of BP, Browne's embarassing departure could have been prevented by earlier intervention on the part of its board. In his analysis for a 2007 issue of *Business Week* of Browne's departure, Yale professor Jeffrey Sonnenfeld blasted the BP board for its tardiness in intervening:

> Painfully, we have seen other boards sit by when the actions of once revered but now underperforming CEOs do not match their rhetoric. Consider when Home Depot's board [members] last year suspended their judgment when CEO Robert Nardelli stopped reporting core retail metrics like same-store sales, dismissed wilting customer loyalty and employee morale, and even recommended directors skip the annual meeting . . . In other meltdowns of Hewlett-Packard's Carly Fiorina and Morgan Stanley's Phil Purcell, boards were slow to act. Now, pious condemnations of Browne's lying about his lifestyle abound, but more-relevant indicators of a need for board intervention were blissfully ignored.

To help immunize you against a future problem, I want you to promise to do five things from this day forward in your interactions with the people who work with and for you:

1. You will interview each new candidate for an executive position at least twice, and at least two people will interview each person in detail so you can compare notes about what was heard and observed.

2. You will conduct a thorough criminal, financial history, and sexual predator background check on each new hire.

3. You will ask a key interview question, which I'll share with you in a moment. I promise it will change the way you look at every candidate.

4. Once you get a "sniff" that someone already on your payroll is a potential problem, you'll promptly investigate allegations with an open mind. If those allegations are found to be true and serious, you'll boot the rascal to the street. If the case merits, prosecute the person.

5. If you sit on a board and signals emerge that a current leader that you employ has possibly engaged in malfeasance or behavior that is contrary to your core principles and stated values, hire an independent investigator to discreetly examine the allegations. If the person catches wind that he or she is being investigated, applaud and reward the person, and indicate to him or her that you are impressed with how he or she is dealing with gutless and anonymous attacks on his or her character. And when you find that you have employed a scoundrel, throw the person out.

Now, that's not a lot to ask, is it?

An Insightful Interview Question

Over the years I have worked to refine a question that employers could use during interviews that may provide unique insight into whether the candidate holds grudges, has any pending grievances, or is a "good fit" for the organization.

It's taken many years and feedback from a number of wonderful companies to come close to perfecting a question that you may consider as part of your interview protocol. Here's the question, and then I'll tell you why so many companies are now using it:

Tell me about a highly stressful situation involving a former co-worker and how you resolved it.

Now, at first glance, this is hardly a magical question. But let's look deeper.

If you find that the candidate says something such as: "I've never had any stress with a coworker in any job, ever!" they're probably lying. Who among us hasn't found some coworker to be a source of aggravation?

If it takes the candidate a few minutes to ponder a response and what he or she says is reasonable (e.g., "Well, I was once mad at my human resources manager because it took him six weeks to fix my relocation expense check"), the candidate might be a safe choice. Decide whether the candidate harbors any animosity (e.g., the candidate adds: "And I'd kill that payroll clerk if I ever ran into him at the supermarket!"). The key point is that you'll receive some insight into what the candidate considers to be a stressful situation. In most cases the responses to this question will be interesting but hardly dramatic. And that's precisely how you want this question to be answered: no surprises, no anger, no drama.

There are two remaining aspects to this question that are important, however. Remember that you are asking the person: How did you resolve it? Was there resolution?

Sometimes you may learn about a grudge that has continued even years after an initially stressful event. But the most interesting aspect of the question appears in its first two words: *tell me*. It's important you phrase it this way because it is assumptive; it implies that each of us has probably encountered some unpleasant coworker with whom we have had some difference of opinion. If you phrased it differently (e.g., "*Have you* ever had a highly stressful situation involving a former coworker? Was it resolved?") you are likely to hear a person say something like: "No, I've been so *blessed* in my career! I've never found anyone to be distasteful." Hogwash.

The magic to succeeding with this question is that it should be embedded into your interview protocol right in the middle of your discussion. Think about it: If you asked such a question at the beginning of your discussion, there is no established sense of trust between you and the candidate and candor will be minimal. If you ask it at the end of the interview, the topic ends the conversation on a potentially sour note. Thus, I'd recommend that you ask it in the middle, after you have developed some rapport, and you may gain wonderful insight into the attitude of this candidate toward work and conflict resolution.

Finally, I just have to share a true example of what you may learn by asking this question. A senior director of human resources who has worked with me over the years called me one day a few years ago, and he relayed to me how an interview from the day before went:

> Larry, you won't believe this. We asked your interview question to this candidate for an assistant store manager job. Most of the time we find the answer is predictable, but yesterday we had a pretty bizarre lady who was meandering her way through the interview. She thought we loved her and that the interview was going so well—she was really convinced she had the job. When we asked the key question, she said she had a miserable relationship with her boss, who was a bully, and over a three-year period, whenever she had the time and opportunity, she pissed in his coffee!

What? Ah . . . how do you extract yourself from that conversation? As that human resources director said, the two people conducting the interview had to compose themselves and find a polite way to wrap up that conversation and move on to their next interview. Next candidate!

Try it . . . ask that question . . . and, just as police have learned through the art of interrogation, the more questions you ask, the more information you may learn. But also remember: If you ask, you had better be prepared for the answer!

I can't emphasize this enough: Be thorough in your interviews. After all, isn't that what your customers, employees, and community leaders would expect of you? Imagine a day sometime in the future when you have to face a barrage of nasty reporters, all of whom are clamoring to ask: "Are you saying you only interviewed your chief medical officer just once?" Or, "You hired a supervisor at your day care facility without conducting a multi-state sexual predator search?" Or how about, "You determined that your admissions officer lied on her resume and you still retained her?"

Just a Nice Country Day School

You've now received several reminders about the necessity of conducting a thorough background check on new employees. But somehow (and I know this will come as a surprise to you) the knuckleheads responsible for budgeting will often tell you that an interview is sufficient and that the $80 cost of criminal checks is just too much money, given the number of applications your company processes each year. I'll agree that it's a lot of money in aggregate, but my suggestion is that you hire firms to conduct these reviews on each and every applicant to whom you are about to make an offer. You're about to begin a relationship that could extend for years, even decades. Do you really want to forgo the opportunity to discover whether this person has a checkered past?

You may want to ask some folks in the Bronx, New York, if they share my views. On May 24, 2007, police arrested an ex-con, Eileen Koranteng, 51, who served as the school accountant for Riverdale Country School, an upscale private institution whose alumni include former president John F. Kennedy.

Koranteng allegedly stole over $500,000 from Riverdale over the course of several years in an "audacious scam by skimming money from tuition checks, fundraisers, donations, the bookstore, and even the cafeteria," reported *The New York Post*. And (I love this) at one point in time during her tenure, she told her bosses she had cancer and needed five months for rest and recuperation whereas, in reality, she used the time to serve a five-month house arrest sentence for stealing about $100,000 in Medicaid funds from a former employer.

My calls to Riverdale were never returned. All I wanted to know was: Do you require that the people who manage your tuition checks and handle cash from fundraisers be investigated and bonded before you employ them? Was a criminal background check ever conducted on this woman? When you began to notice that she was driving two BMWs, a 325i and an X5 SUV, knowing that her annual salary was $61,000, did you ever think about asking her how she managed to fund her enthusiasm for luxury cars?

I loved the school headmaster's press statement; when this alleged swindler was arrested, he said, "This is a very sad day." What I *wish* he had said was this:

> I'm angry, because this is a 100-year-old school that was built on academic integrity and rigor. Parents and students place considerable trust in us. We expect our employees to focus on education and ensuring that students come first. When someone breaks our trust, we get angry, and then we look at ourselves. We should have connected the dots earlier. We should have had better auditing controls in place.
>
> Oh, and also: We should have looked at our parking lot once and awhile, too.

Koranteng isn't alone in her alleged behavior. Many nonprofit schools and charities are susceptible to employing these characters, often because they lack strong auditing controls. In Scottsdale, Arizona, the Unified School District learned the importance of maintaining auditing controls only after police arrested 59-year-old Janet Winkler Rice. Police issued a statement informing the public that Rice had embezzled some $306,000 from the school district in 2007, writing checks from the district's trust account and depositing them into her personal checking account. She allegedly forged the names of officers who were authorized to sign the checks, deposited the money, and then enjoyed her gambling habit at local casinos.

What I really love about this case is that, in a marvelous twist of irony, Rice worked in the "risk management office" of the district. Gotta love it.

When Should a Board Intervene?

In a world where Sarbanes-Oxley and other regulatory standards of care are intended to increase directors' engagement in corporate oversight, a smart company cannot simply wish for a looming problem to go away. For months, even years, after an incident goes public, the

> After an incident goes public, the resulting embarrassment from lapses of judgment can haunt a company and impugn its reputation.

resulting embarrassment from lapses of judgment can haunt a company and impugn its reputation.

Whole Foods' CEO, John Mackey, is an excellent case in point. It was revealed in July 2007 that Mackey had spent thousands of hours during the previous eight years anonymously posting statements on blogs and in Internet chat rooms that were meant to pump up the attributes of his company. More importantly, he used a pseudonym to criticize his competition, which included Wild Oats Market, a company he later acquired; Mackey said that Wild Oats Market had, among other things, "lost [its] way" and was "floundering."

Although Mackey maintained that he never revealed any of Whole Foods' proprietary information, profound questions have emerged regarding the lack of judgment he exercised as he basked in anonymity on Yahoo!. The United States Securities and Exchange Commission (SEC) launched an investigation into Mackey's behavior, but his company and board maintained remarkably low profiles during the initial week of the controversy, even as *Bloomberg*, CBS News, *The New York Times*, and many other reputable media outlets asked numerous questions, including, most particularly, "What will you do about it?"

Among the many options that the board of Whole Foods had at its disposal was placing Mackey on paid or unpaid administrative leave until the SEC investigation was complete. The board also could have issued a statement indicating that, while Mackey's actions were inappropriate, he did not appear to be in violation of any law, and that it was disappointed in his lapse of judgment. Any or all of these statements, if made publicly, would have conveyed the message that the board cared about its consumers and Whole Foods as well. Members of the board also could have issued a collective apology to Wild Oats, indicating that they expected more of their CEO, who was supposed to act as a role model to the rest of the company. Instead, silence prevailed from a company whose entire franchise is built around goodness, greening, and ethical stewardship. It's a bad pun, really, but just where were these yahoos?

Oversight boards need to examine whether retaining an executive during such a debacle is prudent. Any executive in the midst of scandal is owed due process. As we know from the fiasco at Duke University, where several student athletes were inappropriately charged with rape in 2006, sometimes a race to judgment is unfair, and hastily made determinations can be costly. But placing an executive on leave when your publicly traded company is under such intense scrutiny is a feasible option, at a minimum.

An Executive Fight Club

One of my clients called a few years ago for guidance on firing a senior vice president who had engaged in road rage that morning. Although the exec had given more than 20 years of exemplary service to the company, the person he followed at high speed just happened to work in his building. Company surveillance cameras caught the senior vice president just as he was about to take a punch at his 20-something-year-old software programmer. The vice president was properly exited that day for violating the company's code of conduct.

As you've seen elsewhere in this book, don't assume that workplace violence is uniquely American or one that emanates only from young, inexperienced workers. In Korea, for example, people's violent behavior is affecting the country's workplaces, just as it is in China and Japan. When 22-year-old college student Kim Dong-won emerged from a brawl inside a Seoul karaoke bar in March 2007, he needed 13 stitches to close the gash in his forehead. The story might have ended there had his father, Kim Seung-youn, not been the CEO of Hanwha Life Insurance Company, a mammoth conglomerate with over US$23 billion in annual sales. After his son was injured, police accused Kim's father of hiring a dozen brutes to seek revenge on those who reportedly had hurt his son. It turns out that the CEO and his entourage concocted a plan to brutally beat the alleged perpetrators;

eventually as many as 25 people were implicated in the planning of this massive, retaliatory brawl.

Hanwha owns the second largest life insurance company in Korea, as well as numerous hotels and a professional baseball team. After his arrest, the elder Kim called himself a "foolish father," but critics writing on various Korean blogs refused to let him off easy. Soon the media encouraged widespread boycotts of Hanwha, causing the company's finances to nosedive. Perhaps the most important lesson to learn from Hanwha's plight is that negligent retention can occur when any entity retains a problem employee, even if that employee is an executive. What I really love about this story is the fact that between March 2007 and May 2007, while boycotts were being organized and the Hanwha brand was getting trounced throughout Korea, the company declined to comment publicly on the incident and instead hoped that this crisis would pass. Eventually the spokesperson for Hanwha shared this epiphany with *The Wall Street Journal*: "If this lasts a long time, we may need to set up an emergency management system."

Say what?

Effectively Managing the Downsizing Conversation

Psychologists have written that the death of a child or spouse, the loss of a job, and a separation from a spouse are among the worst possible moments of a person's life. You are about to share one of those three messages with one of your employees—that he or she is being laid off. With care, rehearsal, and confidence, you will navigate this difficult task well.

Be sure that any objects that could be used during a moment of anger have been cleared out of the room, including staplers, phones, and paperweights.

1. When you meet with the employee, do so in a room where *you* are located closest to the door, and where a package of severance materials is already laid out for the employee in front of the chair in which you'd like the

person to sit. In front of you should be a pad of paper and a "cheat sheet" of notes for yourself. Be sure that any objects that could be used during a moment of anger have been cleared out of the room, including staplers, phones, and paperweights.

2. If you feel that the person with whom you are meeting could become angry or hostile, ask your security team to wait nearby, within hearing distance of the conversation. The vast majority of separations are civil and sad discussions, but some, although rare, can turn violent. By anticipating a discussion that could become difficult, however, you are being prudent. If you feel, as a result of your discussion, that the person has demonstrated a capability to harm others and is desirous of revenge, promptly alert your security team and the proper law enforcement officials.

3. I have a general standard that all separation discussions should last no more than seven minutes. Avoid any attempt by the employee to engage you in a long conversation or to debate with you. If the person has specific questions that require long answers, you can provide him or her with human resources' number, which the former employee can call with questions after he or she has had time to process the loss of his or her job and think about his or her specific needs.

4. Start the conversation by directly telling the person that the company is undergoing a reduction in force and that you have been assigned the unfortunate task of informing the person that his or her position has been eliminated, effective immediately. Explain and emphasize that economics, not personality or performance, was the driving factor behind this very difficult decision. Be sure to use and emphasize the word *separation* and not *termination*, since termination has a horrible connotation (e.g., terminal = liver failure, something from which there is no recovery). Tell the person that you only have a few minutes to go over the basics of the separation, and that you will be providing him or her with a phone number at the end of the conversation in case he or she is in need of additional assistance.

5. Remember that after this conversation, some people will be in denial, some will be in shock, some may start crying, and some may have no reaction whatsoever. It is virtually impossible to predict how any one person will respond, including coworkers whom you have known for years. This is an extraordinary discussion, and as such, any prior social interaction you may have had with this person can offer no foundation for comfort or predictability.

6. Expect some employees to refer to past or recent performance appraisals as a means of rebuttal during or after a separation discussion. You will want to mention that although the person's past service to the company was very good and appreciated, his or her performance is not considered during a reduction in force; this is, unfortunately, a business decision, not one based on performance.

7. Remember the five- to seven-minute rule. Each minute you spend speaking to the person beyond the seven-minute mark generally works against you. As the time you spend in conversation progresses, so too does the skepticism of the employee you are firing. He or she may attempt to bait you with provocative questions that could lead to an argumentative debate—or worse. You should begin the conversation in accordance with a set matrix of talking points; if your human resources department does not use a standardized set of conversation prompts, I have included a sample set at the end of this section for your use. Go through the talking points included on your matrix and keep a checklist to keep both of you on track. Do not divert from the script your human resources department approves unless it is absolutely necessary to do so.

8. Expect the employee to be angry, and for any number of reasons. Maybe the person has stressors at home, or maybe he or she has recently begun a relationship. Maybe he or she has recently made a large, financed purchase, or is in the midst of some life-changing event. Now, on top of everything the person is dealing with domestically, he or she must seek out new employment opportunities, a process that could take weeks, even months. All of these mixed feelings come together in a blender of "surprise," and for that reason, empathetically listen and be as supportive as possible to demonstrate to the person that you care about what he or she is going through. But be careful not to engage in a prolonged conversation about the person's home life; rather, acknowledge to the person that you recognize how disruptive the reduction of force is for him or her. There is nothing wrong—and potentially much to be gained—from stating, "I feel horrible about this, and I'm as surprised and sad as you are." While some people may retort, "Sure, but you still have a job!" the reality is that you expressed sadness, and that reflects that you're a good human being—period.

9. Some individuals may choose to threaten you—not with a gun, but with a lawsuit. They may make assertions, such as, "You always had it out for me," or, "I'm sure that Janet will have her job tomorrow, since you won't let any women go, will you?" It is very smart to ignore such inflammatory comments completely. If the person hints at an intention to sue you, you may want to say, "This is very hard on everyone involved. You can hire a lawyer, but right now I want to focus on explaining your benefits, your COBRA, and how we would like to try to help you." Stay on track.

10. If you are offering the employee outplacement services, mention this fact a few times, not just once. Astoundingly, studies show that during work dismissal conversations, people are cognizant that they are being fired, but they tend to ignore or gloss over the fact that they are being offered outplacement services. Such consultants are expensive and completely optional for you as the employer, so no matter whether you are providing a modest level of support or something more extensive, you should reemphasize the following: "This is something we worked hard to include in your benefits package, and I'd urge you to contact the outplacement firm right away. It has many resources and tools to assist you, and the consultants there are eager to get started with you." Be as affirming as possible.

11. In the unlikely event that the person with whom you are dealing is very emotional—far more emotional than you had expected or ever witnessed him or her being—you will need to consider your course of action in a timely manner. One option is to remind the individual that your Employee Assistance Program (EAP) is highly regarded, confidential, and skilled at helping people bridge the gap from one employment opportunity to the next during times of transition. Your second option, which should be exercised in those more extreme cases, is to quickly contact your security team to ensure that the person has a "shadow" to escort him or her out of the building. The shadow should carefully observe the former employee's behavior as he or she packs up and prepares to leave the building. After the person has been successfully exited from the premises, the shadow should then inform you if EAP should remain in contact with this person so as to potentially intervene in the statistically rare case that the person seeks retribution through violence. If, however, your conversation with this person leads you to believe that he or she will commit an act of violence, whether against him- or herself or others, you should contact law enforcement officials immediately and then your security team. Do not delay in these encounters.

12. Questions may emerge during your separation discussions that may be difficult for you to answer. They most likely will be legitimate questions, but this does not mean that it is the right time or that you are the right person to address these queries. For instance, a person may ask about how long pregnancy benefits can be extended post-employment, or whether he or she can cash out his or her 401(k) to help pay extraneous household bills. Regardless of the current or future strains on the employee's financial situation, take note of them during your conversation and indicate that you will look into any resources that may be available to him or her. End the conversation by informing the person that someone will call within the next few days with answers or suggestions to his or her concerns—and then be sure someone does follow up with the person. Keeping promises is never more important than during times of emotional distress.

13. A surprising number of impacted employees will demonstrate concern for the well-being of coworkers who are continuing with the company. This type of employee may ask: "How will my team do without me?" Or, "I'm worried about that project we just began. Can you be sure that no one drops the ball on that?" These questions are positive signals and generally come from a genuine person. Acknowledge the specific project and thank the person for bringing it to your attention.

14. You need to decide before the separation discussion how you will answer a very specific and legitimate question: "Who should I call if I have questions?" It is too general to simply answer, "Human resources is best." So, too, is responding, "You can call me any time," which is a very broad promise that implies your 24/7 accessibility. You and your team should decide in advance who will manage the separation questions of impacted employees. Providing the separated person with a specific name and phone number is highly advised.

15. Separating an individual is one of the most difficult tasks that any supervisor will face. To increase your comfort level during the actual separation conversation, I suggest that you role play the conversation in advance. Role playing also will allow you to talk out options and potential best answers to any question or issue that may surface. As such, if you have the time and luxury to prepare in this manner, do it.

16. It is paramount that you thank the employee for his or her contributions to the company as you close out the conversation. It may be awkward to praise someone you are laying off, but it is important that the individual knows that he or she is a good person that made a difference during his or her time with your company. Telling someone that you enjoyed working with him or her does not create any legal liability for you. It's politically smart and humane. Do it.

17. It is important that you address several specific items with the person. For example, in every employee separation conversation, you should mention that you will need to collect the person's key to the building and his or her company identification card. If the person resists, document this fact and follow up with your security team to ensure the company regained this property. This is not a tug-of-war, and these issues are best managed by your security team following the formal separation conversation. You also should inform the person that his or her e-mail and phone line will be disabled, effective immediately. The vast majority of employers disable all IT connectivity during the separation conversation to prevent the dismissed employee from going back to his or her desk and sending a company-wide defamatory note. Work with your IT team to accomplish these tasks carefully, discreetly, and in a parallel fashion.

18. You may be asked by the impacted person if the severance package that he or she is receiving is the same that all separated employees are offered. You need to review your answer to this question in advance with your human resources and legal departments. Whatever it is that you say, your answer should be honest and consistent with the statements of other managers involved in similar discussions. Inconsistencies can—and will—breed contempt by those who are being exited.

19. If the employee asks if he or she can return after work to pack up personal items, it is best to respect such a request. Be sure that members of security are available and nearby as this task is being accomplished.

20. The impacted individual may ask if you will provide a positive reference for him or her. In general, most employers today avoid serving as a reference and only will verify an employee's title and dates of employment. It is best to indicate to the individual that you do not provide professional references to anyone, under any circumstance—and be consistent with this practice. Again, if you break this rule and the person learns that you wrote positive letters of reference for others, he or she could respond negatively—and perhaps even violently. Be consistent and truthful in the management of this request.

> Be consistent and truthful.

Seven Words to Avoid

When separating a person, you must be mindful that the language you employ can be a source of comfort and reassurance, but it can also trigger anger and animosity. You've heard the phrase "choose your words carefully." This has never been truer than during a separation discussion.

In my experience of safely separating several thousand employees, I have found that it is best to avoid the following terms during a separation conversation.

TERMINATION

Refrain from conversations that follow along the same lines as: "Suzanne, I'm afraid we have to lay off several employees today, and you are among the employees that are being *terminated*. I need to go through some items with you. This will only take a few minutes." Instead, try to aim your words in this way: "Suzanne, I'm afraid that we have had to eliminate several employee positions today, and you are one of the people being separated from the company, effective immediately. I wish the news were different, but I am here to help you though the process and to explain the severance package we have designed for you." This is a radical deviation from the way employees traditionally have been separated—a way, I should mention, that has been a source of altercations.

VALUED

Steer away from statements like: "You have been a *valued* member of our team." The impacted employee most likely will feel that this statement is disingenuous. Words like this have triggered such angry reactions in the past: "Valued? Valued? I'm *valued*? But I have no job tomorrow. This is just bullshit!" The following statement is a much more viable way to go: "You have made a difference by being here, and I want you to know that." This is a much more humane way of suggesting to the impacted person that you truly appreciate his or her contributions to your workplace.

SELECTION

During the discussion, the employee may ask you, "How was I selected for this process?" It would be natural for you to respond with a statement like: "Well, our *selection* criteria included factors I can't discuss/I'm not aware of." You have no obligation to share the selection process and your compliance with such a request could even create some liability for yourself and the company. Avoid the word selection and instead emphasize that the process of separating someone is difficult for everyone. To "select" someone is individualized; a process is less so.

CANNOT

It would be natural for an employee to ask, "Can I please go around and say goodbye to everyone on the fourth and sixth floors? I've worked with these people for years." Instead of stating, "I'm sorry,

but we *cannot* allow that," it is better to respond, "We prefer that
you not do that. We need to focus on helping you pack up, and you
should begin reading the severance materials at home so that you can
start the process of moving on to your next phase in life." Try to
avoid firm, negative phrases, such as cannot or will not. "We prefer
not" conveys the same message. If people really push the issue of saying goodbye to coworkers, urge them to do that off-site.

LAYOFF

Interestingly enough, most people understand this term, but it is often associated with "mass *layoffs*"—or, in other words, the harsh decision to fire numerous employees. A further reason to avoid using
this term is that in many layoff situations, employees are given
weeks, and sometimes even a full year (especially in unionized industries), to secure work for themselves after their inevitable separation
from the company. Unless you are giving your employee generous advance notice of his or her impending separation, avoid the term for
fear of confusing the person with the immediacy of this action. If you
are asked, "How many people are being laid off?" you may want to
respond, "I don't have exact numbers in front of me, but a few dozen
people are being separated today." Although you don't want to engage in a debate over terminology, remember that the phrase to use,
if you must rely on any one, is "separation."

POLICIES

While it's true that this conversation is governed by various
policies—including your own and those of the government, for
instance—your employee may perceive your use of the term *policies*
during a separation conversation as harsh. It is common for the impacted person to be in shock during his or her separation conversation. Many won't listen to what you are saying, but when they do
listen, you want them to hear words of support, encouragement, and
empathy. When you treat this conversation as a podium from which to
refer to your company's policies, you sound and look corporate—which
also means that you sound and look indifferent to the very personal impact of this decision. Try to discuss the *process*, not the policies. Not
smart: "Our policy doesn't allow for letters of recommendation.

Sorry." Better: "We have a process in which we will be glad to verify your dates of employment and title, and we can provide more information on that later."

LOYALTY

Every company appreciates and values it, but reminding an individual about *loyalty* during this conversation could trigger an undesired response. Again, it would be natural for you to want to say, "Marilee, you've been really loyal to our company, and we know that. But we have to make cuts, and I'm afraid I have no options here." When the word is used, it is common for the person to retort, "You're full of crap. If you really valued loyalty, someone else would be here as your victim, not me." Once again, if you use this terminology, you are reminding the person that their attributes have zero value to you. Better: "Marilee, we appreciate you as a person and we're going to work very hard to help you in your transition to your next position. We have hired an outplacement firm that you can meet with as early as tomorrow morning. Let's go through some of these steps."

Cheat Sheet for Separating Employees

Make sure that you have this sheet in front of you during every separation conversation you oversee, and check the suggested steps off as you complete them. If the employee makes a specific request or unusual remark that you find disturbing or provocative, write it down to be reviewed later by human resources and your security team.

1. [Insert first name], the company is undergoing a reduction in force today and will be separating you immediately due to economic conditions.

2. This is not performance-related. I need to emphasize that. A number of positions are being eliminated.

3. I am here to help you bridge to your next position. The package in front of you has your COBRA information, details on our severance program, and the phone numbers of job and personal counselors. I'd like you to read them all carefully when you get home, but not now.

4. I need you to pack up after this conversation. You'll find boxes in your work area; let me know if you need any additional help. If you want to come back after hours, I can arrange for that, but I need to know in a few minutes when you prefer to pack up.

5. You have real skills and a real future. If you have questions, please contact the resources at the phone numbers I have provided you.

6. We only have a few minutes. Do you have any questions that I may be able to answer now?

Organizational Rebound

As a supervisor, you want to help the "survivors" of a layoff better comprehend the dynamics of change at your company after such a disruptive event. Here are some recommendations to help you prevent a business crisis from emerging if some of your valued team members resign or begin to search for work elsewhere due to perceived workplace insecurity.

1. Remember that your team will be nervous and anxious after the separations are complete.

2. Bring teams together for a five-minute debriefing session and inform them who was separated, why the company made this decision, and how sad you are about this process. Also remind them that they are members of a team of professionals, that their customers are relying on them, and that they should respect the privacy of those impacted.

3. Do share a verbal list of those who have been separated. Do not distribute the list.

4. Be sure that phone calls, e-mails, and text messages directed to the separated employees are redirected to their supervisors for a reasonable period of time following their separation.

5. Encourage the team to come together and be supportive of one another. Do not say, "There won't be any more separations," as no one can predict the future and your promise is a bond of trust.

6. It is fine to tell the group that each person was provided a comprehensive outline of company benefits, COBRA, and work placement assistance, but avoid discussing the severance packages of individual employees.

7. Encourage your team members to bring to your attention any type of communications they receive that are unusual, threatening, or bothersome. Indicate that if they cannot reach you, your security team is available 24/7 to assist them with their questions.

8. Indicate that you will hold a group meeting within the next few days to discuss the reallocation of projects and work loads, and inform your employees that you welcome their questions in private. Try to minimize groupthink and public discussion during this first group notification. Doing so will give your team time to process loss and focus on next steps.

9. It is highly recommended that you consider hosting a "rebound" debriefing for your team. It is not uncommon for your team to feel sad, distressed, and even victimized by the separations. Many will be concerned that more firings are forthcoming. Anxiety may be high, and some associates may begin to look for work elsewhere. It also is inevitable that some will find the situation amusing or use bad humor as they talk about certain separated individuals. All of these mixed emotions are part of life, loss, and recovery.

5

CRISIS PREVENTION OBJECTIVES DIAGRAM

If you're thinking to yourself, "I know *what* can happen to me, but let's get to what can I do to *prevent* these disabling events from affecting me and my company, already," take heart; in Chapter 12, we delve into a detailed explanation of the many specific measures you can take to ready yourself and your business from terrorism, workplace violence, employee sabotage—you name it. But now that you have some idea of the kinds of threats and crises that have the potential to bring your enterprise to a stand-still—and maybe now that I have scared a bit of sense into you about just how bad these worst-case scenarios can really be—it's time that you start incorporating into your thinking habits those things that you can do on an everyday basis to ensure that when your building collapses, your business doesn't fall in right alongside it.

The time to ponder the potential fallout that can come with any crisis isn't when you're in the midst of chaos; by that point in time, you'll be too busy actually *dealing* with the crisis at hand to derive any benefit from thinking about what else could go wrong. For that reason, I suggest you integrate the following four essential steps to preventing a problem from escalating into a crisis into your daily business mantra. You'll thank me later, when "it" hits the fan.

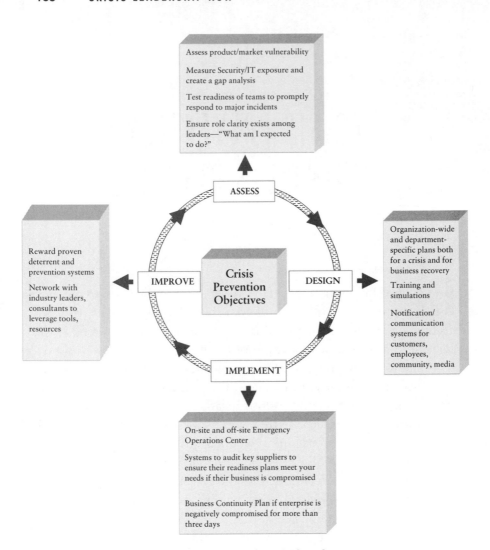

Crisis Prevention Objectives

6

MANAGING HEALTH CRISES: PANDEMICS AND VIRUSES

Most of us live in denial when we consider our vulnerability to possible pandemics: We are aware that flu outbreaks wiped out millions of people a century ago, but we expect modern medicine to rush to our aid in the event of another public health calamity.

If you think global pandemics only happen in developing countries and probably will never hit *your* doorstep, think again. This chapter will provide you with some fundamental realities.

We should look to the past for grim insights on what medical experts say is likely to happen in the future. There have been 10 pandemics over the past three centuries, the most notorious being the global flu of 1918 that killed tens of millions of people. If you fast-forward to 1976, over 400 people died near the banks of the Ebola River in the Democratic Republic of the Congo as a result of a vicious, toxic pathogen. While 400 people may seem pithy compared to the death toll in 1918, it was the *manner* in which the victims of the Ebola virus died that should make you lose sleep; some medical journals reported that the organs of some of the victims poured out of their bodies within days of contracting the virus. Some in the medical community are concerned that if such a virus were to spread again (it had a whopping 95 percent fatality rate), the impact could be unprecedented. If local officials had not immediately burned affected bodies after the initial outbreak, some scientists have concluded that it was theoretically possible that the human race could have been obliterated within three months. This is no exaggeration: It was *that bad*.

Physicians gained tremendous insight from the Ebola experience, but they remain baffled by the virus. "The mystery of Ebola is its yet unidentified reservoir in nature. The lesson of Ebola is simply that there is potential for new pathogens to emerge at any time," notes Dr. Steven Krotzer, a top epidemiologist with the Mayo Clinic. Although Ebola is bad, he adds, "Believe me: There are more horrific examples [of deadly pathogens] in tropical medicine."

There is some good news. Thanks to organizations like Doctors Without Borders and simulations managed by the U.S. State Department and the World Health Organization (WHO), physicians today engage in more cross-continent research that they did a decade ago. Most are concerned that a pandemic could be triggered by a hybrid of the notorious H5N1 virus—the influenza strain commonly called bird flu that recently has claimed victims in Turkey, Vietnam, Singapore, and elsewhere. At the time of this book's publication, the only medication that appears to temper H5N1 is called Tamiflu. Another potentially helpful drug is Relenza, and most Western governments are stockpiling both. But if a global outbreak were to occur, the stockpiles that have been built up of these drugs are most likely insufficient to prevent widespread devastation.

Whenever "it" hits—whatever "it" is—its impact on the companies we own or work for will be devastating. The flu is a virus and as such will necessitate the mass development of a specific vaccine, a process that likely will take months to complete. Antibiotics are useful, but they are only effective in treating secondary illnesses caused by the flu. What's more, their availability would likely be limited only to those who can afford them. Crossing national borders and traveling internationally could be indefinitely limited or suspended. A travel or shipping embargo could be enacted (Canada shut its borders to all international air traffic in 2003 following a bird flu outbreak) once it

Most companies have never taken the time to ask:
What if 30 percent of all of our employees become sick and incapable of working? What if customers simply stop buying our product merely because *they* are hunkered down at home?

becomes clear that the virus has infected an alarming number of victims. Despite their brief yet serious encounters with such trade restrictions, most companies have never taken the time to ask: What if 30 percent of all of our employees become sick and incapable of working? What if our products were impounded at port terminals and held for months? What if customers simply stop buying our product merely because *they* are hunkered down at home?

Even the emergence of a single case of a potentially contagious and untreatable form of tuberculosis (TB) can cause global alarm. When 31-year-old attorney Andrew Speaker, who was knowingly infected with an antibiotic-resistant strain of TB, flew to five countries on his honeymoon in May 2007, his actions potentially compromised the health of the hundreds of fellow travelers he encountered during his travels to the Greek Islands, Prague, Rome, and Paris. Speaker reportedly tried to escape identification at a U.S. airport (his passport had been flagged as a person of interest) by driving into the U.S. through Canada.

Less than two months later, the lawsuits began trickling in. Speaker's fellow passengers on his flight from Prague to Montreal filed suit on July 12, 2007, in Quebec, Canada. Their lawyer, Anlac Nguyen, representing clients from Canada and the Czech Republic, said that although his clients were not yet physically ill, serious medical problems can remain dormant for years before they emerge. "They do not have tuberculosis, but nobody can say that they won't have tuberculosis, either," Nguyen told the Associated Press. "And that will not be known—not now, not next year, but for many years in the future—so the pain and suffering that the people have gone through are real. They continue to suffer now because of the uncertainty."

Several Web sites, including those belonging to the WHO (who.int) and the U.S. Centers for Disease Control (cdc.org), provide continually updated tools to help business managers deal with potential medical crises. These data sources are understandably generic, simply because we don't know what kind of global medical calamity awaits us. Believe it or not, I'm really not much of a doomsday person, but in my interviews with clinicians, most epidemiologists acknowledge that another pandemic is likely to emerge at some point in our lifetime. Your family, neighbors, and community *will* be impacted. Hopefully we'll all survive, but to assume that industry will not be impacted is just unrealistic. It's time for a reality check.

What follows is the best available information from the WHO on how pandemics are monitored.

The left side of the chart is a teaching tool created by the WHO on pandemics, and the right side is designed to help your management team think about how it would respond once an outbreak is suspected.

Pandemic Phases	Your Organization
PHASE 1 **Pandemic Alert Period** Human infection(s) with a new subtype, but no human-to-human spread, or at most rare instances of spread to a close contact.	**PHASE 1** Employees and contractors are not yet sick. Managers begin to identify the need for "back fill" for critical positions. Vendors are asked about their contingency plan to provide critical services if situation escalates.
PHASE 2 **Pandemic Alert Period** An isolated cluster with limited transmission is highly localized. Cross-national studies underway.	**PHASE 2** Management begins to launch a stand-by employee communication plan: If this escalates, how will we manage from off-site locations? Emphasis on Web-based transactions. Telephone call lists are updated for all personnel.

PHASE 3	PHASE 3
Pandemic Alert Period	Leadership informs board of
Human-to-human	stand-by implementation
contamination remains	of pandemic plan to protect
localized but is adapting	organizational assets—
to humans. Media is	human, financial, physical.
emphasizing preparedness.	Heavy reliance on news and
Pandemic risk is growing.	medical advisories.
	Conference calls with key
	customers and suppliers.
Pandemic Phases	**Your Organization**
PHASE 4	PHASE 4
Pandemic Period	Organization implements full
General population is impacted	pandemic plan aimed at
in a significant manner with a	maintaining key functions.
serious impact on trade, travel,	Business Continuity Plans
and customer interaction.	implemented and business
Governments anticipate no	resumption plans readied.
delivery of mail,	
key services; various scenarios of	
"what if?" are publicly debated.	

Source: "Global Influenza Preparedness Plan," World Health Organization, November, 2005.

Crisis Team

A crisis team will greatly benefit your organization, both before and during any major transnational health crisis. That team ideally will be composed of those who can help you anticipate the impact of declining health on your people and operations. A number of Fortune 1000 companies already have developed pandemic plans—just in case. This doesn't mean they are fatalists; rather, it means they understand their fiduciary responsibility to protect their employees in every jurisdiction, their duty to think about how they may deploy aid to expatriates and their families living abroad, and that they likely will be notified of an outbreak only after a significant number of people have become symptomatic.

If a pandemic were to force curtailments in global trade, even for 30 days, imagine the impact: Commerce conducted via ports and worldwide rail stations could be suspended, and truck, tanker ship, and airliner traffic could be slowed or stopped. Products won't be shipped (food rots in storage), services can't be sold (your customers are home tending to the sick), and income will come to a halt (no mail or delivery service; IT servers may be on autopilot—but remember that your data recovery people are also out sick). Yet your employees will still expect to be paid, because somehow—magically!—the banks that oversee our mortgages and car payments will still expect *their* payments. *Oy vei!*

> If a pandemic were to force curtailments in global trade, even for 30 days, imagine the impact: Products won't be shipped, services can't be sold, and income will come to a halt.

How Bad Could It Get?

Pretty bad. The H5N1 subtype, or bird flu, is a contagious disease that mimics pneumonia in many ways and appears to be caused by viruses found in poultry. The virus's high fatality rate among birds alarms scientists because the secretions and feces of birds easily can be spread to the humans who handle them.

Notes *The Economist* in its January 25, 2007, issue:

The disease can lurk unnoticed in domesticated birds for long periods. It may more often be spread, including on the tires of vehicles, when poultry are sent to market . . . Millions of Asians depend on the poultry trade, and far more keep chickens and ducks in their backyards to supplement their diets, so the outbreak is already a big worry.

Now you understand why government officials in China have been paying cold, hard cash in recent years to their ornithologists to hand over dead birds. If one of these strains of H5N1 mutates into something we don't understand—and we barely understand H5N1 right now—the death toll could be catastrophic, especially among the young and elderly, as well as those with already compromised immune systems.

Will there be widespread public vaccination programs? No one knows, but even the WHO admits that there are not enough vaccines worldwide to make a meaningful difference at this time. Can't we just quarantine those who are sick? Yes—well, maybe—if the necessary space exists and if the impacted government admits that it has a pandemic on its hands early enough to forewarn the rest of the world. But you can expect that any given government may fear that once the world is aware that it has a major medical calamity on its hands, its import and export activity and income may cease. Health matters, but economics matter, too.

As is evident, a major outbreak of some strain of influenza potentially could cause more human suffering than any other event short of a nuclear attack. When you hear about an outbreak of a deadly disease somewhere in the world that is beginning to cause alarm, it may be smart to remind yourself, and all of your employees, about the basics of good hygiene. Instruct them to wash their hands frequently and avoid animals, especially birds, when you hear about a flu outbreak. Alcohol-based hand sanitizers appear to make a modest difference in killing most viruses.

Whatever happens, you will need to rapidly, aggressively, and effectively educate your public and employees. The time to think about this issue is now, since most hospitals don't have the ability to stockpile major supplies of anti-viral medications. And remember that if there is a major pandemic outbreak, those in the military, as well as health providers and first responders, such as law enforcement officers, will be the first to receive inoculations so that essential community services can be maintained. Most of us will be on our own.

Anthrax: When, Not If

Since 2004, the U.S. government has been funding Project Bioshield, a study led by a consortium of scientists, pharmaceutical specialists, and public health officials. Its aim is to stockpile upwards to 100 million doses of various vaccines to protect the public against a variety of biological agents and chemical threats, such as anthrax. Although we have seen limited use of anthrax as a biological weapon (former NBC News anchor Tom Brokaw and his senior producer were targets in 2001), an orchestrated terrorist campaign could be directed at entire communities—if not nations—of people.

As article in the June 6, 2005, edition of *Forbes* tells us:

The next attack could be far more horrific. Two hundred and twenty pounds of aerosolized anthrax spores sprayed from a nondescript truck in any U.S. city would wipe out anywhere from 130,000 to 3 million people, the equivalent of a hydrogen bomb. The scenario is considered one of the gravest bioterror threats to the United States. Victims would be utterly clueless. Anthrax is odorless and tasteless and produces early symptoms that can dupe people into thinking they have the common flu.

It's realistic to say that the use of anthrax as a terrorist weapon is likely to be tried in our lifetime. How it will be used again is anyone's guess. Public health officials around the world are actively trying to determine how to rapidly inoculate millions after the first casualties are identified. When it comes to the use of sophisticated toxins such as the nerve gas sarin or a powdered substance such as anthrax, it's fair to say that businesses will be at the government's mercy in terms of what they do, how they shut down, when they reopen, and under what conditions they do so. Other than the principal safeguards articulated here, such as having a business recovery plan and thinking about short-term support to infected employees, there is very little most of us can do other than monitor recommendations from health officials.

Now It's *Your* Pandemic

When pandemics happen in Turkey or Hong Kong, it's their problem. But when you hear the first whispers that the government is contemplating shutdowns of airports near you in response to a global outbreak of disease, then it's your problem. Whether you're self-employed (you won't be able to send a FedEx to Chicago or London) or managing a multinational (your clients are in a state of panic), the time to ponder preparedness is now, in advance, before hundreds of thousands of businesses are scrambling and competing for the same resources to help them manage the health crisis. Here is a summary checklist of issues to consider when drafting your pandemic plan. As you go through this list, be sure to think about *who* in your organization will be responsible for each of these issues and tasks.

- Identify who will "own" the logistics of communicating breaking news about the health issue to the general population so that there is a single channel of communication without contradiction.
- Determine who is currently traveling, where they are today, and whether/how they can get home if they are outside the country.
- Identify one leader who will communicate your plan to your employees and encourage that person to work from home. Then determine how IT will support telecommuting and how customer support needs will be managed. Will *your* company's servers be able to withstand such a crisis?
- If any business traveler has just returned home from an impacted region, he or she may need to see a physician for a routine physical and be advised to self-monitor for symptoms. There will be legal issues regarding what you can and cannot order an employee to do, including work from home, refrain from coming to work, or be temporarily reassigned to another location.

- If products are sent to or received from overseas, a logistics emergency plan is needed that details how you will receive/send future shipments given any embargo that may be imposed.
- Assign a content manager for your company Intranet and public Web site so you can communicate to both the public and your employees key details about your preparedness plan, slowdown, or shutdown in a timely manner.
- Think about the impact that prolonged salary and benefit continuation will have on your company. If you work with a union, engage leaders of that organization early on in the crisis so that pertinent parties are able to reach an accord on major decisions.
- Arrange for regularly scheduled conference calls to your company's various departments so your employees, contractors, and vendors can update one another on key developments, projects, and when they anticipate returning to work.
- Identify succession planning for mission-critical people.
- Update the home, cell, and emergency phone numbers for each employee, key supplier, and contractor, and be sure that multiple leaders have access to this confidential database.

Finally, before offering you a message template that you may want to use in the event of a health emergency, I implore you to recognize that global warming will create complicated health scenarios in the near future. There already is undeniable evidence of a clear link between global warming and the preponderance of outbreaks of certain diseases, such as malaria. If we do not implement globally standardized early detection systems aimed at identifying outbreaks that have been triggered by food, water, or air-related contaminations, such as severe acute respiratory syndrome (SARS), we will have an unprecedented public health and global business catastrophe on our hands. As Dr. Larry Brilliant recently wrote in the May 7, 2007, edition of *Forbes*:

Signs of catastrophe abound. The nonnative tiger mosquito, a vector for diseases including dengue, yellow fever and encephalitis, is expanding its range across North America and is set to displace more benign native species on the back of climate change. Now able to thrive at higher altitudes [due to the warming of the earth's temperature], malaria-carrying mosquitoes, which cause 1.5 million to 2 million deaths a year, are about to spread into northern Europe and the highlands of tropical Africa.

To help you plan for a major health issue, here is a sample letter to your employees that you can tailor to the specific needs of whatever the health emergency is that you may be facing.

Sample Letter

Dear Colleague:

As you know, the news media is reporting that a serious outbreak of a virulent strain of influenza is underway in Mexico City. This morning we learned that this same strain has migrated into Texas and potentially will have a significant impact on U.S. health. Although no one can accurately predict how or when we will be impacted, we have a responsibility to ourselves, our customers, and our investors to be prepared.

We are actively monitoring any updates that are being provided by the U.S. Centers for Disease Control (CDC) and various government agencies worldwide, such as the World Health Organization (WHO). It is important that none of us panic, but we must prepare. If the situation advances, we should expect disruptions. For example, shipments to and from our offices may be held in an embargo, and we may see a suspension of all mail service. It may be difficult for our salespeople to travel to other regions of the country or outside the United States. If the situation escalates further and many become sick, we should expect that a certain percentage of our employees could be sick for days and potentially much longer.

We have a serious responsibility to prudently prepare, at home and at work. The well-being of your family should always be your first priority, and we encourage you to keep your manager informed of any issues that are of concern to you.

Our Web site will be frequently updated as new information becomes available. In the interim, here is some general information that you should review with your coworkers and family members.

WHAT IS THE NATURE OF THIS OUTBREAK?

It appears that a strain of the H5N1 virus has spread from Hong Kong to Mexico. News reports indicate that several hundred people are seriously ill. As you know, the virus can spread and mutate rapidly. Because North America has been impacted, we must remain on high alert because of the migration patterns of this illness.

WHAT IS THE IMPACT ON OUR ORGANIZATION?

At the moment, no employees have reported to our company physician and nurses that they are experiencing any of the symptoms that are commonly seen with this illness. However, some infected individuals do not exhibit the symptoms that are commonly associated with this illness. As such, it's prudent to say that if you are not feeling well, you should contact your physician in a timely manner and then, if you do not feel well enough to come to work, inform your manager. Do not come to work if you are sick.

IS MY JOB AT RISK?

This could either become a major international health emergency, or this challenge could be over within a few days or weeks. We simply do not know if we are dealing with a limited medical emergency or a true pandemic. Members of senior management will work tirelessly to keep you informed about how we will continue to meet the needs of our customers if the situation becomes more serious. We are truly "in this together" as one team.

WHAT IS A PANDEMIC?

The CDC has stated that a pandemic must meet three criteria. It:

1. Possesses a new surface protein to which there is little or no pre-existing immunity in the human population
2. Is able to cause illness in humans
3. Has the ability for sustained person-to-person transmission

WILL OUR COMPANY OFFER VACCINE SHOTS?

If and when immunizations become available for the general population, we hope to have them available to our employees, and the company will pay for all costs associated with vaccination. You should consult with your physician now to determine if it is appropriate to be inoculated, and we will ask that you sign a consent form if we establish a vaccine program. If employers are allocated only a certain number of doses, we will use a lottery system in fairness to all employees. Those who are not selected should contact the Department of Public Health regarding other alternatives.

WHAT ARE SOME COMMON SYMPTOMS WITH THIS VIRUS?

- Aches, fever, cough
- Possible eye infections, sore throat
- Difficulty breathing, lethargy
- Pneumonia-like symptoms

WHAT CAN I DO TO AVOID GETTING SICK?

- Washing your hands frequently is considered a strong deterrent.
- Remove shoes and leave them outside before entering your home.
- Avoid any contact with poultry and birds, since the H5N1 virus may be harvested in these animals.

If you have other questions, please contact Mary Smith at 555-1212.

7

STORMY WEATHER: KATRINA, EARTHQUAKES, FLOODS, AND TSUNAMIS

Katrina was in the cards, forewarned, foreseen and yet still dismissed. That so many officials were caught so unprepared was a failure less of imagination than will.

— *Time*, September 12, 2005

Although natural disasters seem to be occurring more frequently and are causing unprecedented amounts of damage worldwide, the worst natural disaster in history remains a mammoth 1931 flood in China that killed over three million people. That's three *million* people. From a *storm*.

Hurricane Katrina paled in comparison in terms of the human devastation it produced, but for a modern world whose surplus of technological tools is supposed to prepare its citizens for such disasters, the lessons emanating from this particular catastrophe are endless.

When Katrina slammed the Gulf Coast of the United States on August 29, 2005, virtually every trained meteorologist, let alone public official, in the country had

The total financial cost of Katrina exceeded $150 billion.

underestimated its sheer power. Over 1,800 people died, not in preindustrial China and not in 1931, but in a wired, fully modern American city. The total financial cost of Katrina, from mending structure damage to homes and businesses, to financing both rental housing for victims and infrastructure repairs, exceeded $150 billion. The human cost was much greater.

Although parts of Mississippi and Florida also suffered significant damage (with an additional 252 deaths), New Orleans became the apex of public attention, and understandably so; the city's levees, which were critical to the city's commerce because of the hundreds of shipping barges that navigated them daily, were known in advance to be susceptible to collapse. They did.

This wasn't the first time that New Orleans was faced with a crisis as large—and potentially damaging—as Katrina. The crisis "radar screen" for New Orleans can be traced back to 1823, when water crested so far above the Metairie Ridge that nearly 200 blocks of the city were flooded for months. In the almost two centuries that have passed since then, numerous smaller hurricanes and floods have provided engineers with ample opportunity—not to mention evidence of the need—to create a permanent fix to these levees. Although the U.S. Army Corps of Engineers was working on a solution at the time that Katrina hit, their efforts were too little and too late.

The cast of characters that grappled with managing the storm, which originally was labeled a category one hurricane (it quickly zoomed to category three, then five), included New Orleans mayor C. Ray Nagin. Nagin never has been the brightest star in politics. His post-Katrina remarks at a tribute to Martin Luther King Jr. infuriated many: "This city will be chocolate at the end of the day. It's the way God wants it to be. You can't have New Orleans any other way; it wouldn't be New Orleans."

Nagin wasn't particularly swift at decision making, either.

On the evening of August 27, 2005, Nagin spoke with Max Mayfield, the director of the National Hurricane Center; Mayfield advised Nagin to evacuate the city. Nagin reportedly was concerned that if he ordered the public to evacuate and Katrina moved offshore, the city could be sued by businesses for any unnecessary loss of commerce they might experience. Addled by this fear and his apprehensions that New Orleans' tourism industry would decline as a result of any negative publicity the city received in the wake of Katrina, Nagin waited until the morning of August 28 to announce an evacuation. By then, Interstate 10, the area's vital exit route, had been reduced to a parking lot due to excess traffic. To complicate matters, New Orleans' lack of a viable form of public transportation left over 100,000 people stranded; most didn't own a vehicle.

By 5 a.m. on August 29, 2005, floodwalls along the eastern coast of New Orleans collapsed, along with floodwalls protecting the city from flooding from Lake Pontchartrain; by this time, over 83 percent of the city was under water. A cascade of errors and miscalculations ensued. Louisiana governor Kathleen Blanco and Federal Emergency Management Agency (FEMA) director Michael Brown raced to New Orleans's Emergency Operations Center (EOC) at the downtown Hyatt Hotel, but they were too late; New Orleans's communications systems were already nonfunctioning, causing these and other officials to miss a key window of opportunity to respond to the critical facts of the disaster. In the meantime, entire neighborhoods were being washed away; nursing homes were breaking apart with victims inside; and looting and deviant crime was well underway. Some police officers abandoned their posts and never returned.

New Orleans was in complete disarray. As thousands of homes, businesses, schools, and cemeteries were washed away in floodwaters, many raced to save their lives. Those able to climb to the roof of their homes did so with the desperate hope that police or National Guard troops might rescue them. Many died as they crawled into their attics; some would succumb to dehydration, others to heart attack or drowning. As is fairly obvious, many of the principles of corporate crisis management went ignored by the public sector, with the government's most significant act of negligence being its failure to appoint a single incident commander to make key decisions, allocate resources, and link state and federal responders. A subsequent report prepared by a U.S. Senate panel noted that some in charge did not expect the incident to get worse. Requests for intervention by federal officials were slow to be sent—and perhaps even slower to be heard.

In Washington, D.C., CNN seemingly knew more about the disaster than the Department of Homeland Security (DHS). As one of America's largest cities literally collapsed upon itself, DHS secretary Michael Chertoff didn't fly to Louisiana and take command of the situation; instead, he flew to Atlanta to meet with colleagues about— get this . . . *the avian flu.* He later claimed that FEMA chief Brown hadn't kept him properly informed about both the 20,000 residents that were seeking shelter at the Superdome and the other 15,000 who were heading to the Convention Center for safety. Both locations had water; and then no water; food, then limited food; security, then social disarray. Police officers disappeared, allowing criminals to roam freely around the flooded streets with rifles. As *USA Today* reported, "Police chief Eddie Compass said he sent 88 officers to quell tensions (at the Superdome) but they were beaten back by an angry mob." Despite such reports, Chertoff's public statements did not emphasize to the citizens of New Orleans that social order would be restored quickly. What Chertoff's comments *did* do, however, was stroke the feds' egos; Chertoff said that their response efforts were "a source of tremendous pride" to him.

> As one of America's largest cities literally collapsed upon itself, DHS secretary Michael Chertoff didn't fly to Louisiana and take command of the situation; instead, he flew to Atlanta to meet with colleagues about . . . *the avian flu.*

I'd sure hate to see the ones he would have been ashamed of.

Reflections on Katrina

For the first time ever, a major U.S. city was simply taken offline, closed down. Food and water and power and phones were gone; authority was all but absent . . . When Dr. Greg Henderson, a pathologist turned medic, arrived at the Convention Center on Friday, he was the only doctor for 10,000 people. "They're stacking the dead on the second floor . . . People are having seizures in the hallway.

*People with open running sores, every imaginable disease and
disorder, all kinds of psychiatric problems. We have people who
haven't had dialysis in several days.*

— *TIME*, SEPTEMBER 12, 2005

Damage to the eastern coastline was extraordinary. New revelations emerged each day: First, we discovered that the shipping lanes connecting various southern states were badly damaged, and then we learned that over 100 offshore petroleum drilling platforms had been destroyed or floated away, some of them traveling dozens of miles. In Mississippi, water uprooted floating casinos, lifting them across the street and destroying them beyond recognition.

President George W. Bush, who skillfully reassured a frightened nation of its security and resilience after the September 11, 2001, terrorist attacks, was astoundingly aloof throughout this disaster. He flew from his home in Texas to Washington, D.C., on Wednesday, August 31, and although he asked that the plane fly *over* New Orleans so he could see the damage, he never landed at one of several available airstrips in the state. He offered mild statements of concern and sympathy and chatted with Louisiana governor Blanco. He eventually ordered supplies and troops. Yet it took until Friday morning—five days after Katrina hit—for National Guard troops to begin evacuations of New Orleans, and it wasn't until four more days had passed that the president found the initiative to fly to Mobile, Alabama. In addition, *Time* reported that the president praised FEMA director Brown, proving beyond any doubt that he was completely out of touch with reality: "Brownie, you're doing a heck of a job," noted the president.

Oops.

There are literally thousands of lessons that any crisis coach would want to share regarding the Katrina debacle. Here are some of the most profound:

1. Remember that there are three essential requirements for managing your way out of a natural storm: a leader, a strategic platform for decision making, and a means to communicate. With Katrina, the city lacked the first, blew the second, and completely underestimated the third.

2. Make sure that you have adequate supplies, such as long-life batteries for your laptops and cell phones and sufficient generators that can keep your IT infrastructure operating at a functioning level.

3. Think about where victims, including your employees, guests, customers, and others, will be relocated when catastrophe strikes. Ensure that your off-site EOC is equipped with sufficient food, water, and necessities so that people can be comfortable for several days. If you cannot afford such a contingency plan, sign a reciprocal agreement with a local college or university so you can tap into each other's resources in the event of an emergency. Universities are especially useful in a disaster because they often have advanced IT platforms, sleeping accommodations, food and beverage supplies, refrigeration capabilities, and on-site security.

4. Remember that even your security and police teams could be vulnerable in the aftermath of a natural disaster. According to the Associated Press, at least two New Orleans police officers committed suicide and an estimated 200 of the 1,600 salaried police officers abandoned their posts and never returned. Like those around them, most officers lost contact with family members and became instant refugees; for some, their uniform was the only clothes they had at their disposal for several days. Police chief Compass told reporters, "Our officers have been urinating and defecating in the basement of Harrah's Casino. They have been going in stores to feed themselves. They don't have homes. They don't have anything."

So, now that we know the basic needs of any organization in the face of natural catastrophe, let's dig deeper. First, communications.

By the time the New Orleans emergency management team was able to congregate at the Hyatt Hotel, the hotel's generator had run out of diesel fuel and its communications equipment was losing power. Most cell phones died within hours. Scott Domke, a member of the city's IT team, remembered that he had a Vonage account and was able to get an intermittent Internet connection. Thanks to

Domke, that one line of communication remained the city of New Orleans' basic link to federal agencies for the next *five days*.

According to *The Wall Street Journal,* as Domke was trying to send and receive e-mail messages, Compass ordered his officers to break into a local Office Depot and take the single computer that remained; looters had already ransacked the place. For the most part, however, the entire system of communications during Katrina consisted of police authorities passing scraps of paper to one another on the street and in the office: "Tell Olson to get 200 officers deployed to Harrah's Casino." Or, "Find out from Vaughn if we have any body bags in storage. Where is our temporary morgue?"

The police and National Guard also underestimated the frightening power of crowd psychology; about 200 desperate people joined together and stormed the Hyatt, forcing the city's emergency responders to worry at one point that they would be killed. Many of the newly homeless were intoxicated as they roamed the hotel premises with guns and knives. Greg Meffert, chief technology officer for the city, said, "This was when the last parts of the government were about to come undone. It felt like the Alamo—we were surrounded and had only short bursts of communication."

Next, let's discuss the need for contingency decision making in these types of situations. Mayor Nagin designated the Superdome as a last-resort homeless shelter, despite the fact that he and his administration knew from history that this facility was totally impractical. In 1998, the city used the Superdome during Hurricane George, and the sporting arena nearly failed as a temporary shelter under considerably milder conditions. The city did nothing meaningful between 1998 and 2005 to build an alternative safe haven on higher ground for those too poor to leave the city in case of emergency.

With most of New Orleans's streets submerged under 12 to 20 feet of water, about 15,000 people made their way to a sweltering Superdome. Many wonderful volunteers worked tirelessly to line up cots for the elderly, while others prepared and distributed meals. Volunteer members of the Salvation Army, as well as numerous churches and social organizations were especially generous with their time and talent during these challenging hours. The Mormon Church headquarters in

Salt Lake City, Utah, for example, activated a crisis plan and deployed volunteers to New Orleans from a dozen states; some arrived within three hours of deployment to supplement National Guard details. But tensions in the city remained high. Fistfights broke out and assaults were reported in many neighborhoods. At least one elderly man reportedly committed suicide by throwing himself over a Superdome balcony as onlookers watched in horror.

Outside the Superdome, CNN reporters acknowledged on live television that they feared for their own safety. A genuine social breakdown bordering on hysteria was underway. The city couldn't even collect itself well enough to utilize the tools it *did* have at its disposal; as *Time* noted, "A fleet of several hundred [school] buses was left to languish in a lot that eventually flooded," even though, if deployed, the buses could have helped evacuate poor neighborhoods whose inhabitants were aching for aid. To this day Nagin has never specifically addressed the issue of who should have been held accountable for neglecting to deploy those buses.

> Over 51 percent of the U.S. population lives near a coastline and is thus vulnerable to the impacts of a major storm or surge.

What we learned from Katrina is directly applicable to future disasters. According to the University of California at Irvine, over 51 percent of the U.S. population lives near a coastline and is thus vulnerable to the impacts of a major storm or surge. We assume that someone, somewhere, has thought about how we might be affected by the meteorological, engineering, and infrastructure issues associated with a massive disaster, regardless of where we live—but being hopeful is just not realistic. The operations chief of the Army Corps of Engineers, Gregory Breerwood, told *The Wall Street Journal* that their crisis preparedness plans had "never included an event of this magnitude," even though we know the feds designed a simulation a year prior to Katrina's onslaught specifically to avoid the kind of debacle caused by this hurricane.

And finally, let's look at the need for a single voice in disastrous situations. In reality, no one person can be held accountable for a storm—it is classified, after all, as an act of God. But when the

National Hurricane Center warned the city that it was in the direct path of a major storm, New Orleans's lack of a defined communications and decision-making roadmap was painfully evident. This included the failure of Nagin to order an immediate evacuation of the city and the failure of Bush to summon FEMA director Michael Brown to the site (Brown waited five hours after the *landfall* of the hurricane before he proposed sending just 1,000 personnel to the city). It also included the failure of Brown's boss, DHS director Michael Chertoff, to recognize that one of America's largest cities was on the brink of literal collapse. On August 31, 2005, Chertoff (who, like Brown, had no emergency management experience prior to assuming the most important emergency post in the country) said he was "extremely pleased" with the government's response. But others weren't so pleased with *his* performance. As *Time* reported, president Bush, vice president Cheney, and five other congressional leaders participated in a conference call the morning of August 31 with Chertoff, who indicated to them that things weren't nearly as bad as everyone was saying. In fact, he had just spoken to local officials and felt that things were coming together for the city. Senator Harry Reid, the Democratic leader from Nevada, refused to pander to Chertoff and told him that he was out of touch with reality. After asking Chertoff if he really meant what he said, Reid erupted, telling the leader of America's national security: "Turn on your TV!"

Now It's Your Storm

Hurricanes, tornadoes, and earthquakes don't just happen to other people—they may happen to you, impacting your employees and customers. In addition, the disruption they cause could mean that the companies that supply your company with vital goods and services could similarly be disrupted.

Natural disasters are messy, costly, and incredibly burdensome to the people and organizations they affect. Although seasonality plays a role in some disasters (hotels in Kansas test their public address system in the high tornado months of April, May, and June for a reason), other events, such as a freak ice storm or earthquake, are largely unpredictable.

A surprising number of companies are obsessed with weather-related issues simply because it is financially prudent. Wal-Mart often is criticized for its employment practices, but its readiness to keep its stores operating (and customers supplied) during a storm is arguably without peer.

Six days before Hurricane Katrina hit the Gulf Coast of the United States, Jason Jackson, Wal-Mart's business continuity director, was conducting briefing calls for the company's regional leaders throughout the U.S. Suppliers were asked to accelerate orders of dried goods, blankets and bedding supplies, kerosene lamps, radios, and other products that are vital to families in an emergency. Trucks loaded with those supplies, as well as with water, canned food, generators, and Global Positioning Systems (GPS) and Radio Frequency Identification Devices (RFID), were incrementally deployed to states contiguous to Louisiana and Mississippi and ordered to wait until the roads were cleared so they could enter what was now virtually a war zone. Their mission: Deliver and donate desperately needed supplies to those impacted by the hurricane. Mission accomplished.

In fact, Wal-Mart accomplished what the federal government couldn't: It deployed essential resources quickly and efficiently to impacted areas. For a company that often receives criticism for its frugal employee benefits, no one could legitimately criticize Wal-Mart for its superiority at crisis logistics. *Fortune* noted in its October 2, 2005, edition:

> Wal-Mart accomplished what the federal government couldn't: It deployed essential resources quickly and efficiently to impacted areas.

Before the winds died down, Wal-Mart had dispatched members of its loss prevention team—people deployed to protect stores against everything from shoplifting to vandalism. The team was amazed at what it discovered. Looters had cleaned out the Tchoupitoulas Street store in New Orleans. Elsewhere, though, Wal-Mart employees fended off looters and gave away items to the truly needy. In Kenner, Louisiana, a Jefferson Parish town outside New Orleans, a local loss prevention specialist named Trent Ward used a forklift to pop open the warehouse door at his store in order to deliver water to nearly 100 elderly people stranded at a retirement home. In nearby Marrero, Louisiana, Wal-Mart employees transformed their store into a makeshift headquarters for police officers who had lost their homes and had no place to sleep. As ill-equipped National Guardsmen began to trickle into the area, Wal-Mart gave them bullets and holsters.

As is fairly evident, Wal-Mart shined in almost every aspect of crisis management during the Katrina debacle. A week after the storm, Wal-Mart had even located 97 percent of all employees who worked at its 126 stores located throughout the Gulf Coast area. By comparison, Marriott Hotels admitted that it struggled to find its 2,800 workers in the region (weatherman Willard Scott wore a 1-800-MARRIOTT shirt on NBC's *Today Show* to encourage employees to call their employers and let them know where they were). As evidenced by Wal-Mart's success rate in locating its displaced employees, planning, logistics, and even a phone tree with updated emergency phone numbers can pay huge dividends when "it" hits the fan.

Other companies equally shined. *Fortune* noted that, as amazing as it sounds, just one day after Hurricane Katrina hit, 23 of Home Depot's 33 stores that are located throughout the hurricane impact region were open for business. And other businesses lacking the financial strength of Wal-Mart or Home Depot similarly shined, much to the embarrassment of the federal government.

A relatively small company that provided electricity to about 200,000 Gulf Coast residents, Mississippi Power, quickly recruited 11,000 repair people from 24 states and Canada and, harnessing their resources, provided much-needed aid to impacted customers. The company's hurricane manual is four-inches thick, but company executives acknowledged that they really didn't have time to use that document during the catastrophe. What they needed and used more than anything was the basic company telephone directory, which listed all of their employees' names and critical phone numbers. In its efforts to reach out to its 1,256 employees via Nextel cell phones, Mississippi Power employed scenario planning, business recovery strategies, and teamwork to restore power—in 12 days, no less—to virtually every customer whose home wasn't destroyed by the storm.

Hurricane Katrina was not unprecedented in terms of the damage it wrought, but it was noteworthy in terms of the failure of multiple levels of government to conduct a successful mass evacuation in response to it. Over 15,000 business buildings were destroyed, yet not one government agency coordinated efforts to help them recover. Federal agencies debated over who owned which piece of disaster recovery, and in the meantime, no one thought to compile a central database of the victims' statuses and where they had relocated. Some families waited for weeks to hear if a loved one survived. FEMA initially handed out Visa gift cards to aid evacuees in their relocation process, but then suspended the program when some victims were caught using the cards at liquor stores.

The incompetence at both the city and state levels was matched by the total and complete failure on the part of the Bush administration to restore order to the streets. Also among the guilty parties were past White House administrations, whose failure to fix a known, mammoth engineering risk resulted in one of the most horrific American tragedies in recent years. The city previously had ranked as one of the top 10 convention cities in the United States, a status that provided nearly 85,000 New Orleanians with full-time employment. Now, after seeing New Orleans' response to Katrina, some professional organizations have privately indicated that they have scratched New Orleans from consideration for a decade or more, until hotels, transportation infrastructure, and other basic tourist needs are rebuilt, restored, and verified for safety.

When All Else Fails, Send a Text Message

If you examine virtually every major natural catastrophe in recent years—earthquake, blizzard, or tsunami—you'll find that in most of these disasters, vital communication systems have failed, rendering impacted people incapable of using their cellular or landline

> The one technology that works over 96 percent of the time is text messaging.

telephones to receive or send emergency messages to their loved ones. Telecommunications experts tell us that in a major catastrophe, basic telecommunications systems, including wireless Internet systems, are often disabled, although some can be sustained on batteries for a few days. According to *The New York Times*, however, the one technology that works over 96 percent of the time—and the one technology that worked throughout the 2004 tsunami that devastated Sri Lanka and Indonesia—is text messaging. Many governments are now following the lead of countries like the Netherlands and Hong Kong, both of which have embraced Short Message Service (SMS), a satellite-reliant system that can be used to send a text message to any SMS-compatible mobile device. The government of Hong Kong now alerts about seven million cell phone users whenever rumors that the city has had an outbreak of the communicable virus SARS begin to run rampant. It did so in 2003, telling residents that the rumors were false via text messages that were sent to citizens' cell phones and personal digital assistants (PDAs), an action that potentially prevented citywide panic. For more information, check out ready.gov.

What Did We Learn?

If Wal-Mart and a small electric company can get their hands around a crisis, you can, too. Just don't assume anyone from the government will lend a hand—at least not immediately. In the interim, I'd recommend you become ambidextrous.

With regard to Hurricane Katrina, remember that history is rich with comparative lessons. In his brilliant analysis of the 1666 Great Fire of London, one of the most monumental catastrophes to befall any major city, author Neil Hanson (2002) penned several conclusions that I find illuminating vis-à-vis Katrina:

- Most Londoners at the time felt that the inferno that reduced 80 percent of the entire city to ashes was a message from God that a sinful earth needed to clean up its act. A number of devout Southern Baptists took to the media airwaves after Katrina and shared the same observation; this storm, they said, is surely a message from God.

- In London, mob rule prevailed for nearly four days following the outbreak of the fire. Women were raped, stores and homes were ransacked, churches and museums were robbed of priceless artifacts. In New Orleans, hundreds of vandals roamed the streets and unashamedly walked away with stolen stereo systems, flat panel televisions, and cases of liquor. Social order broke down.

- Government records finally estimated that the London death toll exceeded 700 people; because government census records also were destroyed in that fire, the definitive number of deaths has never been ascertained. Even as most Londoners saw major billows of smoke and fire approaching a full day *before* the fire engulfed their neighborhoods, most remained in their homes in the face of impending danger. Many tuned out their intuition to flee simply because they didn't want to lose the few possessions they had. The Londoners' reactions to the 1666 fire parallels the findings of some sociologists who studied Katrina; although some simply could not afford to evacuate, other victims stayed behind voluntarily because they thought *others* were overreacting.

- Residents of London in 1666 were no strangers to chaos; in fact, they were intimately acquainted with the inexorable power of nature. Just a year before the Great Fire, in September 1665, thousands died *each week* after the eruption of one of the worst plagues in centuries. Bodies were piled six and seven deep in the streets of many neighborhoods, and homeowners left their doors and windows open for weeks at a time in the hopes that "airing out" their homes would prevent them from being infected. Despite the fact that they were moderately experienced with catastrophe, Londoners lacked a single point of decision making, communication, and coordination in terms of crisis logistics. Their relative lack of crisis management skills is understandable; after all, it *was* 1666. But there's no excuse for what happened in 2005 with Hurricane Katrina. Most certainly better equipped than seventeenth-century London, New Orleans benefited from advanced meteorology and weather forecasting models, as well as from its experience with numerous prior hurricanes and catastrophes. Nevertheless, it was only when residents looked out their front windows to see their neighbors' homes floating by that they ran to the roofs of their own homes.

- Just about the only radical difference between the two catastrophes from a crisis management perspective was that of accountability. A major investigation by London authorities led to the hanging of Robert Hubert, a mentally ill drifter who admitted on October 29, 1666, to setting the fire. In New Orleans, Mayor Nagin enjoyed a different outcome: He was reelected just nine months later.

The Crisis-Ready Company

If a major storm were to impact your organization, readiness matters. A smart organization will exercise a contingency mentality and have a series of supply kits ready. Here are five essential issues for you and your team to consider when preparing for a natural disaster.

1. Do your employees know what phone number to call to access your company's most up-to-date operating information?
2. Does your public address system have prerecorded messages that can be immediately launched by your security dispatcher to inform employees or guests that a tornado or other storm is approaching?
3. Do you have a readied supply room filled with bottled water, dried foods, radios, flashlights, blankets, and other goods that could provide comfort to those in your facilities for an extended period of time?
4. Do your company's leaders have access to several two-way radios that would allow them to walk the company's premises and communicate back with you in the event that cellular service is lost in the area? Remember, these radios must operate on a different frequency than that used by cell phones in order to be effective.
5. Do you have a medical kit, defibrillator, and other equipment that could be used by nonspecialists to assist anyone who may

be injured by flying glass, debris, or other materials in the event of a violent storm? In many disasters it is impossible to transport victims to area hospitals due to road closures or overcrowded hospitals.

Earthquakes

Chances are that, somewhere in your facilities, you house major pieces of equipment that could spill, rupture, or break. Consider what you can do before an earthquake strikes to prevent such heavy items, including lighting fixtures, signs, HVAC equipment, and various hanging items from falling and injuring or potentially killing one of your employees. In the retail sector, customers are especially at risk because they are relatively unfamiliar with your store and may not be aware that televisions or other heavy items on a rack, even those on industrially "qualified" shelving systems, are known to commonly fall during earthquakes.

Floods

When you are aware that a dam may break or a flood could be triggered by other natural events, think about moving your people and operations quickly to higher ground, preferably to a location at least a few miles away from moving waters. Floods typically do not recede for several days, sometimes weeks. Because you may have some time to prepare your staff prior to evacuation, think about how to back up all your IT needs quickly. You also should inform your employees to work from home and provide them with adequate telecom capabilities. Before evacuating the office, be sure that you secure work areas as best as possible and move key equipment either to higher floors of your building or to short-term rental facilities that are on higher ground.

Tsunamis

Because the tsunami that struck Indonesia and Sri Lanka in 2006 helped us better understand just how damaging these devastating forces of nature can be, remember that international warning systems are improving thanks to ongoing efforts by the United Nations and the World Meteorological Organization. It is prudent to be aware that the impact of a tsunami is typically hardest on the poor living near coastlines. Your company may be able to assist in such a crisis by providing them with food and technical assistance and shipping them products they need to recover.

Benchmarking

Violent weather can impact you if you are managing a manufacturing plant, hospital, hotel, or government agency: no matter what industry you're in, we're all in this together. Similarly, it doesn't matter if your business is located in the United States or abroad—bad weather can happen anywhere, at any time.

For instance, if you visited the EOC at any number of the nation's largest theme parks, you'd see that their weather forecasting technology is extraordinarily advanced. Many companies continuously monitor wind direction, velocity, and moisture for a variety of important reasons. A surge in winds means that canopies must be dismantled, signs must be taken down, and, in the event of a pending violent storm, street parades may need to be postponed or cancelled.

For instance, if you find yourself in New York City at the end of November and stop by Macy's mammoth Thanksgiving Day parade, you might notice that the department store is forced to reckon with the sheer power of wind during its event—and it hasn't always fared so well. Back in 1997, for example, the giant balloon featuring the "Cat in the Hat" tumbled to the ground, seriously injuring two people.

If you take a tour through the Marriott in downtown San Francisco, you'll see how much the hotel's management has learned from history—most notably from California's devastating 1906 earthquake. Sirens, bullhorns, medvac teams ready to deploy the injured, shatter-proof glass doors—all of these and many other features are in place in the hotel for that inevitable major quake that will likely one day destroy much of that city.

Or, for a really fascinating journey, travel to the village of Bad Reichenhall, Germany, and talk with the operators of the Bavarian skating rink. On January 2, 2006, the roof of that rink collapsed following a major snowstorm, killing 10 people. Although management routinely sent workers up to the roof each year after a storm to clear off heavy snow, no one could have predicted that the incremental weight stress from heavy snow would eventually cause the roof's collapse.

Whether you are in Texas, New York, Brazil, or Hong Kong, the impact of a weather-related crisis can be devastating. You may not be able to prevent a storm, but you can discuss how you may react to such a catastrophe. You can anticipate the resources, tools, and supplies you will need in such an event now. Your employees, customers, and investors expect at least that much from you.

The time to think about what your company will require to sustain its operations, including food, portable water, telecommunications, and other needs, is not *when* nature sends a disaster to your doorstop but rather *before* such a catastrophe occurs. Given the kinds of incidents that could impact you, no matter where you are in the world, with little or no warning, think about how you can frame your response and recovery plan in an appropriate manner.

> You may not be able to prevent a storm, but you can discuss how you may react to such a catastrophe. You can anticipate the resources, tools, and supplies you will need in such an event now.

Review Your Coverage

As the chaos of Hurricane Katrina began to wind down, multiple home and business owners filed claims against their insurers for the damages they incurred as a result of the storm, but most did not understand the nuances of the policies they had purchased. Many assumed that their properties were covered by flood damage, but numerous insurers disputed these post-Katrina claims, saying that their damages were the result of pipe breaks versus an act of God. Some companies settled claims and others are likely to be in litigation for several years or more.

Businesses must be especially prudent to purchase two kinds of policies; property and casualty policies that will reimburse you for part or all of the destruction caused by an earthquake, blizzard, or other storm or incident, and business interruption insurance, which reimburses you for the costs of bringing in special damage experts, as well as for the costs of replacing a portion of the revenue you lost while you were closed or under reconstruction. An industry group, Property Claims Services, reports that Katrina alone led to 156,000 claims by businesses (resulting in $20.6 billion in payouts) in the impacted states and 1.2 million claims by homeowners.

As a crisis manager, I hope you understand that natural disasters can overwhelm a small or large business financially. But the greatest toll from these events—blizzards, hurricanes, earthquakes, and others—is on the human psyche. When people feel betrayed by their local or national government because they expected such agencies to approach the crisis more expediently and humanely, their bitterness can be profoundly deep. In the case of Katrina, smart businesses reacted faster than the government.

8

INDUSTRIAL AND ENVIRONMENTAL DISASTERS

nevitably, I find that management teams generally avoid contemplating accidents of an industrial nature. This is for two principal reasons:

1. The scope of damage that can arise from industrial accidents, such as the death of construction contractors on your property or employees that become sick from a serious toxic spill near your site, is incredibly wide. Many crisis managers find it difficult to prepare their management framework for the dozens of potential scenarios that could impact their organization, especially when they manage several locations.

2. Unlike cases of workplace violence or natural disasters, many managers tend to believe that their lawyers will be able to apply the same crisis standards that generally seem to work when other types of incidents arise. As a result, managers often suggest that their lawyers spend less time on these issues because of the (false) assumption that legal counsel understands the nuances of such complicated matters as technological science and construction dynamics, which are unique to industrial accidents. This often is a horrible assumption.

As you begin the process of assessing your company's vulnerability to industrial accidents, you'll want to consider a variety of factors, including:

- The proximity of your facilities to under- and aboveground oil, natural gas, and other utility lines
- How close you are to major highways and rail lines, where a variety of toxic materials are transported daily
- What kind of chemicals your company keeps on-site, who manages those chemicals, and whether you have experienced any industrial incidents or regulation infractions in the past three years
- How many projects may be going on at any one time at your company that require the skills of external contractors, as well as what competencies and equipment those contractors may need (e.g., cutting equipment, forklifts, chemicals)
- How well prepared your local first responder departments may be to major issues involving contamination or a release of a toxic cloud nearby, as well as how adept they are at orchestrating evacuations and issuing widespread alerts to neighborhoods and businesses
- When senior management last spent an hour focusing specifically on issues like waste management, local pollution controls, and how local wildlife would be impacted if there were a toxic chemical spill on-site
- Who is monitoring the driving records of those who operate company vehicles, delivery trucks, and special equipment at your facilities; you should also know who is monitoring and keeping records of their driver's licenses and receiving updates from regulators when any licenses are suspended or revoked
- If you have adequate on-site medical response and safety systems to address the first tiers of an industrial accident; you should check if your company employs a trained nurse or physician, as well as if it has first-aid kits, defibrillators, and other equipment and provides regular training
- Who monitors and investigates when incidents or near-misses occur at your facility

You'll find that different countries use differing terms when referring to industrial accidents. In the United States, regulators such as the Occupational Health and Safety Administration (OSHA) track the most serious incidents and use the phrase "industrial accident" in their reporting systems. Canadians have a more holistic approach that is focused more on prevention than on response and tracking, and their Industrial Accident Prevention Association (IAPA) helps businesses implement training programs and solutions in advance of a critical incident; their process is embedded into a "Workplace Health System." In Australia, you will find that most corporations use the phrase "Workplace Health Management" in discussing how to make companies' workplaces safer. And Japan prefers to avoid negative connotations; the phrase that is commonly used by Japanese employers is "Safety Campaigns," which is suggestive of an ongoing effort that requires continual promotion. Interestingly enough, on a per capita basis, Japan has one of the lowest rates of industrial fatalities inside of manufacturing plants, and there is some empirical data suggesting that this is due to Japan's enormous focus on safety-first themed posters, meetings, and communications.

What Would You Do?

Many sociologists and psychologists who study trauma increasingly believe that most people have one of only two principle reactions when an unpredictable event strikes.

The first group appears to "freeze" in place; the mental state of those in this group is profoundly static, often characterized by a notion of "this can't be happening to me." Those in the second group appear to be cognizant of danger and rally with a remarkable sense of "I need to get out of here quickly." The National Institute of Standards and Technology (NIST) routinely interviews survivors of catastrophes to better understand survival tactics in the midst of danger. The NIST found that of the estimated 15,410 individuals who successfully abandoned the World Trade Center towers on September 11, 2001, most took twice as long to walk down a flight of stairs than normal (about a minute), *but at least they listened to their intuition and moved.* That decision likely saved their lives. However, at least 1,000 people in Tower 2 took the time to shut down their computers before making the same decision. Others in both towers listened to the advice of some 911 operators and stayed in place because they were being assured that help was on the way, even though first responders were actually trapped.

Of similar interest are studies conducted by the National Transportation Safety Board (NTSB) that show that about half of all passengers on commercial airliners that crash survive. Interestingly enough, aviation experts increasingly believe that what survivors do, both emotionally and physically, in those critical moments before the plane crashes is of extraordinary importance. At the Federal Aviation Administration's Oklahoma City training facility, psychologists and engineers study how people respond to a variety of incidents while onboard a plane. Their studies concluded that those who took the time to study the closest exit and rehearse an evacuation strategy were far more likely to rely on that memory base and evacuate before being overpowered by fire or smoke.

> Those who took the time to study the closest exit and rehearse an evacuation strategy were far more likely to rely on that memory base and evacuate before being overpowered by fire or smoke.

There are smart reasons to look for an exit when you sit in a movie theater, visit a nightclub, or work in a high-rise office building. Prior awareness of exit locations could be your lifeboat; in a crisis, your brain must process thousands of pieces of information amid screams, injury, shock, and possibly psychological denial, rendering you unable to identify the best exit route. The majority of people, according to Dr. Thomas Drabek, sociologist and professor emeritus at the University of Denver, engage in this "milling" process before evacuating. *Time* magazine interviewed Drabek and found that some victims may even seek to verify events—by checking with coworkers, a news report, or calling someone. This phenomenon baffles both psychologists and crisis experts.

Management Decisions and Precursors

Let's look at some categories of incidents that escalated from being problems that were under the radar of most management teams to becoming organizational nightmares. You can become a better crisis coach within your organization if you learn from these examples and apply the ramifications of these cases to your own work culture.

Sleep Deprivation

Several years ago, one of the nation's largest fast food chains engaged in a practice that you would never find in any written policy manual. Here's a general summary of what workers were told: "If the demands of our shifts escalate, management may ask that you work overtime. Although you can refuse that overtime, we take that into consideration when it's time to evaluate your performance. Oh, by the way, if you refuse overtime too many times, we may replace you, and we're sure you understand."

The implications of this policy may not sound all that serious, but they were significant when a young person who worked for the chain was charged with vehicular homicide after hitting and killing someone on his drive home from work one morning after a 17-hour shift.

It wasn't the first time, or the second, for that matter, that sleep deprivation has led to a fatal outcome. Months later, after a prolonged and agony-filled trial, the restaurant chain was forced to acknowledge that its employees sometimes worked two, often three shifts in a row, since we live in a world where 24/7 food is demanded and help can sometimes be short. No one, the legal argument suggested, had assessed what happens to that worker when he or she left the company and drove home. The lack of sleep, it was argued, not only compromised the safety of the employee, but it potentially

> Not all work-related accidents occur on your property. You may be held liable as an employer for the off-site actions of your colleagues if your practices or policies are later found to have been grossly negligent.

placed others in harm's way. You can imagine the legal nightmare that ensued. Lesson: Not all work-related accidents occur on your property. In some cases, you may be held liable as an employer for the off-site actions of your colleagues if your practices or policies are later found to have been grossly negligent.

Biological Agents at Work

In addition to preparing for industrial accidents that could take place at or near your property, you should consider meeting with your facilities management team to better understand just how prepared you are to deal with any number of other potential accidents. Many of the most serious ones are discussed on OSHA's Web site at osha.gov, which I summarize below.

ANTHRAX

Anthrax is an acute infectious disease caused by a spore-forming bacterium called *Bacillus anthracis*. It is generally acquired following contact with anthrax-infected animals or animal products. Anthrax has been sent via the U.S. Postal Service to newspapers, public officials, and broadcasters, among others, in recent years.

AVIAN FLU

A highly contagious disease, avian flu (or H5N1) is carried by birds and has been at epidemic levels among some poultry populations in Asia. Despite the uncertainties associated with an infection, poultry experts agree that immediate culling of infected and exposed birds is the first line of defense for both the protection of human health and the reduction of further losses in the agricultural sector.

BLOODBORNE PATHOGENS AND NEEDLESTICK PREVENTION

OSHA estimates that 5.6 million workers in the health care industry and related occupations are at risk of occupational exposure to bloodborne pathogens, including human immunodeficiency virus (HIV), hepatitis B virus (HBV), hepatitis C virus (HCV), and others.

BOTULISM

Cases of botulism are usually associated with the consumption of preserved foods. In July 2007, Castleberry's Food Co., of Augusta, Georgia, recalled more than 80 types of canned chili and other meat products after consumers in Indiana and Texas were hospitalized with botulism. Botulism is a muscle-paralyzing disease caused by a toxin made by *Clostridium botulinum*, a bacterium commonly found in soil. As we think about future botulism threats, remember that the botulinum toxin is currently among those compounds reportedly being studied by terrorists as potential biological weapons.

FOODBORNE DISEASE

Foodborne illnesses are caused by viruses, bacteria, parasites, toxins, metals, and prions (microscopic protein particles). Symptoms range from mild gastroenteritis to life-threatening neurologic, hepatic, and renal syndromes. Although most cases are mild and treatable, there is increased recognition by public health officials worldwide that contaminating our food chain would be easily achievable. A mammoth investment in screening, testing, and enhancing the sourcing of foods is needed across national borders.

HANTAVIRUS

Hantaviruses are transmitted to humans from the dried droppings, urine, or saliva of mice and rats. Animal laboratory workers and people working in infested buildings are at increased risk of contracting this disease.

LEGIONNAIRES' DISEASE

Legionnaires' disease is a bacterial disease commonly associated with water-based aerosols. It is often the result of poorly maintained air conditioning cooling towers and portable water systems. In 1976, some 221 people became ill and 34 died when Legionnaires' disease made its way into air coolers at the Bellevue-Stratford Hotel in Philadelphia, Pennsylvania. In April 2000, 101 people became ill and 4 died at the Melbourne Aquarium in Australia as a result of the same bacteria.

MOLDS AND FUNGI

Molds and fungi produce and release millions of spores that are small enough to be air-, water-, and insect-borne and that may negatively affect human health via allergic reactions, asthma, and other respiratory problems. Molds and fungi typically are caused by water damage. In 2001, the opening of a new tower at the Hilton Hawaiian Village had to be delayed because maids discovered mold during pre-opening inspections. Mold, depending on the type, is no laughing matter. The Hilton Hawaiian Village, after extensive cleaning, re-opened in 2003.

PLAGUE

The WHO reports 1,000 to 3,000 cases of plague every year. A bioterrorist release of plague could result in a catastrophic spread of the pneumonic form of the disease.

RICIN

An easily produced toxin, ricin has been used in the past as a bioterrorist weapon and remains a serious threat because it can destroy the cells in your body if ingested or injected into your skin. It can appear as a powder, mist, or liquid and is thus a "clever" weapon because the routes of transmission are so versatile.

SEVERE ACUTE RESPIRATORY SYNDROME (SARS)

SARS is an emerging, sometimes fatal, respiratory illness. According to the CDC, the most recent human cases of SARS were reported in China in April 2004.

SMALLPOX

Smallpox is a highly contagious disease unique to humans. It is estimated that only 20 percent of the population has any immunity to the disease from previous vaccinations.

TULAREMIA

Tularemia is also known as "rabbit fever" or "deer fly fever" and is extremely infectious. Relatively few bacteria are required to cause the disease, which is why it is an attractive weapon for use in bioterrorism.

VIRAL HEMORRHAGIC FEVERS (VHFs)

Along with smallpox, anthrax, plague, botulism, and tularemia, hemorrhagic fever viruses are among the six agents identified by the CDC as the most likely to be used as biological weapons (osha.gov).

> Hemorrhagic fever viruses are among the six agents identified by the CDC as the most likely to be used as biological weapons.
> —osha.gov

Construction Hazards

You'd have to search really hard to find a large employer that doesn't have a major line item in its annual budget for construction and renovation. Whether you own or lease your property, most companies find that they have to expand space, remove or add walls, install new plumbing, or undertake some kind of reconstruction project on a routine basis. In almost all of these cases, companies will outsource the work to qualified, bonded firms that have all their licenses in place and whose safety records have been verified by the general contractor or project manager.

However, accidents happen to even the best of qualified contractors. It will likely be your company's name, not theirs, that leaps into the headlines if one or more of their workers is injured or killed while working on your project. For that reason alone, it's smart to periodically review the qualitative aspects of your risk management program regarding your fiduciary responsibility for construction safety and the safe management of materials.

When the upscale Luxor Casino and Hotel opened in Las Vegas in 1993, the unique, pyramid-like structure captured the imagination of engineers around the world. It advanced thinking on how bearing walls, support structures, and elevators could be embedded into structures in which they had never been tried before. The project contractors, however, received widespread negative publicity after three workers died during the construction of the property. Allegations surfaced that the project required higher safety direction because of the extraordinary demands inherent to the building's unique design. You should keep in mind that whenever you are managing a project involving people, machinery, or new construction dynamics, the architecture of risk management that has served you well in the past should be revisited to accommodate your groundbreaking venture.

Although the incidents at the Luxor received widespread attention because the public was anticipating and watching as the unique design features of that property were being constructed, even traditional construction projects can be sources of major accidents and multiple deaths on the job. A case in point was the extraordinary accident at the new Hyatt Regency in Kansas City, Missouri. On July 17, 1981, shortly after the hotel opened for business, a ramp way above the hotel lobby collapsed, causing various bolts and floor systems to give way. Many people were pinned under concrete as water gushed into the lobby from water mains; first responders struggled to identify where water main valves were located because the property was new to them. Several respected analysts suggested in public hearings that infighting between local police and first responders complicated the disaster response effort. In the end, 114 were killed and 185 were injured.

The Luxor and Hyatt Regency cases are just two of many in the hospitality industry, and not all cases end with fatalities. On October 10, 2007, the atrium at the Embassy Suites Hotel in Hunt Valley, Virginia, collapsed. Fortunately the noise of ceiling stress and glass breaking alerted guests to run and no one was injured. However, 108 of the hotel's 120 employees were furloughed until the building was deemed safe to occupy again. It should be noted that there is a disproportionate share of industrial accidents at hotels and convention centers because they are continually adding or renovating space. But any facility, from an office or retail space to a nursing facility, can find itself in the midst of chaos when a piece of equipment fails or when safety rules or requirements are not followed.

When you are contemplating beginning a major construction project on your company's property, you may want to consider hiring an independent project supervisor who will examine and verify that contractors have a superb safety record, that all of their records and regulatory requirements are up-to-date, and that your insurance carrier has reviewed the scope of your project.

Whistleblowers

After an industrial accident, it may not take long for current or former employees or contractors to race to the news media or blogs with biting insights on what you should have done better and earlier to prevent harm. One of the U.S. agencies responsible for investigating the 2005 catastrophic fire in Texas City, Texas, that killed 15 people interviewed various employees about their perceptions of what contributed to the explosion. That report concluded:

> Budget cuts were imposed based on the previous year's spending and did not take into account the specific needs of the refinery . . . The prevailing culture at [British Petroleum's (BP)] Texas City Refinery was to accept cost reductions without challenge and not to raise concerns when operational integrity was compromised.

To add insult to real injury, *The Economist* properly lambasted BP's failure to pay attention to prior warnings at its Texas City refinery. A year before this devastating fire, an internal audit at the company found "widespread tolerance of noncompliance with basic Health, Safety and Environmental (HSE) management systems . . . lack of leadership competence and understanding to effectively manage all aspects of HSE . . . and insufficient monitoring of key HSE processes." The tragedy not only spawned 1,700 separate lawsuits, but also resulted in the imposition of a $21 million fine by OSHA.

And what did BP have to say when journalists called the company spokesperson and asked for a comment regarding the disaster in Texas amid an unprecedented joint investigation by the FBI, EPA, and OSHA? "BP spokesman Neil Chapman declined to comment on anything related to the Justice Department's investigation," according to *The Boston Globe*. So much for the BP slogan, "Beyond Petroleum."

Crisis Readiness

Finally, remember that your risk management department will serve you well if you regularly review and update this information in your crisis plan:

- Where your Computer Aided Design (CAD)/architectural blueprints for each floor of your facility are located
- What chemicals are on-site and where/how they are stored
- Which local structural engineers have strong credentials and superb reputations
- Who qualified contractors are that specialize in water, smoke, toxicity remediation, and failure analysis

9

TERRORISM: WHEN "THEIR" PROBLEM BECOMES YOUR NIGHTMARE

A swelling cohort of radicals with boundless anger and a belief in unbounded war, a growing ability to prepare a terrorist attack quickly, the prospect of guidance and technical assistance from a distance—all these add up to a changing threat that may be turning more abundantly dangerous and more difficult to defeat.

— *THE NEXT ATTACK*, BY DANIEL BENJAMIN AND STEVEN SIMON

It comes as no surprise that we live in a world of many dangers. Terrorism is *the* big daddy of them all.

As a business leader, you have a responsibility to think about one profoundly troubling question: Just how would your organization be impacted by a terrorist attack, and how would you respond? To respond effectively, you need to design specific antiterrorism strategies for your organization *now*. Let's think about the magnitude of the issue before addressing potential remedies.

You won't become an expert in terrorism by reading this chapter. Many of the thought leaders that I rely on, such as professor Stephen Sloan of the University of Central Florida, will tell you that even after several decades of studying the history of terrorism as a political and social force, the research journey is never complete. Terrorism is not like medicine, where the hypotheses of science are validated by peer review and tests are used to confirm or deny a diagnosis. Terrorism is interpretative. It is based on some facts, partial facts, known damage, and, most importantly, the desire to create fear.

Weapons of Destruction

We know for a fact that many of the terrorists and alleged perpetrators that have been captured and interrogated in recent years have spent a considerable amount of time analyzing *past* terrorist attacks to help them inflict terror on others. They hoped their research would help them perfect the schematics of their attack and avoid counter-terrorism efforts. With that in mind, let's take a stroll down a perverse memory lane for a minute and consider recent historic milestones in terrorism.

- Palestinian terrorists take control of the cruise ship *Achille Lauro* and throw American passenger Leon Klinghoffer overboard to his death while strapped to his wheelchair (1985)
- Pakistani terrorists kill two and wound three outside the offices of the Central Intelligence Agency in Virginia (1993)
- A well-planned attack by domestic terrorists on the Murrah Federal Building in Oklahoma City, Oklahoma, claims the lives of 168 people, including 19 children; some 674 others are injured by a 4,800-pound explosive containing ammonium nitrate fuel; some 26 buildings in the area adjacent to the building are destroyed or severely impaired; the magnitude of the blast scatters glass and debris over 11 city blocks (1995)
- Hundreds are killed when bombs are detonated simultaneously in the East African cities of Dar Es Salaam, Tanzania, and Nairobi, Kenya; the bombs are intended to kill U.S. government employees, but the majority of the causalities and injured are African (1998)

- Suicide terrorists ram their speedboat into the *U.S.S. Cole* while it is anchored in the Yemen harbor of Aden; the blast creates a massive hole in the vessel, killing 17 and injuring 39 (2000)
- An orchestrated campaign designed by al-Qaeda operatives using attacks on airline personnel leads to attacks that kill over 3,000 people in Pennslyvania, New York, and Washington, D.C.
- Some 202 people are killed after nail- and glass-infused bombs explode at a Bali, Indonesia, nightclub; intelligence reports suggest that al-Qaeda sympathizers planted the bomb as "target practice" for further acts (2002)
- A Moscow theater becomes a surreal home to a disturbing drama of its own as 700 people become pawns in the 29th Division of the Chechen Army's attempt to end the Chechnya War; the army threatened to kill all 700 hostages if the war continued; the Russian Federal Security Service deploys its elite "Alpha" squad to the theater and pumps a mysterious chemical agent into the building; some 39 terrorists and 129 hostages are killed (2002)
- Federal investigators uncover a sophisticated terrorist plot that reportedly targets the MGM Grand Hotel in Las Vegas and the headquarters of *The New York Times* (2002)
- 191 are killed and hundreds of others are injured as the result of three simultaneous bomb blasts on commuter lines and intercity trains in Spain; Prime Minister Jose Anzar initially blames the Basque terrorist group Euskadi Ta Askatasuna (ETA, which stands for, translated from Basque, Basque Fatherland and Liberty) for the killings, but evidence later suggests that al-Qaeda operatives orchestrated the effort; Anzar loses the next national election as a result (2004)
- Fifty-two are killed and at least 700 are injured after four bombs explode on London buses as al-Qaeda operatives seek revenge for British involvement in the Iraq war; most victims are on their way to work or school (2005)
- Several modern-day pirates attempt to gain control of the luxury ship *S.S. Sebourn Spirit* but are thwarted when the

captain acts on his intuition; upon seeing a speedboat armed with cruise missiles racing toward the ship, he rapidly turns, accelerates, and avoids a catastrophe (2005)

Think about the typologies of terror behind these and other serious incidents. For our purposes, we'll focus on the five principal categories of terrorism that could impact any industry, including:

- Nuclear
- Chemical
- Biological
- Violence-inspired
- Technological

As you'll see in a moment, we have witnessed the successful application of four of these five categories against businesses and governments in the past two decades. We'd better pray that we never see the fifth—nuclear detonation—successfully applied. Let's start there.

Nuclear

A nuclear-based attack targeting a major city would likely constitute our worst collective nightmare. You are probably aware of various Armageddon scenarios, but as you contemplate this ghoulish possibility, remember that plutonium, the element necessary for the construction of nuclear weapons, has been stolen several times in recent years. Some nuclear analysts believe that a nuclear device could be used as a means of extortion in the years ahead. Studies by the World Health Organization (WHO), the Brookings Institution, and the Union of Concerned Scientists suggest that the detonation of a "dirty bomb" could claim upwards of 100,000 lives and cause up to $1 trillion in damage—in a single incident. Various intelligence reports suggest that highly potential targets include London, Tokyo, New York, Chicago, Los Angeles, and Tel Aviv.

Chemical

You will recall from earlier in the book that the Aum Shinrikyo domestic terror group successfully used chemical weapons on a Tokyo subway, creating mass panic in Japan in 1995. The Aum attack was relatively limited in scope, as nerve gas is particularly difficult to contain and transport. We must assume, however, that perpetrators are working to overcome these barriers; an aerosol release of these toxins, for example, would be potentially deadly. A coordinated attack of this nature in several locations concurrently could cause a catastrophe so huge that the death toll is unthinkable. It is encouraging to note that police and fire departments in Los Angeles, London, New York, Chicago, and elsewhere have begun to stage simulations in which they consider how they would manage events after a chemical attack; their simulations, grotesquely enough, include the prospect of burning a massive number of corpses to prevent others from becoming seriously ill. Similarly, a massive decontamination of survivors would require that tens of thousands of individuals "strip naked and submit to a brutal shower from a fire hose," according to *Business-Week*. This assumes, of course, that health care workers and other first responders are even capable of reporting to work following such a premeditated incident. In fact, one research study concluded that just 57 percent of health care workers reported that they would actually come to work following a major attack. To achieve this kind of mass havoc, terrorists may not need to be particularly innovative; finding chemicals already located near major cities for use in a terrorist attack is unfortunately rather easy. Bruce Nussbaum of *BusinessWeek* concluded that there are about 700 chemical plants located near or in U.S. cities with populations of at least 100,000; he noted that New Jersey, Houston, Texas, and Louisiana are particularly vulnerable to attack.

Biological

In contrast with avian flu, which is primarily spread through unintentional contact with birds, the intentional release of an Ebola-like virus in a subway station or concert hall is one of the most sinister scenarios capable of dismantling a stable society; the germs would spread so quickly that there would be no hope of containing the virus. The Department of Homeland Security (DHS) estimates that a single attack on a city such as San Francisco or Houston could cost as much as $750 *billion*, and that as many as one million people would perish were the germ to effectively spread and mutate.

Violence-inspired

Violence-inspired terrorism resulted in the loss of nearly 3,000 lives on September 11, 2001. Comparatively, North America was fortunate not to have been victimized earlier, as there have been hundreds of recorded terrorist attacks on civilians prior to 9/11 in Northern Ireland, Africa, Britain, the Philippines, and elsewhere. In assessing how the United States became so vulnerable to attack, Federal Bureau of Investigation (FBI) director Robert Mueller told a closed-door hearing of the 9/11 Commission on April 14, 2004 (transcripts were later released):

> There were no slip-ups. Discipline never broke down. They gave no hint to those around them what they were about. They came lawfully. They lived lawfully. They trained lawfully. They boarded the aircraft lawfully. They simply relied upon everything from the vastness of the Internet to the openness of our society to do what they wanted to do without detection.

Technological

For years and with differing degrees of success, terrorist-hackers have been orchestrating tens of thousands of attacks aimed at dismantling the technology that supports the Internet. They also relentlessly attempt to destroy specific software platforms that are the lifelines of various institutions, including banks, insurance companies, universities, technology firms, and others. Unfortunately, the public doesn't really view perpetrators of technology crimes with the same degree of disdain as that with which they consider political operatives. But I suspect most would change their minds if the ventilators in their local hospitals ceased functioning after a hacker dismantled regional electrical grids.

Law enforcement agencies regard hackers as some of the most potentially destructive terrorists in modern-day society. Intelligence specialists are mindful of individuals such as Kevin David Mitnick, for instance, a hacker who used social engineering methods to steal intellectual property from a variety of companies in the 1990s. Mitnick was convicted for various computer crimes and served five years in prison. Although Mitnick does not see himself as a terrorist and has since become a consultant who teaches companies how to enhance their software security systems, his crimes brought massive havoc to those he targeted. I should know—I was vice president of crisis management at Motorola when he targeted some of our proprietary encryption data. Mitnick's sympathizers would argue that by exposing weaknesses in firewalls and intrusion detection systems, he actually initiated a badly needed investment of time and capital in security awareness that ended up making corporate security stronger. I suspect they're right.

Law enforcement agencies regard hackers as some of the most potentially destructive terrorists in modern-day society.

Typologies of Terrorism

Now let's analyze those categories of terrorism that impact business within the context of the primary drivers behind acts of terror in a modern world. We face:

- **Autocrat-driven terrorism:** The direct application of terror by a dominant force against its own people, such as that committed by Joseph Stalin, Idi Amin Dada, and Pol Pot
- **State-sponsored terrorism:** Funded and designed by governments such as North Korea and Iran
- **Alliance-sponsored terrorism across continents:** Such as that of al-Qaeda operatives and their sympathizers and funders
- **Individual and small-group perpetrators:** Including domestic terrorists who act at home, abroad, or both; for instance, a Sikh terrorist plot to destroy an Air India plane at John F. Kennedy

International Airport failed in 1986 but succeeded in 1995; similarly, al-Qaeda sympathizers attempted to destroy the World Trade Center in 1993 in a bombing that killed six people; they succeeded in 2001 upon a second attempt

On its Web site, fbi.gov, the FBI defines terrorism as:

The unlawful use of force or violence against people or property to intimidate or coerce a government, the civilian population, or any segment thereof in the furtherance of political or social objectives.

Although there are many definitions of terrorism, here is the one I have developed for business leaders:

Terrorism is the threatened or actual use of weapons intended to cause widespread human, political, economic, and social disruption; the physical harm inflicted is significantly out of proportion to the emotional impact on immediate victims because of long-term psychological damage.

It should be noted that these and other definitions of terrorism all contain the following elements, to some degree:

- Violence
- Audience
- Fear
- Innocent victims
- Political/social/personal motives

While we often think of terrorism as a "vocation" (traditional view), today we must realize that terrorism is a "business" (nontraditional view) and that profit is sometimes a motivating factor. As one of my colleagues, Geary Sikich, notes in his work, *Integrated Business Continuity: Maintaining Resilience in Uncertain Times*, definitions of terrorism need to be expanded to include organized crime, drug cartels, and others. Those terrorists that are motivated by a profit, including fringe extremists, extremists, ideological groups, and gangs also have the desire to wreak havoc on their surroundings.

The Cast of Characters

Twenty years ago, the world was focused on threats posed by the Irish Republican Army (IRA), an extremist political organization whose principal aim was to extricate British rule from Northern Ireland. The IRA's tactics—principally bombings—disrupted the fragile state of relations between Britain and Ireland. The IRA was responsible for a devastating bombing in the heart of London's financial district in 1993, as well as for scores of subsequent and random car, home, and office bombings throughout the United Kingdom. As some IRA operatives later admitted during legal proceedings, the perpetrators desired a reward greater than the immediate killing of victims. Their goal was to inflict fear and create post-incident panic; they realized that the bombings caused many people to stop shopping, investing, and sending their children to school out of fear for their personal safety and that of their families. The operatives hoped that their phantom attacks would disrupt social order and proceedings to such a degree that the British government would change its policies in an attempt to ward off future attacks.

Terrorists are refining their methods to increase their rate of success, and they're learning numerous lessons from history books. Indeed, history is rich in lessons regarding acts of terror that have been perpetrated by a wide variety of radicals. Perhaps the most notorious terrorist in history was Pol Pot, the leader of the Khmer Republic in Cambodia from 1976 to 1979, who led a massive terror campaign that resulted in the deaths of an estimated 1.7 million of his own people. Similarly, Vladimir Lenin plays an especially noteworthy role in the history of terrorism because, unlike in prior civil wars, where the destruction of businesses was the result of collateral damage, Lenin encouraged Russian revolutionaries to intentionally destroy any business or agency that stood in his way. Robert Service in *Lenin: A Biography* (2000), writes:

Lenin's solution was to give arms to detachments of workers and students and let them go on revolutionary activity . . . The detachments should kill spies, blow up police stations, rob banks and confiscate the resources they need for an armed insurrection. His imagination ran wild. When it came to street conflicts, he suggested the detachments should pull up paving stones or prepare hot kettles and run to the tops of buildings in order to attack troops sent against them. Another proposal was to keep a store of acid to hurl at policemen.

Not in My Backyard

Remember that terrorists, whatever their specific gripe may be, are not always easily identifiable. You will recall that seven physicians were arrested in Britain and Australia in July 2007 after a firebomb exploded at Scotland's Glasgow Airport, an attack that intelligence experts believe was merely a trial run for a far more sophisticated attack involving biological weapons. You might find it interesting that physicians are especially treasured by terror organizations; doctors can help their coconspirators understand medical vulnerabilities and what specific attack methods would result in the greatest number of human casualties. Noted *Newsweek*: "The most dangerous extremists are not embittered young men without jobs or hope. They are the elites, or more typically, the sons of the elite who are working out some grievance or vengeance and have the know-how and means to find truly dangerous weapons."

As a result, stereotyping terrorists is simply illogical. Sometimes a terrorist will act alone, with no apparent political agenda; such terrorists have proven themselves capable of eluding even the most talented and skilled investigators. For 18 years, a disturbed loner who was enraged over what he perceived to be the dominance of technology in modern life sent mail bombs to a variety of targets, including university professors and airline executives. We now know that Theodore Kaczynski murdered 3 people and wounded 23 others as part of a complex campaign to pressure modern society to reject software, cable television, motorized transportation, and the telephone—all of which are items he deemed unnecessary. Kaczynski baffled the most fabulously talented forensic psychologists in the world simply because he didn't fit the "profile" of a terrorist. He inflicted fear as much as he inflicted death.

An accomplished mathematician, Kaczynski entered Harvard University at the age of 16, received his Ph.D. from the University of Michigan in mathematics, and was awarded a prestigious fellowship from the National Science Foundation. Kaczynski became an assistant professor at Berkley in 1967, but he resigned abruptly only two years later, becoming a loner and drifting from state to state. He eventually moved into a crude, one-room cabin in Montana, where he wrote incredibly detailed "manifestos" on the dangers of technology. Later known as the Unabomber, Kaczynski wrote: "The most dangerous leftists of all . . . avoid irritating displays of aggressiveness and refrain from advertising their leftism, but work quietly and unobtrusively to promote collectivist values."

Kaczynski is the embodiment of his very characterization. In a twist of irony, as psychologists were analyzing the manifestos he had mailed to various groups and individuals, hundreds of corporations raced to purchase expensive bomb detection technologies for their mailrooms to protect their employees from Kaczynski's exploits. Eventually, *The New York Times* and *The Washington Post* agreed to publish his ramblings at the request of the Department of Justice, who feared that if this were not done, more victims inevitably would be targeted. Millions of dollars were spent on the manhunt for this single perpetrator who inflicted nationwide terror. The Unabomber represented a particularly unique terrorist profile; he was not angry with any single person or political policy, but rather was a prolific ideologue with a diabolical mind. By inflicting terror, Kaczynski was able to communicate an obscure message to a national platform that few would have otherwise cared about or agreed with. He was a killer *and* a social extortionist.

Despite the efforts of what went down as the most exhaustive manhunt in FBI history, it was not until Kaczynski's brother David read a 35,000-word essay penned by the Unabomber called *Industrial Society and Its Future* that he recognized a stream of thought that paralleled his brother's beliefs; he contacted an attorney who in turn called the FBI. David Kaczynski recognized very specific vocabulary usage and a unique writing style that was eerily similar to letters he had collected over the years from his estranged brother. Rather than employing a biopsychosocial model to assess the threat, he acted on his *intuition* to identify a terrorist.

The Unabomber's acts impacted victims at a variety of businesses and institutions, including Northwestern University, American Airlines, Boeing, the United States Air Force, California Forestry Association, and others. He was sentenced to life in prison without parole and is serving his time at a federal prison in Florence, Colorado.

No matter whether we're talking about attacks by the Unabomber or by al-Qaeda, remember this: The very dynamics of terrorism have shifted dramatically over the past decade. Whereas businesses were once secondary casualties, now *commerce has become a prime target*. When fear is achieved, the terrorist succeeds. As a result, you must become a student of history as well as a bit of a soothsayer if you are responsible for the people and physical assets of any organization.

> Whereas businesses were once secondary casualties, now *commerce has become a prime target.*

When You're the Target

The face of terrorism is changing. We are in the midst of an unprecedented holy war aimed not only against governments, but also against business. There was no evidence that the Hindu nationalist who assassinated Mahatma Gandhi in 1948 or the Muslim members of the Egyptian Islamic Jihad who murdered Egyptian president Anwar Sadat in 1981 were aiming to disrupt financial markets. But today, raids on alleged terror cells in London, New York, and elsewhere are turning up copies of *The Financial Times* and *The Wall Street Journal*; perpetrators are watching CNBC and monitoring the volatility of oil prices. They are seeking recruits who work in banks, stock markets, and mutual fund firms. And what is their aim? They want to incite economic and social turmoil. These facts are undeniable.

This jihad is fueled by a passion for revenge and religion and is being funded by an alliance of misfits that stretches across dozens of countries. As you will see, various factions have been fine-tuning their arsenal of weapons with increasing skill and deadliness in recent years. But, as was previously mentioned, the terrorists' weapon of choice is fear—especially when they are targeting businesses. They relish the fact that consumers spend less money on an industry after it has been targeted by terrorism. Their strike may be on only a single nightclub in Bali or Jakarta, but in doing so they are able to devastate a resort area's convention business for a decade or longer. Remember that the goal of the terrorist is to create an impact larger and more profound than that felt on *immediate* victims. In this regard, they inevitably win. Business loses.

That is, if we let this happen.

Business leaders are cooperating with governments more than ever in the effort to intercept terrorist plots before they destroy innocent people and institutions. But, as professor Denis Smith of the University of Glasgow told me in a personal communication, unless there is role clarity in advance among investigators and first responders, infighting will occur when we need these professionals' services most. "There are still tensions between organizations about areas of control and responsibility," he noted. Despite this, progress is being made in both the public and private sectors. He added that companies such as Shell and British Petroleum "have invested considerable amounts of time and effort in developing their crisis management capabilities. What companies such as these seek to achieve is an awareness of [both] the issues that allow incidents to escalate into crises and the importance of good information flows and decision-making capabilities in dealing with problems as they occur." He believes that role clarity probably is far superior in corporations than it is between police and fire responders, most notably because corporate leaders have the ability to dictate how—and on what priorities— funds will be expended. In contrast, first responders must respond to all the demands and critical needs that result from a crisis, and thus must listen to multiple demands and many bosses. In the process, they inevitably will disappoint or cause friction with another bureaucrat.

Another reality: Most businesses still believe that antiterrorism initiatives should fall within the domain of the government. But more business leaders need to understand that if they are alert to suspicious people and activities and report their concerns to authorities, they can make a difference. Why? Because whether you have a business in St. Louis, Missouri, or in Taipei, an attack anywhere could significantly disrupt your people, IT, communications, and transportation systems.

If you manage any corporation or agency, you should always act on the assumption that you could be a direct or secondary target in a major terrorist attack. Even if a weapon of mass destruction (WMD) or another calamity does not directly impact your business, historically the impact of terror on business has been profound. As you read through this list, ask yourself: Am I ready? What do I need to do to ensure that our readiness is complete? The impact range includes:

- Immediate loss of life and survivors who must grapple with permanent injuries
- Traumatized employees, customers, and others who witness an attack and must assist those who suffer from massive injuries
- Suspension of transportation systems, including the closing of bridges, highways, airports, and rail and bus systems
- Suspension of mail, including government-sponsored mail systems and those of private vendors, such as FedEx or DHL
- Potential disruption to telephony systems, making landline and cellular communication with family members, hospitals, and first responders difficult or impossible
- Social and criminal opportunists, including looters and others who seek to take advantage of community havoc; this includes the potential exposure of your retail space, warehouses, and other areas containing high-yield items
- Payroll and accounts payable/receiving continuation; you would be amazed at the number of companies that still issue paper checks to employees as opposed to insisting on direct deposit as a condition of pay, so remember that those with criminal records, and this includes potential terrorists, avoid direct deposit because banks and credit unions require passport and birth certificate validation under the Patriot Act

- Temporary suspension of banking, stock trading, and other financial transactions
- Web site and Web-based transactions freezing or suspension for days, including inventory and just-in-time implications for manufacturing and customer service purposes

Remember that regardless of what happens during a terrorist attack, your operation is likely be impacted to some degree.

Your organization should be prepared to provide aid if and when a major incident in which hundreds or thousands are killed occurs in your community. Crisis managers must shine during these moments of tragedy; their singular responsibility will be to assist in coordinating all aspects of incident response and recovery. Among the issues you may have to confront are:

- Locating and identifying missing people
- Providing trauma counseling; we know conclusively that the sooner counseling begins, the less residual the impact, and so highly qualified trauma counselors often are invaluable after a terrorist attack; make sure that a directory of qualified advisors is included as an essential aspect of your crisis plan
- Tracking requests for donations from families, neighbors, and community groups, such as the Salvation Army and Red Cross, that provide relief, and having a "fast track" ability to provide financial and other assistance
- Assisting with temporary camps and relief centers; the homeless and newly homeless will have an extraordinary need for shelter, food, and other basic needs
- Using Google Maps and Google Earth to ascertain the level of devastation if cable television and other technologies are disabled
- Providing aid to community child protection systems, since during and after major incidents, children are especially vulnerable; you will want to consider added security for your child care center and realize that some of the children of those who work for you may now be orphans; counseling, support, and community services will need to be coordinated and thoughtfully implemented

As you discuss these issues with your staff, you'll want to peruse the Business Continuity Plan toward the end of this book for further clarity on how to move your organization from a planning stage to one of genuine preparedness.

Business: The Unspoken Victim

When terrorists strike, the community where that attack occurs often is dismantled. At the very least, it's psychologically traumatized. But another community, that of employers, is similarly impacted, often with devastating consequences.

During the World Trade Center attacks, 700 of financial firm Cantor Fitzgerald's employees perished; insurance broker Marsh McLennan lost 292 employees. The New York City Fire Department saw 345 of its heroes killed. Because so many of these organizations' employees were concentrated in one location, the impact of the 9/11 attacks on them was profound. Other firms also suffered an immense loss of life and talent, but the statistical impact for them was different, principally because of luck and location: Morgan Stanley employed 3,730 people at the South Tower and Five World Trade Center, and yet only 6 died. Sun Microsystems employed 351 people in the South Tower: all survived. Not surprisingly, evacuation worked best for those employees working on the floors below where the jetliners struck.

The list of 9/11 victims represented a mosaic of society: Entrepreneurs, small business owners, single moms, students, Hollywood producers, Pentagon personnel, and priests were similarly affected. According to the National Commission on Terrorist Attacks, it took 19 terrorists less than $500,000 to prepare for and execute a multi-phased plan that claimed the lives of some 3,000 innocent people and that also fundamentally changed the institutions for which the victims worked. Along these lines, I'd like to suggest that corporations can be victims as well.

It is impossible to replace those victimized by the 9/11 attacks; the incurred loss was monumental to the families, friends, and coworkers of those who perished, and people's grief was made worse by their lack of tangible proof of death. As a result, the most massive forensic investigation in history was undertaken by the Office of the Chief Medical Examiner in New York; scientists and other specialists transported almost two million tons of debris to Staten Island, where nearly two thousand pieces of tooth, bone, and other anatomical evidence were recovered and analyzed for their DNA makeup to help identify those who had died. Those families that knew the names of the victims' primary-care physicians and dentists were able to pull their loved ones' records and identify their remains faster.

While the unpleasantness of recovering their family members' remains certainly took a toll on survivors, so too did the discovery that many of their loved ones lacked adequate life insurance. In light of this, be sure that your life insurance coverage is sufficient to protect those you would leave behind if you were to die suddenly. With a sudden death, your family might be faced with the compelling need to fill the gap of decades of lost income; tuition, mortgages, and other major bills still must be paid. You should consult with a Chartered Life Underwriter (CLU) or a Chartered Financial Consultant (ChFC) regarding your specific needs and be sure that your insurance and estate plan documents are in a place that can be accessed by your next-of-kin.

Stages of Response

When a terrorist attack occurs, companies should transition through four phases of response.

- First, business leaders should attend to victims and their families. Thoughtful employers will try to offer short-term financial relief to impacted families to assist them with their medical or funeral expenses. You will want to offer employee assistance counseling to families, witnesses, and coworkers to help them cope with the tragedy.
- Second, you should assess the intellectual capital and business acumen lost. Since you are running an enterprise, you have an obligation to your shareholders and employees to reboot and recharge as soon as possible so that you remain a viable

organization. To do so, your leaders in human resources should conduct a thorough assessment of knowledge and skills lost. You'll need to create a battle plan of how you will recruit new talent to offset those who may need months to recover from injuries. This is one of the key reasons that smart organizations continually memorialize projects, skill sets, and deliverables *before* a terrorist attack occurs. Should you lose an entire facility or team of key individuals, how would you recapture your competitive edge?

- Third, business leaders should examine the impact of the attack on their physical and technological assets and restore operations as soon as possible. It sounds uncaring, but while you are burying your employees, visiting hospitals, and trying to cope with personal and group grieving, your customers have a different set of priorities: Where is my product? When will it arrive? Why is your call center not answering my questions? Right now, in advance, you should be thinking about how you would seamlessly transition your key operations, from telephony to shipping and receiving, to an off-site location. If you wait until your community or country is under attack, it may be too late to locate the many essential vendors that can help you reboot your company. Break ties with any sense of denial you may be feeling. We are living— and *working*—in a different world.

- Fourth, revisit your insurance coverage for business interruption and your terrorism riders now (you should review details of the Terrorism Risk Insurance Act of 2002 on the Internet). Leading organizations that dispute settlement offers from their insurance companies after a terrorist attack typically will need to slug it out to determine how much it will actually cost to rebuild lost infrastructure. Take a detailed inventory of your human and capital assets and retain it off-site. When is the last time you looked at your company's insurance policy? Is terrorism included, and if so, under what conditions? If you don't have a risk management specialist on your staff, invite a member of the Risk and Insurance Management Society (RIMS) to speak to your executive team. Their contact information can be found at the end of the book.

Speaking of insurance, my bet is that you have no idea just what kind of coverage your company has in the event that you lost people and other assets in a terrorist attack. I assure you that the time to review your coverage is now, before one of these calamities occurs.

You can buy insurance from companies like American International Group (AIG) that will help you recover the costs of some of your company's direct losses that result from terrorism (such as a destroyed building), but insurance can never help you recoup your loss of talented people. In some cases, these policies will reimburse you for revenue lost as a result of closing your business for several days or weeks. But for most businesses, the deductible you're responsible to pay will typically amount to $5 million or more. It took years for the businesses in and around the World Trade Center to complete claims with insurers, even after the federal government provided them with direct financial assistance.

As a leader, it is your responsibility to be aware of issues of insurability. The time to learn about your financial exposure is now, before devastating events occur. Large companies have risk management departments that typically work with credible insurance brokers; I encourage you to invite a few brokers to visit your office and provide you with a briefing; in doing so, you will learn in detail what is, and what is not, covered by your plan.

Many insurance companies work in close concert with Lloyd's of London because its underwriters arguably have the best historical, geopolitical, and financial data in the world. If you ever visit Lloyd's headquarters, you'll see rows of hundreds of desks where underwriters discuss and debate their clients' risk exposure. And there, in the middle of the largest floor in the world devoted to risk management, is Lloyd's Holy Grail—mammoth master logs the size of a coffee table. I'm not kidding. These logs go back to 1688. Each day since the one on which the logs were first employed, whenever a ship that Lloyd's underwrites experiences an industrial accident, environmental spill, or storm damage, the location and details of that accident are entered into these logs by hand. The sheer brainpower, mathematical modeling, and geopolitical analysis collected from centuries of experience in just this one industry should give you an idea about how much Lloyd's has learned about the analytics of risk.

Given what we know, who needs terrorism insurance the most? Based on a detailed analysis in *Terrorism and Business*, the industries that suffered the most in terms of market decline in the month following the 9/11 attacks were:

1. Semiconductor equipment
2. Metal mining
3. Photo and imaging
4. Hotels and resorts
5. Airlines

But keep reading. Those are the companies that suffered *immediately* because of nervous investors. Based on my analysis of earnings over the next four quarters after the 2004 Madrid bombings and the September 11, 2001, attacks, here are the industries that suffered the most from a *sustained* loss of revenue:

1. Airlines
2. Hotels and resorts
3. Automobile sales
4. High-end retail clothes
5. Casinos

As you can see, the hospitality and travel industries pay a disproportionate price for terrorism. Because the aorta of tourism remains the airlines—without them, there are virtually no transnational meetings or major conventions—they are, and will likely remain, a prime target of perpetrators of terror.

You probably didn't think much about it, but an estimated 300 small businesses in New York City alone closed their doors permanently after the 9/11 attacks. Most lacked adequate insurance, a Business Continuity Plan, and the liquid capital needed to reopen. Other enterprises that lost some of their employees on 9/11 found the tragedy so operationally disabling that they permanently moved key departments out of New York City, seeking refuge in New Jersey, Connecticut, and elsewhere. Most companies that remained in New York spent considerable time revisiting their notification and evacuation systems because they witnessed a city in panic; highways and bridges were shut down, restaurants closed, and tens of thousands of people had no way to get home after subway and bus systems were frozen in place. They did this only after experiencing a terrorist attack because contemplating disaster in advance would have required them to spend time on the uncomfortable subject of risk management. Some senior executives may have charged that preparing for such an attack would have been too doomsday-like in thinking or would have resulted in too much lost time spent on a scenario that would never impact *them*.

Regardless of your location and the nature of your enterprise, just remember the realities of the age in which we live; there are over 676 identified "hate groups" (tolerance.org) in the United States alone, not to mention the 200-plus internationally based hate organizations. Their membership rolls are increasing. The active supporters and sympathizers of these organizations have begun to infiltrate our workplaces. As a result, our ability to detect and deter perpetrators is becoming increasingly more difficult. Because terrorists have no conscience, we need to be smarter, better resourced, and anticipatory in our thinking. We need to plan.

Terror Awareness, Not Prevention

Unless you're James Bond and have the resources of MI6 at your disposal, your best bet in a dangerous world is to prudently assess four fundamental issues:

1. How exposed is your organization?
2. How you would notify and evacuate your employees in the event of a threat or incident?
3. How will your enterprise achieve its goals and objectives (after all, that is why you are in business)?
4. Do you have sufficient insurance to sustain your organization after a calamity?

Terrorism is a greater threat to your organization if you have human and physical assets in a major metropolitan area or if you rely on key suppliers who are located in or near such cities. The geocentric aspects of terrorism are especially sensitive if you operate in North America, Europe, and/or Asia. Because terrorists seek to inflict the maximum amount of damage possible in the hopes that their actions will elicit a change in governmental policy, they prefer urban targets. There is increasing concern, however, that they are also interested in learning how to compromise the food or medical supply of an entire population. Bottom line: We simply don't know what terrorists are up to. It is often not until the final phase of planning, when a mistake is made or a sympathizer contacts law enforcement officials, that we become aware of a potential attack.

Your single greatest opportunity to make a difference in the lives of your employees during a terrorist attack is in your notification of evacuation. No matter whether your operations are housed in a single building or are in a stream of corporate campuses or warehouses, you have a fundamental Duty to Warn. You may want to read more about the Occupational Safety and Health Act's General Duty Clause to ensure the safety of your workplace.

To accomplish this, you must be able to quickly notify your employees, whether through word of mouth or a public address or e-mail system, that a threat or incident has caused you to suspend operations. You then need to make a decision to advise employees to either stay in place (if an unknown chemical has been released, close your air vents) or evacuate. You'll need to consider evacuation accommodations for disabled, pregnant, and other special-needs employees. In the event of electrical power loss, a simple, battery-operated bullhorn can spread your message effectively, as long as you can communicate the same message to associates in all locations quickly. What people crave in the midst of a critical incident is *direction*: Tell them where to go, what to do, and how to remain in contact with you.

> What people crave in the midst of a critical incident is *direction*: Tell them where to go, what to do, and how to remain in contact with you.

A word of caution on evacuation: Always do your very best to know all of the facts before you make a recommendation. Hundreds of employees who worked in the North and South Towers of the World Trade Center were ill-advised by 911 telephone operators to remain inside and stay calm, even as danger engulfed them. In a major analysis of 103 phone conversations between those trapped on high floors and emergency operators, only two callers were told to evacuate the building; the rest were told to stay in place, put on hold, or told that the city could provide no meaningful guidance. *The New York Times* concluded that the final human contact that many of those trapped ever received was, for the most part, filled with ambiguity and inaccuracy. Operators lacked proper training and guidance, complicating a horrendous nightmare. As reported in the April 1, 2006, edition of *The Times*:

> Overworked, overwhelmed, they were thrust into situations for which no training could prepare them. Yet they kept picking up phones, improvising answers even when they were exasperated, even when they were in the dark about evacuation orders that had been issued by fire and police commanders. Helplessness increasingly defined their predicament and it showed in some of their conversations.

Astoundingly, the very people who most need training in evacuation messaging—our phone operators and receptionists—are often the least trained in emergency procedures. You can address this situation tomorrow by scheduling a meeting of those who respond to security calls at your organization and reviewing what they should do, as well as what template messages they should rely on, if a major incident were to occur. Better yet, include them in your simulations and drills, since they undoubtedly will be called on to act when your leadership is tested with a crisis.

A Sobering Risk Assessment

You may be saying to yourself, "My enterprise wouldn't be of any interest to a terrorist," but sorry—it's not all about you. It could be about your city, or about disabling the electrical grid that serves your region, or about destroying area rail systems or schools, all of which are events aimed at harming civilians and first responders while concurrently inflicting widespread fear. What's even more disturbing is that *terrorists do not generally fear retribution*. The kamikaze method of a surprise attack is now embedded into the minds of tens of thousands of terrorists-in-training.

Writing in *The Art of War*, Sun Tzu offered insight into the value of planning for nonconventional battle more than 2,000 years ago. His counsel is a playbook for the modern terrorist:

> The enemy must not know where I intend to give battle. For if he does not know where I intend to give battle, he must prepare in a great many places . . . If he prepares to the front, his rear will be weak, and if to the rear, his front will be fragile. If he prepares to the left, his right will be vulnerable and if to the right, there will be few on his left. And when he prepares everywhere he will be weakened everywhere.

So doing nothing and assuming that your government will race to the rescue and bring relief to victims, medical assistance to the injured, and immediate insurance relief to your factory or store is impractical. You may or may not rebound from the immediate impact of an attack. But with planning and awareness, you can build a culture in your organization that will help make you more adaptable to the impact of a major incident—and that's a start.

Paranoia

In 1996, the chief executive of Intel Corporation wrote a book called *Only the Paranoid Survive*. The title is magnificent because it's true.

If you are leading an enterprise today, you need to be concerned about and sensitive to many of the subjects in this book. Terrorism should be at the top of your planning list. If you're still skeptical, let me try to motivate you to act by reviewing several of the more nasty events that could cause havoc for you, your employees, and customers.

First, let's look at anthrax. An aerosol release of anthrax inside a stadium or hotel convention center would be devastating for victims.

It would unquestionably paralyze commerce for a sustained period. Two Washington, D.C., analysts who study terrorism, Alexander and Alexander, estimate that tens of thousands of people would die if just 100 kilograms of anthrax spores were released inside a large facility.

Second, let's consider the prospect of terrorists unleashing an outbreak of smallpox. The U.S. government has organized several simulations to test community and first responder effectiveness against such a scenario. In the summer of 2001, the government funded a project in Oklahoma City, Oklahoma, called "Dark Winter"; the results of this simulation suggest that millions of people in dozens of states could be sickened—and millions could die—if terrorists pursued such an attack. If smallpox became virulent in Los Angeles, for example, and spread throughout Orange County and beyond, about one-sixth of the American population could be compromised within a month.

Third, let's turn to the container industry, as our shipping lanes are really highways of global commerce. Stephen E. Flynn, former senior fellow at the Council on Foreign Relations, observed at an international forum after 9/11 that if terrorists were to compromise containers used to ship products—which is incredibly likely, by the way—the resultant destruction would be unprecedented. In its summary of that meeting, the Japan Society reported that "there are no barriers to access, no controls across the chain of custody and it is infinitely scalable" because several million maritime containers enter the United States annually. Flynn's research shows that upwards to 500 trucks a day bring 160 boxes *an hour* onto ships headed for the West from Hong Kong and Singapore: "Checking the contents of each container is practically impossible," he noted. Given that America's port security is lax and our maritime borders are not aggressively patrolled, a WMD could easily be transported inside a container on a ship. "Why develop a missile?" he asked. Gulp.

As a leader who must assess the risk tolerance of your organization, it is essential that you:

- **Watch the markets.** There tends to be a "freeze frame" effect after a terrorism-related event; regulators sometimes cause this freeze frame by suspending market trading to minimize the likelihood that investors will trade all their stocks on impulse and cause a market crash. Intended to minimize profiteering, market suspensions have rarely been used. But desperate times call for desperate measures, as in the case of 9/11, when U.S. financial markets did not reopen until September 17. The 9/11 Commission in the United States speculated that members of al-Qaeda contemplated purchasing equities before the attacks in order to financially profit from their plan, but this theory was never proven.

- **Watch organizations on the brink.** We now have conclusive evidence that companies struggling before a terrorist attack may see an accelerated decline in profits after a terrorist incident. When a major terrorist attack occurs, investors in Asia, Europe, and North America tend to embrace "safe haven" investments, such as bonds. As Washington, D.C., insiders Alexander and Alexander wrote in *Terrorism and Business*, the following companies that were struggling to survive financially pre-9/11 found that events *after* the terrorist attacks led to the demise of their investors' confidence: Renaissance Cruises, the Aladdin Casino and Hotel in Las Vegas, Polaroid, Bethlehem Steel, and Burlington Industries. All of these companies either closed their doors or filed for Chapter 11 bankruptcy, most likely as an indirect result of the 9/11 attacks.

- **Watch for opportunists.** After a major terrorist incident, a variety of self-proclaimed "experts" will make their way onto CNN, BBC, and other global networks and blogs spouting proclamations about how *their* staff had been monitoring the group responsible for the attack and how *their* clients benefited from their unique insight. I have intense disdain for most of these people because those who take terrorism studies seriously recognize that the time, location, and impact of a specific attack is unknown, often even to perpetrators, until the moment that the event actually occurs. This is especially true in the case of suicide bombers. Conversely, I admire the insights of such serious scholars of terrorism as Professor Sloan of the University of Central Florida, who has spent years studying the tactics and motives of terrorists. His bottom line: Governments remain the only entities that have an arsenal of intelligence and other resources that is strong enough to prevent or mitigate a terrorist attack. Instead of wasting time trying to predict when and where the next terrorist attack will occur, leaders of corporations should focus on *adapting* to this new world.

Instead of wasting time trying to predict when and where the next terrorist attack will occur, leaders of corporations should focus on *adapting* to this new world.

We simply can't wish that this problem will go away.

So, if terrorism is an ongoing threat to industry, what can you do to minimize your exposure to terrorism events?

- As a leader, your ability to conduct internal audits or implement travel policies gives you a considerable amount of control over restricting the number of executives traveling together at any one time. TJX, owner of Marshall's and T.J. Maxx, lost seven buyers and executives when American Airlines Flight 11 crashed into the North Tower of the World Trade Center on September 11, 2001. For TJX, this tragedy was a human—as well as business—catastrophe.
- You can create a redundancy plan for your IT systems so that your customers are not adversely impacted for a prolonged period. Virtually every business in the world is reliant on IT to one degree or another. Ask your key vendors for a copy of their crisis plans—if nothing else, doing so will assure you that they have one.
- Ask yourself: If our facilities became a place of refuge for employees and neighbors, could we accommodate them with food and water for a prolonged period?
- Push your teams for specific answers: Will our exit plan be effective enough to ensure the safe evacuation of all of our employees if officials warned that a threat is imminent?

Let's consider other avenues.

Although the terrorist organization that you should be most worried about is al-Qaeda, because it is unrivaled in sophistication and financial backing, numerous other internationally based terrorist groups are pursuing their own agendas with increasing velocity.

There are also hundreds of domestic terror groups seeking to dismantle governments in parts of Europe, North America, and Asia. Let's hope they don't secure a group discount and hold a convention in Las Vegas.

Looking Ahead

When the next orchestrated attack occurs, we should expect it to be monumental in scope. Intelligence sources have warned us that "splinter" groups embedded in Afghanistan, Iraq, and elsewhere are now cooperating with one another, supported by unprecedented secrecy and renewed financial strength. Unlike street gangs that often attack at random, terrorist organizations are willing to invest many years in designing a single attack that inflicts massive injury on people and organizations. To be successful and create a sense of insecurity worldwide, they increasingly target commerce, as well as embassies. Unlike conventional warfare, where the general consensus is that targeting schools and hospitals is unacceptable, terrorists reject standards of civility. Everything connected to the enemy is game. There are no rules, no warnings; nothing is "off limits."

Reports published after the attacks of September 11, 2001, informed us that terrorists and their sponsors will spend thousands of hours learning and assessing the vulnerability of both the people and the systems they are targeting. The 9/11 hijackers, for example, carefully studied and practiced their routine; they even analyzed the seating charts of various airliners, eventually picking the one that allowed them to remain in eye contact despite sitting across the aisle from one another. They literally rehearsed their routine on prior American and United Airlines flights. We know that they visited Maine's Portland International Airport and Boston's Logan International Airport several times as part of an intensive surveillance program aimed at detecting the alertness of airport personnel to knives and other weapons. They took flying lessons, practiced navigating an aircraft on flight simulators, and read numerous books to learn the amount of gasoline needed to ignite a fire that could burn through steel and cause building fatigue. They were not only terrorists; they were students of risk management and business vulnerability.

Harsh as it may sound, your security guards aren't much of a match for these guys. Placing concrete barriers in front of your building may help deter a car bomber, for sure. But for the most part, our collective well-being is in the hands of experts who continually analyze communications, infiltrate organizations, study financial transactions across borders, and engage in counterterrorism tactics. The people who do this for a living are incredibly underpaid, underappreciated, and often misunderstood. We frequently hear about the mistakes they make at a Congressional hearing, but we never hear about their valor and success in interrupting the unthinkable.

Many of the most respected names in corporate security and Western intelligence believe that we should anticipate future orchestrated catastrophic attacks in several cities. The events that are being planned may be designed to pressure various governments, such as those in Britain, Israel, and the United States, to change their policies.

While al-Qaeda failed completely in its 1995 plan to blow up a dozen transatlantic planes simultaneously over the Pacific, its success on 9/11 was only partial (at least four other concurrent plots may have been foiled when all commercial planes were grounded in North America). Its next major attack is expected be even more monumental in scope than anything we've experienced before. It will be designed to generate momentum and attract new participation for the organization.

Speaking of momentum, you can't have it without chatter. Scotland Yard hears it, the Japanese National Police processes it, the CIA leaks it—everyone processes chatter, including civilians. *The Philadelphia Inquirer* even uncovered a woman in Montana who every day scans blogs written in Farsi pretending to be an extremist Muslim so she can infiltrate discreet chat rooms and report her findings to government officials in Washington, D.C. Just as they did in World War II, citizen soldiers such as this woman can make a real difference. I just wish there were more of them working inside our food companies, hotels, nuclear power plants, and Amtrak.

Although I'm sure several catastrophic events have been disrupted because the people at the North American Aerospace Defense Command (NORAD) or the woman in Montana intercepted critical information early enough in a potential plot (and I'm mighty glad they did), we cannot rely solely on their good efforts. As a result, *we* have to become radar-screen operators inside our own companies. If we have strong IT firewalls, more astute surveillance, more detailed background checks on new employees—if we create a culture of "if it seems out of place, tell us"—we may make a difference. Bring this up at staff meetings. Encourage law enforcement officials to speak at a meeting of senior executives. Monitor threat assessments by credible sources on the Web.

Now comes the hard part. Even though you may not be able to singularly prevent a future terrorist attack, you still need a comprehensive plan to help your people and customers rebound if one occurs. When you engage those affiliated with your organization in talks about terrorism, however, I'd recommend you keep the discussion theoretical and nonspeculative. Terrorists win by creating widespread panic and paranoia. Thus—and this is really important—leaders *have* to be paranoid. But since you want your employees to show up for work tomorrow, share your concern, show the roadmap in broad terms, and move on. Your job is to manage the art of crisis preparedness while also mastering the science of fear reduction. It's not easy, and it's not pretty—but by God it's important!

> Your job is to manage the art of crisis preparedness while also mastering the science of fear reduction. It's not easy, and it's not pretty—but by God it's important!

Planning

I mentioned chatter with a dose of sarcasm, but it's not a joking matter. Wherever you live, whether it's in Dublin or Los Angeles, the good news is that some extraordinary people who are skilled at foreign languages and geopolitics continually sift through leads. Their efforts often are shared with leading security companies that counsel corporate directors on the security of their enterprises through daily advisories covering trends in kidnapping, piracy of data, and other terrorist threats. If your company cannot afford these briefings, sanitized hybrids are frequently updated on the U.S. State Department's Web site.

In addition to monitoring government advisories, you can invite various thought leaders who are skilled in terrorism studies to speak at your executive roundtables. These terrorism experts often are embedded in the faculties of some of the most prestigious schools around the world, many of which train members of the intelligence community. These include the Fletcher School of Law and Diplomacy at Tufts University, the School for Advanced International Studies at Johns Hopkins University, and the Hoover Institute at Stanford University, among others. You can find other leading geopolitical programs at Brigham Young University, Thunderbird/the American Graduate School of International Management in Arizona, and the University of Glasgow, Scotland. Ask leading scholars from these institutions and your government agencies to provide you with terrorism briefings. Be specific about what you would like to know. Then encourage your teams to use the terrorism preparedness programs of those companies that are reported to be best-in-class within your industry as a benchmark for your own.

In his article, "September 11, 2001 Aftermath: Ten Things Your Organization Can Do Now," Geary Sikich recommends actions that companies can take now that will lower their vulnerability to risk:

Ten Actions	
Action # 1	Make your enterprise an unattractive target
Action # 2	Revise employee screening processes
Action # 3	Validate business, community, and government contacts
Action # 4	Assess Business Continuity Plans
Action # 5	Train and educate your workforce
Action # 6	Equip your workforce
Action # 7	Review leases and contracts for risk exposure
Action # 8	Assess value-chain exposure to supply disruptions
Action # 9	Review insurance policies and conduct cost/benefit analysis
Action # 10	Communicate commitment

Here is what he recommends for each step.

Action #1: Make Your Enterprise an Unattractive Target

If your enterprise presents significant physical barriers to access, it is less likely to be targeted. The application of active, as well as passive, security measures serves to deter the perpetrator. You can introduce "target hardening" measures, such as concrete barriers, cameras, perimeter lighting, and access badges. These measures act as passive deterrents to unauthorized entry. You can also add active barriers to access, such as manned guard emplacements with gates, tire spikes, and reinforced fencing.

Action #2: Revise Employee Screening Processes

More than ever, employers need to identify employees and potential employees who are at risk of being exploited, compromised, or coopted by terrorists or criminals for information, access, or passive cooperation. The better you know your employees, the less likely your organization will be targeted. You can accomplish this by performing more detailed background investigations on potential employees.

Action #3: Validate Business, Community, and Government Contacts

You should learn as much as you can about the critical infrastructures your enterprise depends on:

- Electric, power, supplies
- Gas, oil
- Telecommunications
- Banking, finance
- Transportation
- Water supply systems
- Emergency services
- Continuity of government

Action #4: Assess Business Continuity Plans

Use an "All Hazards" approach when formulating your Business Continuity Plans. An "All Hazards" plan will take into consideration life safety, emergency response, event management, operational events, workplace relocation, and external events, all of which can have a negative impact on your organization.

When broken down into its basic elements, the "All Hazards" approach consists of only six parts:

- Preparation and prevention
- Detection and classification
- Response and mitigation
- Reentry, recovery, and resumption
- Training and resource development
- Information management

Action #5: Train and Educate Your Workforce

Consider developing programs to educate your employees on basic life safety skills (first aid, CPR, evacuation, assembly, and accountability), what to do if an event occurs, and what to do after the event. In addition, a community outreach program can enhance coordination with local emergency response and law enforcement agencies, put your organization in a positive light in the community, and provide your employees with more information on community resources.

Action #6: Equip Your Workforce

You need to equip your workforce with the appropriate emergency response equipment, such as:

- First-aid kits and a defibrillator
- Fire extinguishers
- Event response kits
- Evacuation, assembly, accountability procedures

Action #7: Review Leases and Contracts for Risk Exposure

Every organization needs to completely assess its risk exposure. In addition to the standard risk assessment methodologies currently employed by your enterprise, your organization should review all leases and contracts for potential risk exposure while keeping in mind the specific issues of terrorism and terrorism-related events.

Action #8: Assess Value-Chain Exposure to Supply Disruptions

Study your vulnerability. For example, let's say you are a distributor and are concerned about matters pertaining to critical inventory. While your information systems may be able to accurately assess your inventory, if you were to lose access to your inventory supply location or no longer had the ability to move the inventory to market, it would not matter how accurately you could determine the number of products your company is holding in inventory, as you and your customers would not be able to access the items. "Vulnerability" can therefore be defined as the potential for any degradation, interruption, or nonrecoverability to such an extent that the consequence is likely to result in harm to the organization, harm to others (suppliers, customers, etc.), and substantial negative financial impact.

Action #9: Review Insurance Policies and Conduct Cost/Benefit Analysis

Many organizations will find that a cost/benefit analysis aids in decision making, strategy planning, and the development of risk reduction solutions. Changes in insurance coverage for many organizations in what are deemed to be high-risk/high-exposure areas potentially will be financially burdensome for many organizations. This could lead to adverse effects on the organization's ability to maintain its business orientation, retain or increase staff, and continue to operate from its current locations.

Action #10: Communicate Commitment

It is extremely important for your company to have both primary and adequate backup systems in place that can help you identify, catalog, prioritize, and track issues and commitments relating to crisis management and response activities.

Worst Fears

As you know, Western government agencies employ very smart people who work tirelessly to protect us, but their success often is heavily dependent on tipsters who inform them of data relating to perceived or detected threats. Without those leads, law enforcement officials don't have much of a chance to protect us at home or work.

Since it's prudent to be at least partly paranoid, let's look at a few examples of what *could* happen to you, your organization, and your employees. In June 2007, law enforcement agencies reported that they had uncovered a plot orchestrated by sympathizers of Osama bin Laden that would have caused fuel lines leading to and from John F. Kennedy Airport to blow up in a series of extraordinary, successive detonations. Had the plan been carried out, the world might have witnessed the most deadly terrorist attack in human history. Somewhere between 10,000 and 100,000 people could have been killed (the numbers are purely speculative). Considering the sheer volume of fuel stored in the area's underground pipes and aboveground tanks, all of the passengers and staff at the airport—plus the population of adjacent neighborhoods—could have been destroyed; the loss of life could have been staggering. Had the terrorists succeeded, the very fabric of New York and much of America would have changed—overnight.

If you're one of those folks who complain about the Patriot Act, or maybe you've hurled some insult at a Transportation Security Administration agent who confiscated your bottled water at the airport, you may want to think about what will happen to travel restrictions after *this* kind of attack. We'll be lucky if we can carry a boarding pass.

So, you're probably saying: "Yeah, yeah, heard about JFK. Give me another one." Well, grab another Jack Daniels. Get ready for a doozie.

About 70,000 nuclear weapons have been built in the United States since the outbreak of World War II. Remember that these weapons contain plutonium, a lethal substance that is highly prized by terrorists because it can be used to construct dirty bombs. If deployed in any number of urban areas, such explosives would cause a massive loss of life.

A former Department of Energy employee named Rich Levernier went public in 2003 with his admission that once a year, he orchestrated scenarios as part of his duties in which he and other mock terrorists tried to gain access to Los Alamos National Laboratory in New Mexico, where a considerable stockpile of plutonium is stored. He told *Vanity Fair*: "In more than 50 percent of our tests of the Los Alamos facility, we got in, captured the plutonium, got out again, and in some cases didn't fire a shot because we didn't encounter any guards." What?

The magazine's investigation found that plutonium isn't the only weapon that terrorists are after. Starting in 1966 and for the next several years, a security specialist with the Federal Aviation Administration named Bogdan Dzakovic tried to bring fake bombs and other weapons on various planes headed to North America. He succeeded 31 times . . . in 31 attempts. Dzakovic thinks that another 9/11 is inevitable because our airports are protected by ill-trained, poorly equipped personnel working in environments that are designed to keep planes flying—but not secure. "It makes the flying public think it's being protected—you know, all the theatre of standing in line at airports and taking off your shoes—but it doesn't do much to deter serious terrorists." He's right.

So, let's go back to the example of Los Alamos. Although whistle-blowers such as Levernier have been able to bring attention to our risk exposure to terrorism, the reality is that our government has done comparatively little to construct meaningful safeguards against terrorism and other known security risks. Meanwhile—you may have missed this one—two more vials of plutonium were reported "lost" at Los Alamos in June 2003.

They've never been recovered.

10

SABOTAGE:
THE UNDISCLOSED CRIME

*A Forbes, Inc. computer technician deliberately caused five
of the publisher's eight network services to crash as retribution
for his termination from a temporary position. All of the
information on the affected servers was erased and no data
could be restored. As a result of this one act of sabotage,
Forbes was forced to shut down its New York operations
for two days and sustained losses in excess of $100,000.*

— *ARA* CONTENT

*I'm currently working on a $30–$50 million fraud against a major
manufacturing company with what we believe has the objective to
force the corporation close to bankruptcy. Once near bankruptcy, the
company would be vulnerable to a corporate buy-out. This is an
example of planned economic sabotage on a very large scale.*

—FORMER FBI AGENT FRED GRAESSLE, PERSONAL COMMUNICATION
TO AUTHOR

I have a friend who years ago told me that his dry cleaner had ruined one of his prized suits with a chemical stain; the company
had a great reputation, and this was the first time my friend had ever
encountered a problem with the service he was being provided. When

he asked the manager to rectify the situation, the manager was in-
credulous and insisted that the company was not responsible for the
issue. "After all," the manager pressed, "the suit is made of linen,
and we simply have no obligation to take responsibility for this." My
friend asked again about a fair accommodation. He wasn't asking for
the moon; he simply thought a credit toward future dry cleaning was
the least the dry cleaner could offer.

"No dice," he was told, "that's our policy."

"Hmm . . ." he said to himself. "Well then I'll come up with *my
own policy* toward dry cleaners that screw with customers who have
been loyal for years."

So this friend (who gave me permission to share this story because
he still hates his former dry cleaner) asked his wife and children to
ransack the house, garage, and attic. "Find the nastiest and oldest
clothes in your closets. Find the stuff that even the charities wouldn't
want." They did, and they were able to fill several bags with tattered,
unsalvageable clothing. Next my friend cut a few of the dresses and
coats, pulled off buttons here and there, and basically made the
clothes as unusable as possible. Then he walked into the dry cleaner
and handed over the gigantic bags during the second shift (so the
original manager he confronted wouldn't recognize him) and, after
handing over his order, he provided the name and phone number of a
particular neighbor he couldn't stand.

"Oh, I got him back. We had a cleaner house because of this. The
dry cleaner had several hundred dollars worth of product he couldn't
give away or trace, and my neighbor was probably taken to small
claims court for a bill that he didn't even incur. I loved it."

Now, I know this story isn't supposed to be funny, but I almost
spilled a glass of wine when I heard him tell it because I was laughing
so loud. My friend probably would have wanted me to take my
stained clothes to his former dry cleaner.

Every day around the world, people engage in acts of retribution
and sabotage. The incident I just recounted is miniscule in comparison to the thousands of acts committed daily by employees and customers against businesses that they feel have wronged them. And if a
business experiences enough acts of sabotage or revenge, it can be financially damaged, especially if it is small or family-owned.

Banks, technology companies, public agencies, and the retail and hospitality sectors often are faced with far greater, more complicated, and more costly incidents. Chances are we all know someone like my friend who found solace in "getting even" with a business. The problem is that sabotage isn't funny. It isn't a victimless crime.

A Different Kind of War

Sabotage between individuals is just about as old as civilization itself, but it became something of a science with the advent of modern war.

Sabotage between individuals is just about as old as civilization itself, but it became something of a science with the advent of modern war.

Historians note that generals leading their respective regiments in World War I would routinely engage in post-battle discussions about casualty statistics, but they would just as often analyze new tactics of sabotage. They would study, for example, how the enemy blew up fuel tanks or poisoned fresh water supplies to stall their advances. Two decades later, during World War II, Hitler's generals spent years perfecting their plans to infiltrate foreign governments and place informants and saboteurs inside factories, supply depots, and ports in order to delay or mysteriously destroy key shipments or parts.

Similarly, the Allies recognized that sabotage was a weapon of enormous strategic significance, and they engaged a former Medal of Honor winner and New York City lawyer William J. Donovan to lead the Office of Strategic Services (OSS), the progenitor of today's CIA. The OSS did its job well. World War II historian Ronald Spector notes that the OSS became the Allies' premiere agent "for sabotage, espionage, and psychological and guerilla warfare" during World War II. To defeat the dual threats of Nazism and Japanese air supremacy, for example, the OSS forged alliances with the Chinese and other operatives, including "agents, thugs, and assassins that were daring, ruthless, and effective." As the United States' implementation of the OSS suggests, by the end of World War II, the world was aware of how disabling well-planned sabotage could be for an enemy.

Today's saboteurs take many forms and are not always easily identifiable, but they can cause genuine security risks when they infiltrate air defense or public safety systems.

While the majority of modern saboteurs have chosen the Internet as their playground, sabotage is more than bringing down technology platforms and airplanes. Several leading agricultural science scholars remind us that the lessons mastered by some during wartime could easily return to haunt us in this era of heightened terrorism. John Shutske of the University of Minnesota has written extensively about such threats, noting that whether their weapon of choice is manure or snake venom, saboteurs using bioweapons can cause illness, death, and the devastation of crops. His work also reminds us that attacks on crops and animals extend back thousands of years. The Germans tested and deployed numerous schemes to poison the water and food supplies of their enemies during World War II, and the Soviets "developed and stockpiled anti-agriculture weapons" throughout the 1940s and 1950s, he adds.

Today at work, the rules of engagement are the same, minus the political intrigue. Your enemies may include former or current employees and contractors, competitors, or investors who are eager to manipulate chat rooms and blogs in order to profit from a significant movement in your stock price. You might say: "Oh, come on, that's not sabotage—that's just business," but when you consider how much of an impact cyber crime, competitive intelligence, or related acts can have, it will become clear that these tactics are aimed at impairing you, your reputation, and your market position.

Unlike cases of robbery, which typically are reported to local law enforcement officials, sabotage is a different kind of crisis for a business. Supervisors often are hesitant to report incidents because they fear that local newspapers will publish the incident, causing the company embarrassment and potentially further economic loss. In some cases, the leaders of a company may not even know that their databases or equipment have been sabotaged. Upon suspecting sabotage, many companies will hire investigators who sometimes engage in social engineering to try to track down and prosecute the perpetrator. There is no science to combating such threats; sabotage is a crime that is downright complicated, and, as you will see, its impact on a business often is significant—and sometimes deadly. If the employer knew—or even should have known—that these risks existed, a crisis can emerge in your company.

The Inside Job

Sabotage is not the result of a spontaneous act of revenge; it requires planning, knowledge, access, and usually some self-exposure on the part of the sabo-teur. A catalyst or motive is always present, even if the acts are driven merely by self-gratification. An individual who has access to your systems and controls generally has a far greater chance to penetrate the safety of your core business operations.

> Sabotage is not the result of a spontaneous act of revenge; it requires planning, knowledge, and access.

For example, a disgruntled Fidelity National employee stole sensitive data on almost 8.5 million of the company's customers in July 2007 and sold the information to direct marketers for an undisclosed (but suspectedly hefty) amount of money. The company originally said that the number was close to 2.4 million customers. According to *Computerworld*: "The stolen data included names, addresses, birth dates, bank account, and credit card information, the company said. The database administrator worked for Certegy, which provides a check-authorization service to help merchants decide whether to accept checks as payment for goods and service." As I've stated, a successful inside job requires access and motivation; this perpetrator had both.

Chances are that your business has property and casualty insurance, director and officer insurance, errors and omissions coverage—but do you also have cyberinsurance? If not, you may want to read a white paper by Kevin Kalinich, national director of risk for the insurance company Aon. You might lose some sleep when you realize that your failure to protect sensitive data about your employees, customers, and others could be a violation of the Gramm-Leach-Bliley Act. Some litigator out there will likely want to know if you ever contemplated the possibility of sabotage in your shop.

None of this is really new; it's just that sabotage has been broadened from tampering with machinery to far more sophisticated efforts to destroy companies. In 1993, I completed a research study for the Institute of Industrial Engineers that concluded that the industries most susceptible to sabotage at that time were manufacturing and utilities. Numerous documented cases emerged of employees who knowingly destroyed key equipment at some leading manufacturers of tool and power equipment, and prosecution of these individuals forced many business leaders to ask themselves: "Could one of my employees or former coworkers seeking revenge do the same thing?"

Possibly. But before we discuss how sabotage can blossom into a business crisis, let's place the issue in its proper context.

Most employees are genuinely honest people whose efforts contribute to the overall productivity of the organization for which they work. Let me be clear: Most employees do not engage in acts of retribution or sabotage. But we need to realize that some employees are immature, regardless of how old they might be. Their lack of cognitive maturity may incite them to act out their anger, not with a gun or a clenched fist, but by engaging in incidents aimed at damaging the operations of your company. And there are others who are quite mature but who may have a personality disorder that fuels an appetite for sabotage; thus, we have hackers and highly skilled technicians who seek to disable entire IT systems in order to harm a company they don't like, an industry they find offensive, or a political cause they disagree with.

Because not all sabotage cases blossom into true business crises, let's push aside the example of the dry cleaner for a moment and focus on what you as a business leader need to worry about when managing your organization through sabotage attempts. There are four principal categories of sabotage that we'll focus on, principally because they impact the business and government sectors:

- Human resources related
- IT and mechanical
- Economic
- Reputational

Let's take a look at these more serious—and far more complicated—cases of sabotage and revenge.

Human Resources Related

When employees and contractors intentionally seek to harm your business because they have been upset by a poor evaluation, the denial of a merit raise, or for some other reason, many will openly express their discontent prior to acting. "Getting even" is a priority for some people, and the methods they employ to do so can be costly and often difficult, if not impossible, to track. Let's look at two cases, one involving an individual and the other involving a group of employees.

In January 2003, Randy Jay Bertram, a 39-year-old supermarket worker in Michigan who police later labeled as a disgruntled employee, intentionally contaminated about 250 pounds of hamburger with a pesticide at Byron Center Family Fare Market; some 148 people became sick as a result of his act of sabotage. Prosecutors said he brought a bottle of insecticide to work and poured it into the machines that processed the ground beef; his acts were intended to get his boss in trouble. Instead, he got in trouble. He was charged with a nine-year prison sentence; his victims included 40 children, a pregnant woman, and an elderly man with heart problems.

In a personal communication to me, here's how former FBI agent Fred Graessle looks at these acts:

> Many acts of sabotage, like other acts of fraud, have signals that precede the act. These signals are often missed or ignored. The [human resources] department, and all levels of management, needs to be aware of these signals. This process starts with recognizing problem employees, knowing if they are in over their heads, knowing what the employees have access to, and assessing the organization's exposure. Employees [that are] in over their head[s], for instance, may sabotage internal reports, financial figures, production records, etc., to cover short-falls. Some may sabotage production capabilities or other processes to cover for their incompetence.

We know for a fact that some saboteurs target the food and agricultural supplies of a nation; in fact, the Extension Disaster Education Network, which represents a consortium of agricultural experts at universities throughout the United States, published a report indicating that European and American military investigators have found more than 700 translated articles and documents in Afghani caves in recent years related to how animal and plant products can be contaminated. And if you think I'm providing free consulting to terrorists, I'm second banana to the former genius that ran the U.S. Department of Health and Human Services, Tommy Thompson. He once told reporters at a news conference: "For the life of me, I cannot understand why the terrorists have not attacked our food supply because it is so easy to do."

Good move, Tommy.

Individuals can sabotage food, like Bertram did, or they can destroy equipment that is expensive and time-consuming to repair. They can also bring a business to its knees, if they are so inclined.

Let's look at other sectors. By 1977, the cruise industry had evolved into an affordable yet luxurious vacation vehicle for middle-class individuals worldwide. Companies like Royal Caribbean and Norwegian Cruise Line even benefited when ABC television introduced *Love Boat*, despite the fact that the hour-long weekly program showcased the joy of a cruise vacation on Princess cruise ships.

At the lower-price tier of the cruise industry was Carnival Cruise Lines. Carnival's owner, Ted "Micky" Arison, was a daring, make-it-happen entrepreneur who sometimes bought rough ships that had seen better days and then converted their storage spaces into staterooms and put them afloat. As author Kristoffer Garin writes in *Devils on the Deep Blue Sea* (2005): "The competition boasted of white-glove service and formal nights. Carnival went the other way, bringing belly-flop contests and beer pong to the high seas . . . every spare penny had been channeled into Carnival's future, first to upgrade the ramshackle *Mardi Gras* and then to buy other ships from [its] bankrupt owners in Europe." The company was going gangbusters and had added a new ship called the *Tropicale*. The crew of that ship, recruited from islands around the world and paid pennies for tolerating demanding, overbearing, and often drunk passengers, was considered more of a nuisance than an asset by many in management.

On Easter Sunday of 1981, Carnival learned about sabotage the hard way. With both ships filled with passengers and about to set sail from Miami, some 300 crewmembers went on a wildcat strike. To be fair, the strike was understandable. Those who made beds and served meals and cocktails often worked 12-hour days and slept six to a room; they were mostly from Honduras and often were peppered with low racial slurs by officers. They had had enough.

The strikers gathered at the bow of the ship to form their strategy; fastened heavy lines between the two boats to prevent towing; and strung thinner ropes across the gap in order to pass notes back and forth between the ships. Inside, gangs patrolled the vessels, "making sure that no one else worked." In the meantime, the strikers enjoyed their newfound power in an environment where powerlessness had always defined their experiences.

The strike became a national embarrassment for Carnival in the midst of *Love Boat* popularity, and Arison's first crisis as a CEO involved passengers being kicked off (often without their bags and passports) two ships that were now grounded. His only assets were now controlled not by captains, but by busboys. Arison feared that the busboys would burn the ship.

According to Garin, Arison was hearing "all sorts of talk about sabotaging the ship, breaking the toilets, lopping pipes, and everything else . . . Everyone felt things slipping out of control . . . By the end of the third day, everyone was haggard and frightened."

In response, Arison hired Wackenhut, a security company that patrols prisons as well as retail and office buildings, to helicopter in a mini-SWAT team onto the ships while he met with the workers' representatives on shore. The strikers thought they were being visited by news crews but learned otherwise when the "security officers," brandishing guns and knives, landed on the ship. They led the workers to Miami-Dade County police officers, who were waiting at the port, and the strikers were immediately bused to the airport and deported home.

Carnival had experienced three kinds of sabotage in a single episode. First, its core business was compromised when two of its ships were taken offline. Second, angry workers damaged parts of the ship. Third, the news media highlighted Carnival's horrible working conditions, damaging its reputation. The cruise industry, meanwhile, learned an important lesson: Viewing your employees as company chattel that you can abuse according to your every whim certainly can place your business at risk. In response, most cruise companies diversified their hiring efforts and improved working conditions and pay for their help.

IT and Mechanical

It's pretty difficult to cover up a case involving 300 of your workers holding a few thousand passengers hostage on a cruise ship docked in Miami. But companies are pretty hush-hush when they know or suspect that a worker has tampered with company equipment. Examples of this kind of sabotage might include anything from a disgruntled mechanic who intentionally breaks a key piece of equipment inside an auto plant during a period of peak production, to cases of intentional damage to a company's computer systems. The impact from one act of IT or mechanical revenge can cost you millions of dollars in lost production due to equipment malfunctions and time delays. If your saboteur is particularly devious, he or she may rig a piece of equipment in such a way that a coworker might be seriously injured or killed; this is not uncommon in the construction, forestry, and steel industries.

> The impact from one act of IT or mechanical revenge can cost you millions of dollars in lost production due to equipment malfunctions and time delays.

It is increasingly difficult to engage in sabotage of this nature in some workplace environments today because of the increased presence of surveillance cameras. As a result, more saboteurs are attempting to negatively impact computer and software systems. In July 2007, for instance, NASA acknowledged that a subcontractor had deliberately cut wires to a computer system inside the *Endeavor* space shuttle just as the vessel was about to be launched; the person also had attempted to sabotage a second system used at mission control. The agency, which has a documented history of a lack of candor regarding employment gaffes, would not offer any explanation as to how such incidents could occur, let alone why someone would be motivated to commit such an act of sabotage. The incident at NASA may not have compromised the lives of astronauts and the launch proceeded as scheduled, but it speaks volumes to the fact that causing intentional damage to IT and mechanical systems is comparatively easy. If it can be done to NASA, it can be done to your company, too.

Cyber crime, the sabotage of corporate systems that is most often committed by IT workers, is rapidly becoming a global crisis for both businesses and government agencies. Carnegie Mellon University researchers have concluded that it doesn't take a rocket scientist to identify perpetrators—they're typically "disgruntled and paranoid, generally [show] up late, [argue] with colleagues, and generally [perform] poorly." According to *TechWorld*, about 86 percent of cyber crime is committed by tech workers, 90 percent of which had privileged access to systems; about 41 percent were employed by the company when they damaged systems, but the majority of cases was committed by former employees who knew enough about hacking to master the very intrusion detection systems they had installed or previously used.

> Cyber crime, the sabotage of corporate systems that is most often committed by IT workers, is rapidly becoming a global crisis for both businesses and government agencies.

When it comes to safeguarding your IT and mechanical systems, remember that sabotage is not always as simple as someone throwing a wrench into a sophisticated piece of printing equipment or breaking into a database and crashing your system firewalls. Some experts I interviewed told me that the more conniving saboteurs at work avoid "hard crashes" of company systems and prefer a "slow bleed" approach, which creates unplanned interruption or dramatic slowdowns in IT performance and frustrates customers, driving them to the competition. Sometimes the competition plants saboteurs in your company; these individuals relish the opportunity to scratch their heads as they try to figure out "what happened and who's trying to harm us?" when they are, indeed, the perpetrators. The financial damage these individuals bring to your organization can be significant. Forrester Research estimates that it costs a single airline about $90,000 an hour each time it experiences system failure, and that number soars to $150,000 per hour for a pay-per-view television network. Companies that depend heavily on Web sales, such as L.L. Bean, Scottrade.com, and Buy.com, declined to answer my research questions about their methods of preventing potential system exposure. As a business leader, you will want to ask your IT team what its recovery time objectives (RTO) are, especially because reducing your RTO to 30 minutes or less is considered a best practice standard today. If you employ smart hiring and investigate worker complaints and grievances early, you may be able to prevent misunderstandings among workers from growing into cases of sabotage.

Sabotage is a crime, and companies such as TJX, owner of T.J. Maxx and Marshall's, learned this lesson the hard way in 2007 after detailed credit card information from millions of its customers was systematically stolen. The company was widely criticized by consumer groups, the news media, and regulators for its failure to both notify customers expediently and answer their questions, by phone and in stores, thoroughly. What's more, TJX used "confidentiality" shields to avoid publicly acknowledging that it lacked the proper systems to prevent widespread fraud. Phil Levy, an accomplished television news editor at WCVB TV in Boston, told me in a private communication that in his 30 years of covering corporations that found themselves in the midst of media scandal as a result of sabotage, he never witnessed a company that displayed such blatant disregard for public concern. "Here I am, an editor, and I told their spokesperson, 'Get out there. Tell your story. Apologize. Do it now,' and they just wouldn't listen. The story grew out of control and they were slammed by the media. They had a chance to be contrite and show that they were a victim, but by being silent, they looked quite guilty."

IT system compromises, whether caused by a current or former employee, have occurred at virtually every type of enterprise worldwide—police organizations, retail and manufacturing entities, small businesses, and so on. More organizations are employing vaulting services, which transmit confidential information in high-data volumes, thereby reducing the exposure of precious company records to hackers, a situation that has disrupted employers for years. Johns Hopkins University in Baltimore, Maryland, probably is still haunted by the day in February 2007, when it realized it had no choice but to notify about 52,000 employees and 84,000 patients that it had lost nine tapes worth of sensitive information. Neither Johns Hopkins nor its contractor could identify how the tapes were lost, and those individuals whose personal information was compromised experienced real anxiety. Again, as a result of a crisis, we learn how much of a competitive advantage protecting your IT can be. While saboteurs can and eventually will learn how to target vaulting systems, these IT platforms still appear to be your best bet for reducing your exposure to incidents such as those experienced by TJX and Johns Hopkins.

If you are worried about technology-based forms of sabotage negatively affecting your company, you may want to purchase insurance from specialized companies like Assurex International, the largest company in the world that specializes in private risk management. The president of Assurex, Thomas W. Harvey, has said in various articles that e-sabotage is one of the most misunderstood risks a company can face. "Cyberinsurance policies help mitigate losses resulting from business interruption, lost productivity, computer viruses, fines, theft, embarrassment, and other e-risks," he notes. Purchasing cyberinsurance might be worth considering at budget time.

Even if you're highly confident that no one would want to sabotage you and your organization, be wary of those who may seek to undermine your suppliers; if they succeed, your company could be affected as well. In a personal communication to me, professor Denis Smith of the University of Glasgow said it best: "Consider the landscape of suppliers and customers, and consider the fragility of supply chains and networks—then consider the stages through which a crisis might pass, and the task demands that would be generated as a consequence." Bottom line: We're all interconnected. It's time you begin to ask those companies that you do business with for a copy of *their* risk management plan.

Economic

Several years ago, I was invited to speak at the national conference of the Society of Competitive Intelligence Professionals (SCIP) about the tactics some companies use to steal data from their competition to advance their margins of profitability. SCIP insists that its member companies only engage in ethical intelligence gathering about their competitors—which means that they do anything that's within the law if it adds to their bottom line. The program was fascinating.

Some of the most seasoned product managers working for venerable brand names have admitted to reading, scanning, and listening to anything and everything the competition has to say in order to stay one step ahead. Because shareholders and financial analysts evaluate the leadership performance of publicly traded companies every 90 days, the argument holds that companies have more pressure than ever to discuss not only their recent performance, but also what new projects, design, products, and markets they're working on. As a result, ethical intelligence gathering is "a gold mine," one executive from Intel Corporation told me. "If you listen to enough downloads on iTunes, and scan enough of the technical literature, and sit in the back of a university classroom where their engineers are giving a lecture on what they're working on, you can sew a lot of pieces together." It's perfectly legal and potentially high-yield. That's capitalism.

Economic sabotage isn't quite as kind to its victims. It's hardball, and nowhere near ethical. This is an arena in which, as you'll see, former Russian spies, current Korean government ministers, and many other characters find a way to get themselves on the payrolls of the companies they are seeking to destroy. They're not likely to attend an SCIP meeting because they're too busy going through your corporate trash (they hired the driver from your waste management company to make a detour before heading to the dump) or giving your assistant financial officer two weeks of paid vacation in Hawaii to determine how much you're spending on research and development. These actions might not seem like sabotage at first, but the intentions of the saboteurs become apparent when the information gained is used to destroy your product launch or to bad-mouth the safety or efficacy of a clinical trial on which you are working. This is not child's play;

there are millions, sometimes billions of dollars at stake when information based on incomplete or manipulated data is leaked to regulators and customers.

There are many companies that will help you collect corporate intelligence, and most of them do it legitimately and legally. These are the firms that you should contact if you suspect that vital company information is being leaked on various blogs or other forums. A number of retired Russian spies now work for a company called Trident, which is based in Virginia. One of Trident's many responsibilities is to help the Motion Picture Association for America ensure that American films are not illegally duplicated and sold as DVDs in Russia for the equivalent of US$2 before they are even shown on the big screen. In doing this, Trident helps prevent attempts of economic sabotage against major film studios. Similarly, some American companies are hiring ex-CIA agents to protect their core interests against competitive intelligence and sabotage. *BusinessWeek* reported that Lehman Brothers promoted a veteran CIA operator, Ted Price, from director of corporate security to director of operations at the firm's Mumbai, India, location. Several other CIA veterans have started a company called Prescience, based in New Canaan, Connecticut, that helps hedge fund companies avoid economic sabotage and related data leaks.

Finally, remember that you don't need to be a former spy to understand how basic theft can quickly become economic sabotage and destroy a store, a factory, or an entire company. Various anarchist Web sites encourage workers to post stories about how they have stolen or engaged in the damage or destruction of company property to "get even" with their employers. In a December 29, 2005, posting on libcom .org, a former employee of Kmart store 3399 recounts in considerable detail how he stole nearly $100,000 in merchandise while unsuspecting store managers fumbled around in their attempts to figure out Loss Prevention 101. "The same people who were stealing were doing the inventory, so we were able to cover our asses real good," the author notes. "The job was boring. Everyone who worked there hated being there; it was drudgery." Saboteurs will act on any number of reasons to damage you, from boredom, retribution, and political or social disagreements, to absolutely no reason at all.

Reputational

Sometimes you get the reputation that you deserve. Let's look at another example from the hospitality sector.

Regency Cruise Line branded its ships as graceful and high-end, but the company was pretty much a sham operation from the beginning. By the time it was shut down in 1995 for leaving about 30,000 passengers to fend for themselves in various ports, according to Garin, author of *Devils on the Deep Blue Sea*, crew members hadn't been paid in weeks, food suppliers stopped their deliveries, and the ships' mechanical systems were failing due to a lack of repair. To make matters worse, Regency's no-refund policy meant that those passengers who were already onboard were stuck in a hellish vacation, and the global media reported that its reputation had been virtually ruined. Things weren't much better when Premier Cruise Line left about 1,500 passengers and 450 crewmembers stranded in Nassau, Boston, and Nova Scotia when it declared bankruptcy in September 2000.

Almost a year later to the day that Premier shut down its operations, another cruise line, Renaissance Cruises, declared itself insolvent, and many passengers and crew *once again* were screwed over by a company who accepted reservations and deposits when it knew (or should have known) the cruise line couldn't even meet its payroll expenses. You may want to travel only on reputable cruise lines with brand names you trust, whose parent companies are financially strong, and who rank consistently well on satisfaction surveys. In fact, apply this methodology to all of your corporate purchases, including incentive trips and other needs.

Let me be clear: A bankruptcy is not an act of sabotage. Actually, it's typically an act of mismanagement. But there's no question that when a company is on the brink of failure, competitors, eager to build market share, may spread rumors, increase their attempts to poach top talent, or engage in other acts that will accelerate that company's decline. *That's sabotage.* It has existed for years, and it continues to exist in virtually every industry imaginable.

> Corporate sabotage can become a crisis when you realize that the risk to your reputation is spiraling out of control.

Corporate sabotage can become a crisis when you realize that the risk to your reputation is spiraling out of control, that someone out there is working with extraordinary zeal to injure your profitability and market standing.

Procter & Gamble (P&G), the world's leading manufacturer of consumer goods, including Crest toothpaste, Tide detergent, and numerous other well-known products, painfully learned this lesson in 1997. After more than a decade of researching thousands of leads, rumors, newsletters, and petitions falsely claiming that P&G was an agent of Satanism and that company profits were used by Satanists to advance their cause, the company filed a series of lawsuits against Amway Corporation and a number of Amway distributors. Amway subsequently renamed itself Quixtar.

P&G argued that Amway, and specifically distributor Randy L. Haugen, knowingly spread false and malicious statements about the company and its alleged allegiance to Satan. In its complaint, P&G argued:

> Defendants, individually and in concert, have made the false, defamatory, and product-disparaging statements contained in Exhibit F to increase their economic gain, to enhance their Amway distributorship, and to sell Amway products, all to the detriment of Plaintiffs.

Although Amway and four distributors said that they were merely sharing information that they believed to be true on internal voice-mail systems that they had received from others, a federal jury in Salt Lake City, Utah, ruled in favor of P&G and awarded the company $19.2 million in damages. Because it feared further propagation of the ugly allegation that it supported and funded Satan worshipping, P&G has never publicly acknowledged the full extent of damages that were done to its fine reputation. It is widely assumed, however, that P&G lost millions of dollars in sales because gullible (that often means stupid) consumers bought the tale about Satan living in P&G's Cincinnati, Ohio, headquarters.

Sometimes allegations are aimed at people, not companies, and this merits some analysis as well.

A case in point: Three Caucasian members of the Duke University lacrosse team were accused of raping Crystal Gail Mangum, an African American exotic dancer, following her performance at a college frat party the men attended in March 2006. Mangum reportedly provided conflicting accounts of her alleged rape to the police, but her story nevertheless rallied many of the campus community to take up her cause.

District Attorney Mike Nifong prosecuted the three athletes with unbridled tenacity and insinuated in public statements that their alleged acts were racially motivated. Despite statements made to police by the lacrosse players' fellow partygoers averring the athletes' innocence, Nifong accelerated his charges. To make matters worse, Duke University's school newspaper published a letter to the editor that brought further allegations against the young men before they were even tried in a court of law; the letter was signed by 88 members of the campus community.

A year later, after an exhaustive investigation, state attorney general Roy Cooper exonerated the athletes of all charges and accused Nifong of recklessness in his investigation and prosecution tactics. Yet the serious reputational sabotage already was done, not only to the three young men whose identities were publicly—and permanently—linked to a crime they never committed, but also to lacrosse coach Mike Pressler, who resigned amid death threats just days after the case went public. The fact that some members of the Duke campus community would be so hasty as to launch a campaign amid unproven allegations demonstrates that Nifong was not alone in his race to judgment. Nifong resigned on June 15, 2007, and then was disbarred the next day for unethical conduct. The chairman of the legal disciplinary committee blamed "political ambition" for Nifong's downfall.

Similarly, the world news media gathered in 2006 in Bangkok, Thailand, in a rush to hear the details after John Mark Karr confessed to playing a role in the brutal rape and murder of six-year-old JonBenet Ramsey. Once again, the collective "we"—the news media, police, prosecutors, and society—were quick to assume that Karr had committed the crime; after all, he shared with authorities little-known and extensive details pertaining to the 1996 crime. After weeks of detailed forensics and police interviews, however, it was determined that Karr fabricated his involvement in the crime, and all

charges against him were
dropped. Psychologists on television who had previously come
close to indicting Karr based
solely on his self-incrimination
and with no basis for fact now reported in media interviews that
Karr's statements and behavior were baffling. Remember, before you
race to judgment, make a monumental decision or accusation, or
allocate resources: Validate all the facts.

> Remember, before you race to
> judgment, make a monumental
> decision or accusation, or allocate
> resources: Validate all the facts.

Applying Strategic Standards

I've hopefully convinced you by now that sabotage can happen to individuals, groups of individuals, small companies, and large corporations. Most acts of sabotage are committed by those close to you,
notably current and former employees. Although you may not be able
to prevent all vengeful acts that are aimed at your company, by God,
you'd better try hard to prevent the ones that could immobilize your
operations.

In recent years, I've had a few opportunities to work with former
FBI agent Graessle. On one of these occasions, the chairperson of the
board of a privately held company called to alert Graessle and me (of
course, it was during Christmas week) that the company recently had
become aware that its CEO had a criminal past. In fact, the CEO not
only had boasted to a few colleagues that he had been involved in
some capital crimes, but he also admitted to being incarcerated for
those crimes. To make the situation even more intriguing, the CEO
acknowledged that his son had committed suicide and that he came
from a family with a hefty history of violence. The company that
contacted us had not conducted a background check on this character, and now he was engaging in a pattern of bullying that was causing widespread concern. The company feared that if it terminated his
employment, he could sabotage the company and spread malicious
rumors that could undermine the viability of an otherwise strong
organization.

Graessle and I worked with a licensed clinical psychologist to create a plan that resulted in smart case management. The problem employee was separated and we minimized any chance for sabotage—but we only were able to reduce the company's exposure by working well together to bring the case to resolution. As Graessle has pointed out to me on numerous occasions, there are three components to managing instances of sabotage: detection, deterrence, and prevention. Because he's led numerous investigations into cases where fraud and sabotage cost companies millions of dollars and untold hours of productivity spent tracking down the saboteur, his expertise is extensive. Graessle recommends a five-stage approach to preventing sabotage:

1. **Assess your risks and look at your internal controls, including your human resources practices.**
   Be candid about your vulnerabilities and be ready to commit resources to improve and expand the quality of your background checks.
2. **Design policies and procedures that recognize that it's a new world.**
   Distribute and discuss ethics manuals and be serious about compliance as a strategic objective. Remember that even the "strongest" organizations have been damaged by saboteurs. Have a contingency plan to reboot your IT systems.
3. **Embed an antifraud program into your culture now.**
   Monitor and test processes to determine if someone can steal data, products, patents, financial projections—anything that may be of genuine value. Hire an outside auditor or forensic firm to attempt to gain access to your site and assets. Be ready to terminate those who had a responsibility to protect and who were asleep at the wheel. Set a high example.
4. **Engage all stakeholders in discussions about retribution and sabotage.**
   This isn't out of a Matt Damon movie—every employee and contractor needs to understand that you won't tolerate attempts to maneuver or manipulate systems. Fraud awareness training is essential: Explain what's happening to others both in- and outside your industry and how you're learning from them.

5. **Create a robust investigative process.**
   Have a model so that employees and contractors can discreetly and anonymously report their suspicions that someone may be seeking to damage your reputation, product line, or bottom line. Consider outsourcing the investigative piece of the effort if you cannot afford a full-time detection and deterrence department in your organization.

Now, stop looking over your shoulder. We're not done.

11

COMMUNICATING WHEN IT'S CODE RED

*Sad to see David Neeleman lose his CEO job at jetBlue Airways.
I truly hate it when entrepreneurs are tossed from their own
companies. My guesses are, one, that jetBlue will someday regret this
decision, and, two, that Neeleman still has another act or two in his
brilliant career. Of course, if you were one of those poor souls trapped
in a stuffy, bathroom-fouled jet for eight hours, you might be toasting
Neeleman's sacking. Who could blame you? Had it happened to me,
I would have filed kidnapping charges.*

—FORBES.COM, RICH KARLGAARD

nce touted as the shining star of Wall Street, jetBlue learned the hard way that effectively communicating during and after a crisis is one of the most complex and serious responsibilities of any management team.

When companies with large public relations departments find themselves in a code-red situation, they have the luxury of turning to a large team of writers and trained spokespeople who have a variety of tools at their disposal to help the company achieve business recovery. But most organizations don't have a large image-building team or adequate crisis management tools. Even when they do, the demands of the unique situation they face—a chemical leak or the kidnapping of an executive, for example—will stretch the skill sets of even the most accomplished professionals.

Executives are largely uncomfortable with crisis communications. In a typical day, your senior management team is working in a known world where customers, products, the supply chain—all of which constitute the principal ingredients of business—are predictable.

There's no way to know when a crisis is about to hit. Events are disruptive. The damage caused can last for weeks, even months, and most likely will be costly. As a result, management teams are often overwhelmed by the velocity and disruptiveness of corporate crises.

"When executives are running a business, they're focused on growth—they're confident, almost to a fault, that nothing will go wrong, and virtually all of their planning, presentations, and efforts are upbeat and forward-looking," noted Kris Davidson, a former Motorola manager who helped create the company's crisis communications plan, in a personal communication. "Our business was growing 20 percent a year for about five consecutive years, but there were signals that we were now operating in unknown territory—growing by huge leaps in India, China, and Latin America—and we were relying on contractors and suppliers as the engine of our business," he added. "We had to convince senior management that when you employ 150,000 people and you're earning more than $30 billion a year, those teams throughout the company needed to understand what to communicate during a crisis. If an incident happened in China and corporate officials were at home asleep in Chicago, we probably couldn't mobilize quickly enough to keep anyone satisfied."

Davidson helped create a crisis communications kit that later was shared with Motorola managers worldwide. The kit contained draft statements about caring for victims and cooperating with local authorities, as well as statements for the phone operators that would be answering questions from customers or loved ones who worked at a Motorola facility. And because Motorola operates in more than 60 countries, the crisis communications plan also included detailed information on how to quickly engage foreign language translators or representatives of the State Department if the crisis at hand involved casualties that presented cultural or political challenges.

Diagnostics: Asking Questions before Communicating

Let me share an example of a crisis that at first glance appeared to be business related but that actually required extensive reputation management. I recently received a call from the chairperson of the board of a major bank. I had worked with him on a prior occasion, when one of the bank's top officers needed to be terminated due to serious performance issues, but it was obvious from the tone of his voice that a new and different kind of dilemma was surfacing.

He explained that the bank's president was involved in some potentially embarrassing activities outside the office and that her actions would likely compromise the bank's reputation—and possibly its license to operate—if swift action was not taken. He needed me in his office the next morning.

On the plane ride to his city, I drafted an outline of a due diligence and crisis communications plan to present to an emergency meeting of the bank board. When I arrived, we began by reviewing the three principal questions that would come to define our crisis communications plan:

1. What do we know?
2. When did we know it?
3. What are we going to do about it?

I pursued a number of questions with the bank's legal counsel, its vice president of human resources, and several of its board members:

- Did the person engage in inappropriate or *illegal* activities? The ramifications of that answer are immense. Were her actions a violation of a specific standard in the company code of conduct? The difference between inappropriate and illegal activities is profound in terms of how the bank might communicate any decisions about her future.
- Is the bank president well known in a community that extends beyond the bank's high net worth clients? Was she a high-profile member of any community and charity groups, for example?
- Because the bank is publicly traded, the SEC, the FDIC, and the state banking commissioner may have questions about due

diligence and whether this individual broke any laws. Did the bank hire a private investigator to verify whether the allegations against her are true? What did that investigation determine? Is the report from the investigation discoverable if her behavior leads to legal action?

- Did any bank employee engage in whistle blowing that led to the initial allegations and the need to hire an outside investigator? If so, what protections will the bank provide that person? Could there be additional facts that will be disclosed in the days to come that could make this situation worse, further impairing the reputation of the bank?
- Are there any major events (such as a quarterly earnings report or the opening of a new branch of the bank) scheduled for the next few weeks that could or should be reconsidered if these embarrassing allegations—even if they are false—become public?
- If the president is terminated, could she sue the bank, and if so, on what grounds? What is the bank's succession plan for leadership personnel?

Just like a physician will analyze X-rays and blood test results to help detect whether you have a symptom or an actual illness, diagnostics also are used in assessing how serious an issue may be and whether current events could blossom into a crisis.

In any crisis, a smart communicator will ask these and other questions to help frame his or her crisis communications plan. Twenty years ago, an institution facing the same situation might have issued a news release indicating that an executive was simply departing his or her company "to pursue new interests." Although there may have been a few inquiries, the majority of management time was spent managing rumors, not preventing speculation. Today, in a world where the spirit of disclosure places a high value on ethical management and organizational culture,

> Today, in a world where the spirit of disclosure places a high value on ethical management and organizational culture, companies must anticipate provocative, legitimate questions from their numerous stakeholders.

companies must anticipate provocative, legitimate questions from their numerous stakeholders. They also must design a robust crisis communications plan to minimize damage from the fallout of a looming crisis.

My Q&A session with the board during the initial stages of the bank's crisis proved invaluable when I went back to create the crisis communications plan for the debacle. Here is what was adapted to fit the bank's dilemma.

Stakeholders Analysis

- Who has an immediate need to know about this incident?
- What categories of stakeholders exist? This might include regulators, elected officials, board members, investors, employees, neighbors, business partners, customers, advertising agencies, and others.
- How much can we share during the first stages of crisis management? Have all the facts been verified to ensure that we are acting on sound information?
- Will stakeholders have an opportunity to ask questions or seek more information from us? Are we adequately staffed via phone or the Web to manage their inquiries so that a unified response can be offered across all communication platforms?

Content

- How quickly can we draft a message that at least acknowledges the incident and offers insight as to why the organization is taking action (e.g., "The board of directors has met and, after careful deliberation and a comprehensive independent investigation, separated Sandy Perkins [fictitious name] as president due to a breach of our code of conduct . . .")?
- Will anything that we say or do be construed as an admission of guilt? How can the legitimate concerns of our insurance company or legal counsel be addressed in a manner that also allows us to be ahead of any criticism we might receive that suggests that we are "ducking" the issue?

Listening

- Since teams often feel they are insulated from facts, how can we be sure that we are listening to the needs of those immediately impacted? This may include a conference call, launching a focus group of consumers or investors, or a Zoomerang! survey of employees to help us measure how effective our communications is at achieving the desired objectives.
- Should we contact financial analysts in New York, London, Geneva, or Hong Kong who make recommendations about our stock in advance so they have the courtesy of knowing what decisions we are about to make? In some cases, they may offer sound insight that we have not considered.

The bank board used the communications roadmap we created so that news of the exiting president was received in a mostly neutral—rather than negative—manner. Key stakeholders learned of the news via personal briefings. Exhaustive Q&As were prepared and shared with branch managers. In the end, what could have been an embarrassing incident was managed properly and turned into a *transition* of leadership rather than a dismissal for cause—which would have been a true crisis.

They Have the Most to Lose

When "it" hits the fan, there are two kinds of organizations that negative publicity damages most—those that have a premium brand name that resonates with consumers across the globe; and, on the other extreme, small businesses that are highly affected by criticism and boycotts due to their reliance on positive word of mouth to draw in and retain customers. So, whether you work for a multinational or a local bank, remember that it is key that you avoid—at any and all costs—betraying your stakeholders. If they feel as though you have betrayed their trust, it could take months, even years, to recapture their goodwill.

Not surprisingly, some small businesses have not survived crises in which their customers felt betrayed; their customers simply take their business elsewhere. A case in point: Friendly's Ice Cream Restaurant in Arlington, Massachusetts, faced a major crisis when, in 2004, one of its workers was diagnosed with hepatitis. A major health scare emerged and, eventually, thousands of customers who had eaten at the restaurant needed immunoglobulin shots. The greater Boston news media created a sense of panic with its emphatic announcements that anyone who had eaten at the restaurant in the weeks preceding the worker's confirmed diagnosis was potentially at risk.

After the physicians had injected their shots, lawyers stepped forward to inject litigation. Seattle attorney William Marler of Marler Clark, the law firm that represented Jack-in-the-Box's customers after the fast food chain's alleged E. coli contamination, led the class-action suit against Friendly's. Marler is a tenacious attorney who, according to press reports, garnered an $11 million settlement from both BJ's Wholesale Club and its meat supplier on behalf of a child who became seriously ill after consuming E. coli-tainted beef that had been bought at BJ's.

"I've taken food companies for well over $100 million in the last 10 years," Marler notes on his Web site. "We do what we do for a lot of reasons—to make money and also to try to change people's behavior. We've been successful at getting the meat industry to do the right thing in E. coli cases."

With its customers worried about the safety of its store and with radio talk shows brimming with criticism aimed at the company for its lack of urgency when responding to questions, this Friendly's quietly and permanently closed its doors forever.

When your crisis hits, remember that neither the number of years you have been in business, nor the high degree of customer loyalty you enjoy, nor the coveted location of your business matters very much if your customers feel you lack common sense, compromised their well-being, or engaged in business practices they believe to be offensive or unethical.

On a broader scale, remember that these multinationals, rated by Interbrand, likely have the most to lose in a corporate crisis based on variables that include earnings, market leadership, stability, and global reach:

1. Coca-Cola
2. Microsoft
3. IBM
4. General Electric
5. Nokia
6. Toyota
7. Intel
8. McDonald's
9. Disney
10. Mercedes-Benz

A Debacle at HP

Brands can be impaired by an industrial health scare, but they also can be negatively affected by a series of horrible management decisions. A case in point is when the good name of Hewlett-Packard (HP) was subjected to one of the nastiest and most prolonged media spectacles in years in February 2005, when the company fired its CEO, Carly Fiorina.

Prior to her termination, Fiorina had been widely praised as the innovative force behind HP's resurgence as a technology leader, but shareholders were increasingly concerned about the aggressive manner in which HP was competing with Dell and other market forces. Fed up with the recurrence of news leaks divulging how the HP board released Fiorina at a corporate retreat, board director Patricia Dunn turned to the company's legal counsel for advice on combating the problem. He, in turn, reportedly asked security experts to determine why HP was experiencing so many embarrassing leaks to reporters. According to California investigators, the company began to engage in data mining and pretexting, a process in which company representatives call individuals associated with the company pretending to be someone else to gain information important to their investigation. In its decision to engage in pretexting, HP colossally failed to consider one very important question: How would members of the public feel if they discovered that HP authorized spying on private citizens?

As news broadcasts around the world zeroed in on the mystery of who ordered what spying upon whom at HP, the company's brand was being tarnished. New accusations and revelations emerged each day. Customers became anxious about whether the company might even survive the debacle. Eager to capitalize on another Enron-like scandal, Congress called for hearings when it learned that HP admitted to spying on the phone records of reporters at *The New York Times* and *The Wall Street Journal*. Some senior executives quit. Blogs lit up each day with new rumors related to the case.

According to *Newsweek*, HP's external legal counsel, Larry Sonsini, acknowledged that security consultants "did obtain information regarding phone calls made and received by the cell or home numbers of directors," but that it was unclear if such a practice was *illegal*. Illegal or not, the practice made a great company look petty. Magazine headlines about Dunn, such as *Newsweek*'s "The Boss Who Spied On Her Board," damaged HP's reputation and immersed the global media in a battle over who could publish what on the presence of alleged lies and spies in Silicon Valley.

In the midst of any corporate crisis, executives have the opportunity to share their story in a logical manner—even in the midst of chaos—if the company has embedded several management tools

> Spokespeople must be credible and reliable, their facts must be verifiable, and they must have the authority to speak for the organization as executives with weight, not as marketing chumps.

into its infrastructure *before* the crisis occurs. Spokespeople must be credible and reliable, their facts must be verifiable, and they must have the authority to speak for the organization as executives with weight, not as marketing chumps. When I was the spokesperson for Motorola, I didn't have to race to the CEO and ask for permission every time *The Wall Street Journal* or a trade magazine wanted our opinion on the claims of a competitor or a market rumor. I spent many hours getting to know the reporters that covered the company, and when I spoke with them, we both knew that my credibility was on the line. This was hardball; if members of the press made an outrageous claim or knowingly published a false rumor, I'd embargo their access to our executives for several months. They had their rules. We had ours.

As HP was in the midst of its worst scandal in company history, its crisis communications framework seemed fractured beyond anything I've ever seen in a Fortune 500 company. The nature of the scandal created an unprecedented degree of suspicion among board members and executives, and allegations were flying almost daily about who was spying on whom. It was virtually impossible for HP communicators to speak effectively and share a key message: Our company will survive this storm . . . our people are working harder than ever . . . our customer satisfaction is extraordinary. Because the company froze communications, public speculation shifted to: Did Dunn sabotage Fiorina's career, or did Dunn properly exercise her fiduciary responsibility? When the California attorney general publicly acknowledged that a crime had been committed at HP but that he wasn't sure by whom, how should the company have reacted to *that* allegation? When company heroes are slinging mud, newspaper and magazine headlines are obsessing over pretexting, and the press is suggesting that the scandal at HP could potentially trigger a hostile takeover of the company, competitors smell opportunity. HP's communications machine seemed frozen in time.

In terms of size and market value, the bank I discussed earlier had nowhere near the kinds of resources that HP enjoys, but it excelled at the science of crisis communications. It only takes one executive to recognize that no matter how innocent a company may be, if the news media believes you are guilty—or at least culpable—you have a potential crisis on your hands. Be that executive.

Crisis Communications Essentials

As you have seen, communications crises don't only happen to large companies.

When governor Don Carcieri of Rhode Island took to the microphones on February 21, 2003, the situation that he was about to discuss was one with which he had absolutely no experience. He wasn't announcing his reelection, and he wasn't touting a new piece of legislation that he was hoping the state legislature would approve.

Rather, Carcieri found himself in the unfortunate position of discussing a tragic incident that had occurred the night before; with about 200 people crowded inside a popular local nightclub called The Station, something had gone horribly wrong. Testimony would later suggest that an individual associated with the band Great White had lit pyrotechnics at the beginning of the rock group's show at The Station. The nightclub had recently passed a safety inspection but was exempted from the general requirement to have automatic sprinklers due to the old age of the building.

When I teach executive crisis management training programs, I typically play three brief videos related to this fire. The first is actual footage taken by a patron's cell phone of the fireworks that ignited the ceiling tiles of the nightclub and created a fireball that killed 100 club patrons. The second video features statements from band representatives indicating that they had nothing to do with the use of pyrotechnics during their show. The third, and by far the most illuminating, includes segments of the news conference held the next day by Governor Carcieri.

I'm sure the governor was in shock the day of the press conference, and I'll bet his constituents were, too. Governors are comfortable when it comes to budgets and regulatory affairs, but rarely do they have to visit a morgue or meet with dozens of parents who cannot identify their sons and daughters because they have been burnt beyond recognition. The governor is a human being, and he was in shock, so let's cut him some slack, right?

Wrong.

This is the governor—the CEO of the state. When crisis hits, the public expects its leaders to become commanders, to take charge of the facts, to issue a call to action—to offer a definitive roadmap to recovery.

Governor Carcieri blew it. In his press conference, he often referred to the individuals who had been killed as "bodies," rather than "victims." Rather than starting the news conference by assuring the public that his prayers and thoughts were with the victims and their families, he rambled for more than eight minutes about how he wanted to hear from dentists because having access to the dental records of victims might accelerate the identification process. Rather than saying, "This fire is beyond anything I've ever seen, and you have my promise that I will devote the full resources of the state to help us discover the cause of this tragedy and ensure that another similar event never occurs," Carcieri looked dazed. His own staff was caught on live national television in the background looking puzzled and seemingly asking themselves: "Where is this guy going with this?"

When crisis strikes, a smart organization expects a barrage of interest and inquiries from reporters, regulators, family members, and others. It selects the appropriate spokesperson, hopefully one who is seasoned at delivering difficult messages. It rehearses key phrases with that spokesperson until he or she has high comfortability with the content of the message he or she will be delivering. That spokesperson will need to participate in several mock interviews so they can answer complex questions succinctly. And the spokesperson should never—ever—refer to victims as *bodies*. In crisis communications, every word counts, every nuance matters. Even the location where you hold your press conference can have a considerable impact on how your message is received.

> In crisis communications, every word counts, every nuance matters.

Every time I show the video of the governor's press conference, my audiences almost always become angry that the one person who had the opportunity to publicly express emotions of loss and rally his constituents instead drifted into a world of dental records and babble. I'm sure his intentions were good. But during his defining moment as governor, Carcieri was a rank amateur at the microphone.

Many people blame reporters for how stories "get twisted" in the news media, but my experience suggests that reporters aren't to blame—managers often are. As a crisis leader, you can prepare for, rehearse for, and inoculate your organization against potential assaults by the news media if you follow several basic lessons. But before we get to reminders about what to do and say, let's briefly review some of the war stories from the crisis communications hall of shame.

- Although Wal-Mart's CEO David Glass had a tough act to follow after company founder Sam Walton died, few retail execs would question Glass's acumen as a business leader. In 1992, NBC's *Dateline* invited Glass to take part in an interview that purportedly would be part of a laudatory report by the news station tracing Wal-Mart's remarkable international growth. During the interview, however, reporter Brian Ross alerted Glass that NBC secretly had taken video crews to Pakistan and India to film children as young as eight years old sewing clothes in horrific conditions in Wal-Mart's subcontractors' sweat factories. Some of these clothes were later sold in U.S. stores on racks under banners that misleadingly read: "Made in America."

  On camera, Glass watched the video carefully. He looked baffled as the video continued, and then replied: "Terrible things happen in this world." A better response might have been: "Brian, I don't know anything about what you're showing me, but if it's true that Wal-Mart hires subcontractors who employ young children, I promise you that I'll look into this tonight and get back to you tomorrow. This is absolutely unacceptable to me and to the values of this company." Instead, the vice president of public relations for Wal-Mart walked onto the *Dateline* set and summarily ended the interview. NBC included that abrupt intervention by the public relations honcho in its story, and I'm glad it did. Wal-Mart not only looked guilty, it looked shamefully culpable. Why else would the CEO have needed to be muzzled?

- Cunard Cruise Lines is a well-regarded name in the cruise industry. When the *QE II* ran aground off the coast of Cape Cod in August 1992, Cunard's spokesperson drove from New York to meet the dozens of reporters who had quickly assembled. It was a scary scene—the cruise ship listed and passengers had to be evacuated in case the ship took on water. The spokesperson for Cunard had little time to prepare a statement, let alone rehearse questions and answers. But she goofed. She alleged that the accident might have been the fault of the U.S. Coast Guard guidance vessel. Ah—not so quick. Maritime law is clear on this: The captain of a ship is in control and responsible under any and all conditions. That afternoon the spokesperson for the U.S.

Coast Guard decided it was time to set the record straight, and, in a rare public rebuke, he corrected the spokesperson. He reminded her of the basic rules of the high seas: The captain, not the U.S. Coast Guard, is always in charge of a vessel. Ouch!

- Similarly, Sago Mining Company in West Virginia faced an enormous crisis when word spread on January 2, 2006, that 13 miners were trapped after a mine collapsed. News stories emerge in any industrial accident involving trapped people; apparently, the specter of drama amid an atmosphere of hope and limited time elevates television ratings and newspaper readership. Company president Bennett Hatfield assured families and reporters that "all 13 miners" were safe, a statement that elicited tears of joy in those who had panicked about the status of their loved ones. Three hours later, Hatfield said he deeply regretted "allowing the jubilation to go on longer than it should have." Sadly, he had to completely reverse his earlier statement: twelve miners had died. The credibility of the company was tainted because it spoke too early, without verifying the facts.

- Arthur D. Little (ADL) isn't around anymore, and for good reason. Thirty years ago ADL was a highly regarded consulting firm that, among other things, served as a design and testing lab that performed trials on everything from new cereals to sophisticated nuclear warning systems. In the 1980s, ADL was contracted by the federal government to create antibodies to counteract the effects of deadly nerve gas. Some officials feared then (and now) that the release of even a quarter of a cup of soman, the most lethal known chemical in the world, could kill thousands of civilians within minutes if it were released into the atmosphere near a major metropolitan area.

  Without notifying local authorities in Cambridge, Massachusetts (home to some of the world's best scientists at MIT and Harvard), ADL built a lab featuring rigorous security controls where soman was secretly introduced. Understandably, community protests erupted when the lab's employees alerted *The Cambridge Chronicle* that nerve gas was secretly transported into Cambridge by tank late at night. The spokesperson for ADL didn't help things. During an interview on ABC's *20/20*, she dismissed concerns about soman and said that the "little old ladies" (her term, not mine) at the bowling alley next door who were complaining about ADL's testing lab basically didn't understand science. The spokesperson may have understood science, but she desperately needed a crash course in diplomacy. Lesson learned: Choose your words carefully, especially when they're directed at well-intentioned citizens who have every right to voice their opinions about your company.

And, by the way, ADL's contention that nerve gas really didn't pose a threat in nonmilitary settings is not credible. In 1995, a miniscule amount of similar toxins were released by a complex domestic terror organization called the Aum Shinrikyo cult on a Tokyo subway, killing 12 and seriously injuring hundreds of others.

- Sampoong Department Store in Seoul, South Korea, learned the hard way that no matter what you say during a crisis, you had better add a dose of humility to your message. On June 29, 1995, one of the most horrific construction accidents in modern history ensued when this mega store, located in what had been designed as an office building, collapsed. Hours before the catastrophe, walls began to tear apart, and employees who told supervisors that they saw water streaming from ceilings were instructed to ignore these signs and go back to work. In actuality, the building was never designed to withstand the weight of hundreds of tons of furniture and other items that were incrementally added to the building's top floors. By the time the building collapsed, an astounding 501 people died and nearly 900 others were injured. Because the company was owned by a variety of investors, Sampoong had no predesignated crisis team. There were no spokespeople that could speak to the global press. The company literally went "dark" for hours as the global media converged on Seoul. In the interim, victims and concerned loved ones angrily blamed the company for its lack of sensitivity. Employees blasted Sampoong for failing to heed warning signs, and politicians seized the moment to criticize the company for failing to adhere to basic building and evacuation standards. A complete lack of candor and communications cost the company what could have been its greatest asset at the apex of the disaster: its credibility.

Drink Up!

Watch some of the world's platinum brands manage rumors and you might learn a thing or two about assessing whether a story has "legs." Take Coca-Cola, for instance, which was the brunt of one of the nastiest rumor campaigns in recent years.

Using its provocative Web site, killercoke.org, a group that is sympathetic to labor unions posts its grievances against Coca-Cola online in an effort to damage the company's reputation. The group alleges, among other things, that Coca-Cola manipulates its workers and is using up the few remaining clean water sources in the world to produce its products (to the detriment of the poor). Now, Coca-Cola may be a lot of things, but it's probably one of the most philanthropic companies around, something the union organizers fail to mention. Smart campaigns, in order to be credible, will often acknowledge at least a few token initiatives of a target company to demonstrate that not everything associated with a company is devious. Not this campaign: It alleges that Coca-Cola *kills*.

On the other hand, the hostile approach by the organizers of killercoke.org appears to be working to some extent, primarily because they have successfully motivated activist groups on college campuses. In urging campus administrators and students to boycott Coca-Cola products, the union organizers have succeeded in getting several dozen colleges around the world to ban the sale of Coca-Cola products altogether from their campuses. Should Coca-Cola have taken this group more seriously before the boycott effort spread to four continents? The company wouldn't respond to my inquiries, but you can make your own assumptions.

There must be a sadistic connection between soda manufacturers and poor crisis management skills. Not to be outdone, Pepsi also has been managing multiple attacks on its reputation in recent years. Pepsi has become something of a villain among many environmental activists around the world due to allegations that the company, like Coca-Cola, takes excessive amounts of precious groundwater to produce its products, most notably from India. If you are aware that only 1 percent of all water in the world is safe to drink, and that global warming could further diminish limited supplies, then you know that this is no small matter. It's especially damaging to poorer populations, who desperately rely on this limited resource of clean water.

Pepsi also has been facing an orchestrated campaign in India since 2003 in which citizens break hundreds of bottles in the streets to protest Pepsi's alleged practice of using pesticide-ridden water in its products. Leading the effort to correct false allegations is a fascinating Pepsi executive, Indra K. Nooyi. As profiled in *BusinessWeek*, Nooyi's job is to make sure that Pepsi doesn't face a campaign in which her product and that of her rivals becomes synonymous with danger and death.

Since the United Nations has said that the quality of water in India is the single worst of any country in the world and because it is in such short supply and is so highly valued (it is often unsafely recycled by families for personal use), the issue will weigh enormously on Pepsi's shoulders if the company cannot prevent this perception problem from blossoming into a business crisis. *BusinessWeek* noted in its June 11, 2007, issue:

> Nooyi recognizes the delicacy of being so closely associated with water in her native land. But she points out that soft drinks and bottled water account for less than 0.04 percent of industrial water used in India. "If we get attention, it's not because of the water use, it's because of what we represent," she says . . . "What we don't want is for people to think that industry is taking out of the ground God-given natural resources and depleting that community of its livelihood or requirements for existence."

Pepsi actually joined with Coca-Cola and hosted a rare joint news conference to protest the serious allegations that the water both companies use in their products may be contaminated. We're likely to see more cooperative communications efforts by competitors in the same

> Your radar screen must be on 24/7, and as issues emerge, someone needs to ask: Could *this* become a crisis?

lines of business—oil, copper, electrical, and others—as issues regarding social responsibility move from venues like college campuses squarely into the broad public domain. Pepsi is in a no-win situation: Unless the company can address these allegations in an aggressive way with a comprehensive program of issues management and crisis intervention, it is likely to see a diminishment in brand value in a growing and lucrative market. Your radar screen must be on 24/7, and as issues emerge, someone needs to ask: Could *this* become a crisis?

The beverage campaign gained enough momentum to trigger an independent investment firm, KLD Research & Analytics, of Boston, to drop Coca-Cola from its Broad Market Social Index (BMSI), the firm's comprehensive list of socially responsible companies, in July 2007. As of this writing, the firm has taken no action against Pepsi.

Now, the divesting of targeted stocks may not mean all that much to the average person, but if you're the CFO of a company, you probably will take notice if thousands of shares of your company's stock are divested in a short time span. I'm pretty sure Coca-Cola's CFO noticed when, after KLD dropped Coca-Cola from its BMSI, TIAA-CREF, the largest pension fund in the world, reportedly divested 1.25 million shares of Coca-Cola stock. As the largest beverage supplier in the world learned, the ramifications of these campaigns can be profound over a several-year period.

Why Communication Matters

Enough about soda. I'm hungry. Let's turn to tacos.

When Taco Bell was forced to close several of its restaurants in late 2006 due to E. coli–contaminated lettuce sickening dozens of people in the Northeast United States, the company acted quickly. Emergency managers contracted specialists to trace the origins of various meat and agricultural products to determine how the bacteria had entered its food chain. Only then, after determining which product distributors were assigned to the specific locations where customers who became ill had eaten, could Taco Bell determine if it faced a national or regional problem. Acting on the diagnostic results of its study, the company closed several more of its restaurants after consulting with state and federal food experts.

Taco Bell encountered what is arguably the worst challenge of any restaurant chain—a loss of public confidence. The restaurant was managing the health scare swiftly to prevent others from becoming ill, and in terms of operational diagnostics, Taco Bell's crisis management teams seemed to move quickly in the face of a pending national crisis. But when it came time to communicate with the public, the company appeared to be *overwhelmed*. Few spokespeople could be reached. Reporters had plenty of questions, but answers seemingly were nowhere to be found. Local managers were ordered to redirect press inquiries to headquarters.

Lacking proper information from Taco Bell headquarters, cable news networks escalated the story. What actually was a crisis that spanned only a few states turned into the "Taco Bell Illness" story; the national news media speculated that the illness had shifted from New Jersey to Pennsylvania. Who would get sick next, and where?

The company, one of several chains owned by Yum Brands, began to draft an advertisement that they later would run in national newspapers to reaffirm the public that its food was safe. However, national sales at Taco Bell, even in areas totally unaffected by E. coli, were plummeting. With consumers wondering if they were safe to eat at Taco Bell, it became apparent that Taco Bell was missing a core ingredient of communications—who was the physical face of this company? Did that person really care about people, or was he or she just worried about a potential nosedive in profit margins? A SWAT team of messages—with a human face—was needed. A full two weeks into the crisis, a frustrated network anchorperson for Fox News, Neil Cavuto, echoed the sentiments of many when he went on the air and slammed the company for its failure to communicate:

Your World with Cavuto

What do Taco Bell and Johnson & Johnson (J&J) have in common? Nothing. One knows how to respond to a crisis, and the other hasn't a clue. Taco Bell's the one without a clue. Only now, weeks after 70 diners at its East Coast restaurants fell sick with E. coli poisoning, is the company's president coming out and talking to the press. Weeks!

This is a far cry from what his counterpart at Johnson & Johnson did more than two decades ago after the now infamous Tylenol tampering scandal. James Burke didn't waste a nanosecond taking to the airwaves to update Americans on the latest news—as he got it, when he got it. Like the Taco Bell crisis, the Tylenol crisis wasn't the company's fault. In Taco Bell's case, it looks like a lettuce supplier. In J&J's case, it looked like a lone nutjob lacing Tylenol capsules with cyanide.

A lot of people got sick in this Taco Bell case. People died in the Tylenol case. Sales fell at Taco Bell. Sales fell at Tylenol. I don't know if Taco Bell's sales will recover. I do know Tylenol's did. Precisely because its CEO was so on top of a crisis, removing old capsules and replacing them with the kind of tamper resistant pills and packaging we're all familiar with today. Burke did that at great cost, and against great financial advice. They told him it would be too costly. His famous reply: It would be too costly not to. Burke was everywhere, talking to everyone. Far from trying to bury a crisis, he was on top of the crisis. End result: Tylenol's share of the pain reliever market went up. Lesson learned. It takes more than a press release to solve a crisis, or a chat with the FDA to end it.

Try talking to your consumers directly. Immediately. The ones who eat your food. And the ones who were getting sick from your food. You owe them more than a press release. Or a weeks' late public assurance. You're the president, for God's sake. Act like it. Take a lesson from Tylenol. They know a thing or two about headaches. Only difference: They know how to deal with them.

As you ponder the Taco Bell crisis, consider how the radar screen could have been managed differently, and at what point in time you would have stepped in to counter the crisis.

Timeline of the Taco Bell Crisis

- November 19, 2006: First cases of sick customers reported in New Jersey
- November 20, 2006: Cases escalate to 70 victims across five states; 48 people are hospitalized
- December 4, 2006: Taco Bell closes 60 stores in New York, New Jersey, Pennsylvania, and Delaware, reopening most of them the next day; confused customers tell reporters that they are not sure if the food is safe in their community
- December 6, 2006: Based on speculation and past incidents at other restaurant chains, green onions are ordered removed from all 5,800 stores nationwide; in communities where the Taco Bell story had not previously been reported, now a "local story" emerges in places ranging from Florida to parts of Canada
- December 8, 2006: Health experts complete their diagnostic and conclude that lettuce, not onions, is the likely source of the E. coli contamination
- December 9, 2006: A comprehensive examination is undertaken by company experts on the sources of lettuce by region
- December 14, 2006: The Centers for Disease Control (CDC) indicates that the outbreak is over and that eating at Taco Bell is safe; company president Greg Creed speaks to the press, triggering criticism from reporters and industry analysts that it is too little, too late

The Eight-Hour Window

When a crisis is confirmed, the wheels of response should begin turning—phones are ringing, updates are needed. Decisions must be made regarding victims and their needs, how those impacted can be comforted, and how the business will adjust to the disruption. This is

When a crisis is confirmed, the wheels of response should begin turning—phones are ringing, updates are needed.

a chaotic and unsettling time, no matter whether the organization is facing the impact of an earthquake or a gunman who returns to work to shoot a former supervisor. Regardless of the scope of the incident, the communications demands can be overwhelming. They must be managed well.

Companies such as Procter & Gamble (P&G), British Petroleum (BP), Kraft Foods, and others recently have begun to standardize the process of harnessing key organizational resources and bringing definition to their crisis communications plans *within the first eight hours after an incident arises*. Decades ago, companies looked at crisis communications in terms of the "news cycle," believing that updates only would be shared with reporters before the three principal television newscasts of the day at noon, 6 p.m., and 11 p.m. There was a sense of predictability in those schedules, especially because spokespeople and their teams could draft statements and test messages with focus groups before each news cycle.

Our Web-centric world has effectively ended the news cycle.

Blogs now allow employees to go home from work and criticize their employers for not doing enough to help employees after a hurricane. Password-protected chat rooms allow union activists to plan their protests outside of a company's headquarters without tipping off company IT or security personnel. Travelers on a cruise ship can photograph bloodstains onboard after a passenger is found to be missing—as was done on a Royal Caribbean ship in 2006, when passenger George Smith mysteriously disappeared—and send them to a television network within minutes. Three news cycles? No. Now there are dozens—everyday—as the barriers preventing global communication erode. A multinational such as BMW or Virgin Atlantic realizes that customers in China or India care just as much about the company's response to a crisis as those in Houston or Glasgow. Business blogs such as digg.com can move you from obscurity to front-and-center with investors overnight.

The eight-hour window is a general standard, not an Olympic-timed event. Yet this time frame is a credible goal that many crisis communicators seek to achieve. If you can capture what has happened, who is impacted, and how you intend to communicate your response with a clear plan of action within eight hours, you have the foundation for an excellent recovery plan.

Also realize that in the midst of a crisis, some Web advertisers like Reprise Media will take advantage of your misfortune with breathtaking speed by charging a premium price to have advertisements placed alongside news reports of your disaster on sites like Google, YouTube, and Yahoo! When the Virginia Tech massacre was first reported on April 16, 2007, advertisers paid as much as five dollars per click to have their ads displayed at the top of anyone's Internet page when "Virginia Tech Massacre" was typed into a browser, according to *BusinessWeek*. A week later, the same ad cost about five cents.

To help you get ahead of the headlines, here is a roadmap to effective crisis communications.

- Create a fact sheet on the scope of the incident, including the names of victims and next-of-kin, as well as a list of witnesses and a timeline of how events unfolded. This fact sheet should be updated each hour—or as needed—during the incident.
- Verify all facts with law enforcement officials and company security members and determine who should make contact with victims and family members, as well as whether someone from your claims or legal department should partake in personal visits to affected families.
- Begin to outline a draft response to the "big three" questions discussed earlier: What do we know? When did we know it? What are we doing about it? Continue to refine all answers based on new information.
- Remember that your telephone operators will receive inquiries from stockholders, employees, and others asking legitimate questions about what happened. Quickly prepare a brief statement for them so that they have a clear understanding of what they can and cannot say. Emphasize that they should refrain from speculating or making any statements beyond the key messages that are provided in their script. All media inquiries should be directed to the appropriate spokesperson.

The voicemail system of all senior leaders and spokespeople should be checked continually, as new facts may emerge. Rumors may be shared. Regulators or elected officials may be calling.

- In most organizations, you will want to communicate known facts with employees first (such as when a plane crash claims the life of a senior executive), but in other cases consumers may be the first to notify (such as during a toxic chemical leak near or at your facility). Remember that the local officials and regulators who provide you a license to operate will expect to hear from you—not from the local media—if you are experiencing a crisis.
- Each shareholder category may have unique crisis communications needs. For instance, employees may want to know if they will be paid even though they were asked to remain at home while your facility is cleaned following a major chemical spill. Customers don't care about paychecks: They need to know when their products will arrive. The news media will have yet a separate set of questions. As a result, your communications team should designate one individual per category of stakeholder to "own" the company's communications process with that category; doing so will reduce the risk of contradictions or omissions.

These cases aren't isolated ones. As you ponder crisis management, don't think just about the damage that a fire or explosion can do to your company; think about how rumors and social policy controversies can blossom into corporate nightmares. Nestle reportedly lost millions of dollars in sales after it knowingly sold baby formula that had been deemed substandard in the United States to mothers in Africa; even after the company reversed this outlandish decision, the damage wrought by the ensuing boycott was profound. Comparably, because its logo featured the moon and stars, P&G, another strong corporate citizen, suffered from years of false allegations that the company was a "front" for Satanists. It took P&G more than a decade of tracking down leads before it prosecuted the individual responsible for a single rumor that turned into an ugly urban legend.

Preparing Your Spokesperson

I am not aware of any company in the world that retains a full-time public relations professional whose work is devoted solely to crisis-related events. Because companies don't leave room on their payrolls for such a position, marketing and public relations professionals, who typically spend the majority of their careers promoting product launches, may find themselves managing corporate communications after their company experiences an industrial accident, a massive fire, or the arrest of a senior executive for embezzlement. These are complicated events for which most marketing and sales leaders have not been formally trained. For this reason, ensure that someone—anyone—who is skilled at persuasion mounts your crisis communications program.

To gain the confidence of reporters and, inevitably, the public, it is essential that you rehearse how you will manage a news conference or media interview during a crisis. It's amazing how many spokespeople will return a phone call to a reporter before thinking about the complex questions that could be hurled at them. When I wrote the crisis management plan for BP, I included a standard process that I termed "the worst 20"; under the terms of this procedure, BP spokespeople wrote down the 20 most disturbing questions they could imagine being asked after a serious incident in order to prepare themselves for when the questions actually came.

"That dramatically changed us as a company, and it helped us rehearse what we would say whenever there was a spill or an industrial accident at a refinery," noted Joseph Liska, retired director of crisis management for BP, in a personal communication. He added:

> When we knew the 20 worst questions that could be asked, we could rehearse answers with our spokespeople and test the

credibility of our response. Many times we would change an answer two or three times because we wanted to be accurate, and we knew that reporters were incredibly adept at knowing if we were hiding anything. So we would often hold a mock news conference before we did the real thing, and a group of employees would sit and listen to our spokesperson and help him clarify, explain things in greater depth, or be less technical with jargon.

The Taco Bell incident should remind you that even though you may not be aware of all of the dimensions of a crisis during the first eight hours, your organization has an incredible opportunity to be one step ahead of criticism by acknowledging that it is *aware* of the problem and is actively addressing it. You can post updates on your Web site and change your switchboard messages to offer pertinent information within minutes after a crisis becomes known. You can communicate that you are interested in feedback; are available to answer consumer questions via your toll-free number; and are eager to speak with family members of victims. No company should delegate crisis communications to an outside public relations firm; you can rely on the counsel and recommendations of external consultants, but in the midst of a disaster, only a company leader can effectively speak on behalf of the name on the door.

> Even though you may not be aware of all of the dimensions of a crisis during the first eight hours, your organization has an incredible opportunity to be one step ahead of criticism by acknowledging that it is *aware* of the problem and is actively addressing it.

Jet Black and Blue

Sometimes companies just don't get it. Sometimes Murphy's Law—that axiom that whatever can go wrong will—applies. And sometimes these and other dynamics collide in a single week. That brings us to jetBlue.

In early February 2007, professor Jeffrey Sonnenfeld of Yale University published a fascinating book, *Firing Back,* in which he extolled the virtues of several CEOs who had been fired in prior jobs, only to see their careers resurrected through ingenuity and innovation. On the very day the book was being touted on business television, one of those he profiled, David Neeleman, CEO of jetBlue (who was exited in the mid-1990s by Southwest Airlines), was interviewed live on CNBC. During this confident interview, Neeleman traced his magnificent comeback to executive stardom. jetBlue was on top of the world, and Neeleman smiled as he shared stories with the CNBC anchors about what he had learned from his departure from Southwest. Then . . . poof!

Murphy's Law descended on Neeleman and his company. On February 14, 2007, an incredible ice- and snowstorm blasted the Northeast United States, forcing jetBlue to find space for 52 airplanes at a terminal designed to accommodate half that number at New York's John F. Kennedy Airport (JFK). Other airlines at JFK responded swiftly and directed their aircrafts to return passengers to the gates; airlines that chose this course of action often did so after only a few hours. However, about 1,000 jetBlue customers aboard nine planes remained stranded on the tarmac. The airline's entire network clogged as a result, leading to about 1,150 cancelled flights and an estimated $40 million in lost revenue.

There are good reasons why an airline will play what only can be described as a variation of roulette during a storm: Quite simply, it isn't prudent to bring an aircraft back to the gate, since the jet would lose its position on the runway if the tower alters its decision about the weather conditions and clears planes for take-off. But while competitors watched as reports surfaced that the weather conditions were deteriorating rapidly, jetBlue experienced a colossal breakdown in crisis response—and in common sense.

Some passengers were left on a plane, less than a few hundred feet from the gate, where they could have enjoyed the comforts of working bathrooms, food, and circulating air. Instead, they found themselves on a plane with poor air circulation and clogged bathrooms for—get this—up to *11 hours*. That's 11 hours on a runway, from which you can see people inside drinking their Starbucks lattes and making alternative plans. Eleven hours on lockdown, until jetBlue finally decided that it would return planes to the gates.

Several other jetBlue planes remained on the runway for as long as nine hours.

The media had a field day with the incident, and the February 17, 2007, front-page headline in *The New York Post* bemoaned the "Jet Blues." Callers on talk shows all over the country asked: "Who are these people? Don't they have any compassion or common sense?"

The jetBlue incident is a classic case of crisis *mis*management, which I'm sure I'll be talking about in executive seminars for years to come. But to make matters even more curious, and to help you understand why communication and apologies matter so much in the midst of chaos, read on: After managers at jetBlue realized that they had an obligation to communicate with the public, the company bought full-page ads in select newspapers with a genuine, sincere message acknowledging that it had blundered. Neeleman was CEO. But guess who *signed* the letter to the public? No one. One ad featured a jetBlue logo only.

Accountability was, well, left on the runway—just like the airline's passengers.

jetBlue's renaissance CEO was criticized for underestimating the importance of the initial stages of a crisis. You can blame Mother Nature for snow and ice, but you can't blame her for poor crisis response. The company offered refunds, free flight coupons (just what an irate passenger wants!), and Neeleman did eventually affix his name to subsequent ads. I actually think he felt horrible about what had happened. But the brand was tarnished. Employee morale tanked. Neeleman went on the *The Late Show with David Letterman* to bring some levity to a very public fiasco, and he seemed genuinely contrite. But even David Letterman couldn't turn the public's indignation around. On May 13, 2007, company directors removed Neeleman as CEO and named him "nonexecutive" chairman. *USA Today* reported that within a few weeks of being removed as CEO, Neeleman sold nearly a quarter of his shares in jetBlue for about $27 million. And, *four months later*, jetBlue still wasn't returning press calls on this subject, according to *Investor's Business Daily*.

Wow. I can't wait to see who Sonnenfeld will select as his model CEO in the next edition of his book.

Summary

A crisis communications plan benefits every organization, ranging from nonprofits to multinational hedge funds. Because a natural disaster, case of embezzlement, kidnapping of an executive, or product recall could impact you at any moment, the time to create your roadmap to communications is not post-incident—it's before crisis strikes.

To achieve a high level of preparedness, your organization should have a basic communications inventory.

1. The communications plan must outline the hierarchy of who will speak for the company. The document should include all office, home, and cell phone numbers of the crisis team, crisis counselors, legal counsel, and any insurance company you may rely on.

2. You need to designate where you will meet, who owns the telephony aspect of your response, and who will activate your crisis alert system.

3. A simple outline of core crisis messages should be embedded into your crisis plan as templates that you can customize. You'll want to remember that in almost every crisis, you will never have all of the facts immediately. You may be told that a fire destroyed just one part of your factory in China, only to learn a few hours later that the entire factory was destroyed. As a result, you'll want to qualify all key remarks with statements such as, "Based on what we know at this point," or, "We are continually in contact with our folks on-site." Remember the case in West Virginia where the family members of the trapped miners were told incorrect information? Once you make a definitive statement and later have to reverse your message because your fact-finding was inadequate, your credibility is compromised.

4. Have your team identify the 20 worst questions you could be asked during any Q&A session with the press or public. When a company calls me in the midst of an incident, I'll often develop those questions for them, and then we conduct a mock news conference on the phone prior to their taking to the microphone. If he or she knows in advance the worst possible questions that could be asked, your spokesperson will be more confident in the midst of chaos. Keep your opening statements to two minutes or less. Allow members of the press to ask their questions. Take a moment to reflect on your answers. You are not on *Jeopardy!*, where a clock is ticking. You are allowed reasonable time to reflect on your answers.

5. Be ready to publicize your crisis resolution actions through media distribution networks like PR Newswire. These networks have accomplished teams that know how to reach reporters and assignment editors quickly.

6. Always frame the crisis properly. Is it an *incident*? A *crisis*? Do you have all of the facts at your disposal? If not, say so. Admit what you know and what you don't know. Remember that stakeholders will have abundant sympathy for you during a crisis if you acknowledge that your colleagues are working feverishly to gather all the facts pertaining to the incident. Tell them that you have deployed teams to the site and that you promise to return with additional information in a timely manner. When Ralph Erben, CEO of Luby's Cafeteria, learned on October 16, 1991, that there had been a mass murder at his restaurant in Killeen, Texas, he immediately flew to the scene to speak with victims' families and reporters. Erben was a gentle and kind leader. He brought a human face and compassionate voice to subsequent interviews. Rather than delegate the responsibility of crisis management to a senior vice president of marketing, he chose to "own" the company's message. In doing so, he gained credibility. Engaging in speculation or placing—or even accepting—blame will, I assure you, impair how the public receives you and your organization.

7. Ask the media to help you. Airlines do a wonderful job after a plane crash because they have learned from over 600 tragedies that have occurred in their industry over the decades. Spokespeople after a crash inevitably begin with statements about thoughts and prayers. Then they explain the facts of the itinerary, the type of aircraft involved, and their unofficial count of the number of crew and passengers onboard. They avoid confirming the names of victims or survivors until law enforcement officials have notified next-of-kin.

Typically, a company representative will accompany police officers when they visit victims' families. And then, early in the news conference, the airline shares an 800-number so that loved ones can call and ask for more information.

The airline industry knows the drill: They use the first several minutes of a news conference (the ones most likely to be carried on live television) to frame what they know, as well as what they *don't* know. They then request that impacted families contact them by sharing a toll-free number. You'll notice that in these news conferences, companies remove any company logos from the conference room in which they hold their news conference. This is a tactical move to protect their brand, as photos of their news conference may appear in tomorrow's *USA Today* or *The London Daily Telegraph*, and the last thing they want is for their logo to be forever associated with the word "disaster." Then they will typically withdraw paid advertising from all media for at least seven days out of respect for the victims. That's the science of crisis communications for the airline industry.

Now you need to research the best practices in your industry and embed them into your crisis plan.

12

CRISIS PREVENTION AND RESPONSE: PICKING A CONSULTANT

You might wonder why a chapter on preparedness would appear toward the end of a book about crisis management. The answer: You've already invested time in thinking about what could happen to your enterprise, and now it's time that you ensure that your business is ready for the variety of nasty, disabling incidents that could come your way.

Assessment

Most executives have no idea what crisis preparedness tools their businesses need until a crisis strikes. That is why they often

> A consultant can evaluate your existing preparedness plans.

contract outside consultants, some of whom are quite good. Among the services that a consultant can provide are:

- Evaluation of your existing preparedness plans
- Assessment of worst-case scenarios based on your industry and market position, who should respond, and how customer support would continue

- Refinement of notification and decision-making processes, as well as resource allocation; this is especially useful during weekend and after-hours incidents, when connecting with your leadership is more difficult
- Preparation of a comprehensive list of response tools, including medical and telecommunications needs, that your enterprise may not currently have access to

Finding a Crisis Consultant

Be wary of consultants who are eager to offer you much more than an overview of their credentials and capabilities. When you interview a consultant about the crisis assessment that he or she may perform for your enterprise, ask him or her:

- How detailed and customized the final document will be
- Whom he or she intends to interview in the preparation of his or her proposal
- The types of questions that he or she will ask
- How many risk or crisis plans he or she has created in the past

Some consultants love to list off their credentials to you, and their accreditations can range from CBCP to CPM, MBCP to FBCI, and CEM to CISA. Hiring a consultant with any or all of these "designations" does not guarantee you a better end product. Why? Some experts feel the need to boost their resumes with accreditations that are not from colleges and universities, but rather from "professional organizations" that run three-day seminars in hotels. Do not select a candidate solely for his or her credentials.

Research the Web for crisis consultants who preferably have experience working in your industry. First, conduct a detailed phone interview. A competent professional should be willing to give you at least a 30-minute overview of his or her knowledge and services. Here are 10 question sets to ask your potential crisis consultant, as well as why I want you to ask them:

1. **Clients: Who are some of your clients today? What services do you provide for them? How long have you been working with them? Are you on retainer, or are you paid on a project or daily basis?**
   Consultants love to wave around the names of the major brands they have worked with as though they were at a cocktail party. Dig deep. The individual may have been one of *several* people who worked on a single project for that company a decade ago. I want you to find out which companies they have worked with in the past few years, who they work with today, who their references are, and whether those companies used them for major projects or for a simple assignment that lasted only a few hours. If the crisis consultant tells you that his or her work is "highly confidential" and that he or she cannot provide references because of the super-secret nature of his or her analyses, take your super-secret budget to another consultant.

2. **Research: We've briefly told you what we think we need. Given that overview, how would you go about creating a proposal for us?**
   If the consultant is smart, he or she will tell you, "This is merely an introductory call. I would like to collect my thoughts, engage in more research, and return with a thoughtful analysis of your potential needs based on what I learned from speaking with you." Think about it: The consultant is being asked to identify major potential risks to life and property. You are entrusting the person to be accurate in his or her initial impressions, and your budget and crisis planning may be predicated on the consultant's findings. Respect a consultant who asks for a day or two to thoughtfully construct a document that outlines goals, objectives, and milestones.

3. **Skill Set: Are you more adept at research and diagnostic issues or at identifying business risks? Is your strength more on the prevention or response side? Over the years, where have you spent most of your professional time: prevention, response, or business recovery?**

This last question is potentially the most challenging of all. In reality, most crisis consultants have completed projects in all three arenas—prevention, response, and business recovery. However, many pursue a specialty within disaster preparedness. The smart ones will tell you when a project is not suitable for them based on their credentials and experience. I would be leery of any consultant who tells you that he or she is equally outstanding in all arenas. On the other hand, if the person's broad experience and consulting style are compatible with your company's culture, it may be perfectly acceptable to hire him or her.

4. **Persuasion: Have you ever given a presentation to a company's board of directors? When, and where? What was the nature of that presentation? What kind of questions do board members ask about potential disasters?**
   In most cases, you will want to hire a crisis consultant who is able to relay the message to both senior officers of companies *and* members of boards of directors that the time to make critical decisions has arrived. Your crisis consultant also should be able to inform your company's leadership when new investments in crisis preparedness and response are necessary. My dad once told me that you can always hire someone to write for you, but you can never hire someone to *speak* for you. That's proven to be incredibly smart advice. A truly first-rate crisis consultant is articulate, confident, and capable of speaking about the lessons he or she has learned. If the consultant is a technician with deep expertise in water or smoke damage, roof collapses, or salmonella poisoning, but he or she isn't the best presenter at a board meeting, hire him or her and a savvy spokesperson. When your company is in crisis, you need a change agent with proper damage-control skills who is compelling, clear, and who "nails it" in the boardroom.

> When your company is in crisis, you need a change agent with proper damage-control skills who is compelling, clear, and who "nails it" in the boardroom.

5. **Experience: Have you actually managed incidents while working at your company or for clients? What kind (e.g., environmental spill/biohazard, facility collapse, sustained electricity outage)? What did you learn from these experiences?**

    This is, of course, the area in which you must listen most carefully, because rhetoric can sometimes run deep in the DNA of consultants. Naturally, I want you to enlist a seasoned pro to help your company prepare for crisis—someone, for instance, who has actually received a call at 2 a.m. and been told that a major facility has been destroyed in a fire. If the consultant you hire boasts this kind of experience, he or she will be more effective at connecting the many dots of your crises. More often than not, this person also will know who among your stockholders should be informed first when tragedy strikes your enterprise— like your insurer and the Merrill Lynch analyst who covers your stock, for example. Sure, it is nice to talk with academics who love to lecture about the stages of a crisis and who have created fancy paradigms and written dozens of articles on the effects of crises on victims and stakeholders. But you are paying for experience, not models; insight, not hypotheses. If the consultant has never managed victims or families in the midst of chaos, find yourself another "expert."

6. **Accountability: Who will we actually work with if we were to engage you? Do you have a staff of researchers and project managers? What percentage of your time would you devote to us if we selected you for this initiative?**

    There are many crisis consultancy companies out there, so, just as you might take special precautionary measures when buying a major appliance for your home, be guarded and take time to research the consultancy groups you are considering contracting. There are a few firms out there that are notorious for bringing in their top presenters to wow you at your conference table but then, after the contract is signed, turn your company's crisis management over to a junior "project manager." I have a rule that you may want to consider: Could you defend this person and his or her credentials if you ever had to give a deposition? If so, congratulate yourself on a great choice. If not, cut your losses and find a rock star that is crisis savvy.

7. **Depth: Let's say the project we assign you is one that focuses on business recovery. What is the typical length of a business recovery plan (BRP) that you prepare for a client?**
Alert! This is a classic case in which more is not better. "Oh, I'd say our typical BRP is about 300 pages. We cover so much and in such great depth, from utility outages to IT recovery hot sites, and from medical evacuations to weather-related alerts—you'll be blown away by how lengthy it is!" Now, think it out. A tornado has wiped out a portion of your building, or a HAZMAT spill on a local rail line has made it impossible for your employees to come to work; local roads could be closed for days, possibly weeks. Are you really going to read 300 pages in the midst of all of the phone calls, interruptions, news media inquiries, and demands on your time? I advise clients that a BRP should never exceed 100 pages. If the consultant's crisis plans generally exceed the weight of most phone books, chances are good that this "expert" has bought a template and is filling in the blanks, billing you for "customization" that, I assure you, is minimal. Buyer beware.

8. **Candor: Name a client who was meaningful to you but that you have lost. What happened?**
I know, I know. Admitting that you lost a client is like admitting that someone you used to date broke up with you—and no one likes to acknowledge a broken heart. The reality, however, is that sometimes even the best consultants lose clients, either because a new company leader wants to bring in resources he or she knows and trusts, or because budget cuts bring about the elimination of the consultant's position at the company. I would not hold any of these excuses against the professional you are interviewing. Be sensitive to the individual's candor and whether his or her explanation is credible. A consultant in this complex field that tells you that he or she never lost a client is either desperate, lying, or both.

9. **Global: Have you ever lived or worked in another country? Tell us about that experience if it has direct applicability to crisis-related issues. What lessons did you learn that you could briefly share with us?**

   Although your company may not have overseas facilities, chances are that your colleagues travel out of the country, or that you import products from overseas. Maybe you outsource some of your needs, such as your call center, to locations abroad. Whatever the extent of your company's overseas inter-actions, certain crises—such as pandemics—can connect the world's population to an unprecedented degree. For this rea-son, I prefer crisis consultants that have some expatriate or global experience, even if it was only for a few months. This adds to their depth of understanding of the role of the State De-partment, import-export controls, and port and customs issues. It also means that they will be more sensitive to several complex international issues, such as language and cultural differences, which most certainly will play roles in any global crisis.

10. **Bottom Line: Do you typically charge by the day or by the project? Do you charge for travel time to and from clients? If we were to place you on a one-year retainer that gives us 24/7 access to your counsel, what would a monthly fee look like?**

    Again, a smart consultant will answer this question candidly, but he or she also will explain that his or her charges may vary, depending on the circumstances of the crisis, and that is per-fectly fair. You may begin your search for a crisis consultant thinking that you need him or her only to conduct a risk assess-ment but then later realize that you need to expand the scope of his or her work to include training programs, presentations to employees, or a BRP. If a consultant tells you that he or she charges a fee for travel to and from your facility, don't balk: These people are hopping planes and flying sometimes from four to eight hours (thus a lost day of income) to come visit you, so nominally reimbursing them for their time is not outra-geous. Shop around and realize that, like most things in life, you get what you pay for.

Do I Have a Software Program for You!

When I first began working with one of my long-standing clients a few years ago, its global crisis readiness was dismal. The company had no crisis plan, no Emergency Operations Center (EOC) capability, no 24/7 way to connect key decision makers during a crisis, and no post-crisis roadmap to business recovery. In the years since then, all of these issues have been addressed, and I have designed and managed about a dozen simulations for this company in locations worldwide to test its preparedness for potential scenarios that could compromise its people and brand. Bottom line: My work with this client has been an incredible opportunity for me, and our mutual respect is high.

Then, a new manager entered the business dynamic, and I was eager to work with him because of his impressive background in crisis management. The next few months, however, were pure hell. Just when we had completed the development of a crisis plan that the company's divisional leaders around the world were aware of and understood, he began to extol the virtues of this wonderful software program that he insisted should be installed on the laptops of members of the crisis management team. But, wait—there's more. He wanted the EOC reconfigured so that the company's entire crisis management system was dependent on this fabulous software that he saw at a trade show. He basically told his CEO: "This software will not only help us ramp up during an incident, but if we embed it in each of our factories and distribution centers worldwide, voila! Our crisis problems will be solved."

Uh, I don't think so. Patiently, calmly, in four different conference calls with project managers, I explained why software is *one* tool in crisis management, but it is not a panacea. I explained that when serious incidents strike, your team needs several tools at its disposal:

> Software is *one* tool in crisis management, but it is not a panacea.

- Updated phone lists
- Accurate and up-to-date site plans with architectural drawings and predesignated "safe haven" areas

- An EOC that has the technology to help you connect with your teams, document milestones, and anticipate whether the crisis could escalate further
- A strong crisis communications plan

Anything and everything beyond these four items is a luxury—nice to have, but not essential when responding to the initial stages of a crisis and getting you on the path to recovery.

Now, I'm not anti-software. There are some wonderful programs out there that can help you better understand disaster management. Some of them can help you track the costs of your recovery effort—information that insurers surely will ask for when you approach them for reimbursement funds. However, many of these programs are loaded with weather maps and traffic sensors. These tools are nice to have, sure, but here is what I want you to remember:

- If you lose electricity, these programs are of low to no value after your laptop batteries or power supplies run out.
- Inevitably, you will be buying a system at a premium price (because it's not an open-platform solution) that must be upgraded as new versions are released, which vendors typically do every year or two.
- Customization is where considerable profit is derived by programmers because of the size of hourly billing. Software companies *love* to customize.

I am prepared for hate mail from software companies telling me how their software has saved their clients hundreds of person-hours and brought precious food to the homeless during some hurricane, earthquake, or other calamity. Maybe the software played a role, but I suspect that it was volunteers who brought the food—not their program.

> In a crisis, you need a first-rate team of crisis leaders who are ready to assess the damage and make a decision.

In a crisis, you need a first-rate team of crisis leaders who are ready to assess the damage and make a decision. You need a roadmap. You need a cheat-sheet to help you remember what your lawyers want you to say and do when it's your turn to take the microphone. You need speakerphones so that you can connect vital people and ascertain what is happening. You need a great communicator that will help you respond quickly to unfolding events and that will move your company ahead of rumor and reporters. You may need foreign language translators. In addition, you continually will need to measure how much what you are doing and saying is being heard, and whether your actions are having a beneficial impact on victims and their families.

Inventory of Must-Have Resources

Remember that you may be able to save a considerable amount of money on crisis preparedness if you pursue a consortium arrangement with other local businesses. You also should check to see if your local emergency preparedness agency might have some of these items in storage, ready to be deployed, if there is a local emergency.

- Air-filtration systems
- Carpet damage extractors
- Portable heaters, refrigerants, and dehumidifiers
- Emergency generators
- Pressure washers to hose down chemicals, toxins
- Fire and smoke recovery tool kits
- Mold remediation plans
- Vital records recovery
- Satellite phones
- Medical kits and face-masks

These are just a few of the tools that smart crisis consultants will insist your company have on hand as they create a diagnostic overview of your enterprise's crisis readiness. You have my promise that when a disaster strikes your organization, you will need these items, and a trained crisis team, much more than any software. When you are in the midst of chaos, I promise you that you will not be reaching for your laptop. You will likely be caring for people with wounds, extracting trapped employees or customers, evaluating the fallout from water and falling debris, listening to angry neighbors, and juggling calls from the news media. Focus on those immediate needs, and you'll be able to stand tall.

13

THEY DID IT RIGHT: THE CRISIS-READY COMPANY

Many will argue that we should not only identify the stumbles that have been made during various debacles, but that we should also identify exemplary behaviors and actions during crisis-filled times. I agree. So here are a few case studies of leaders who, in the midst of chaos, used candor, imagination, and other traits that typify true leadership.

John F. Kennedy

John F. Kennedy had been president for just 84 days when a U.S.-led invasion of Cuba, intended to dethrone Fidel Castro and restore democracy to the island nation, became a fiasco of military logistics and poor planning. Kennedy inherited the invasion plan from his predecessor, president Dwight D. Eisenhower, but Kennedy didn't use Eisenhower as a scapegoat, even though the poor planning tools that led to the botched invasion were Eisenhower's, not Kennedy's.

A small but mighty Cuban army had defeated the American military just 90 miles off the coast of Florida. Although Kennedy had little experience as a crisis manager, he sought the counsel of Washington, D.C., insiders, and, with the help of his brother, Robert F. Kennedy, press secretary Pierre Salinger, and others, he crafted a remarkably honest speech to the American people. If you read the text of this speech, you will see that the 44-year-old Kennedy acknowledged that

the invasion was a flop. Thanks to Kennedy's sincerity, his public opinion ratings unexpectedly soared following the national address. Executives don't typically acknowledge that they could have performed
better; they usually blame someone else. As Graham Allison and Philip
Zelikow point out in his remarkable book *Essence of Decision*,
Kennedy applied the lessons he learned from the failed Cuban invasion
when he was again tested during the Cuban Missile Crisis. In that four-
day, anxiety-filled, potentially Armageddon-inducing standoff with
Russia, Kennedy rolled up his sleeves, led conversations in his Emergency Operations Center (EOC) (the White House war room), and encouraged his team to identify alternative scenarios to motivate Russia
to withdraw its hidden nuclear warheads from Cuba. The result was a
combination of remarkable tenacity, grace under pressure, and superb,
measured crisis response.

Johnson & Johnson

James Burke is often credited with having mastered the art of crisis management when, as CEO of Johnson & Johnson (J&J), he faced a pharmaceutical manufacturer's worst nightmare. In 1982, it was discovered
that Tylenol capsules were being laced with poison, and J&J needed to
quickly comprehend the enormity of this incident. Burke smartly assembled a team of scientists, public affairs specialists, and lawyers. One of
this team's first tasks was to conduct a rapid exercise in reverse engineering: Is it possible that someone inside one of Tylenol's plants could
have had the time, given the company's rapid manufacturing processes,
to stop individual Tylenol pills in mid-production, inject them with poison, and recap them? Within days, the company realized that the poisoning was no inside job; it was the work of an extortionist. The
Tylenol brand was under assault, and Burke determined that all Tylenol
products had to be voluntarily recalled.

Long before books on crisis management existed, Burke and his
team acted swiftly, communicated frequently, and—this is often
overlooked—relied on law enforcement officials to target the location
of the perpetrator of the crime. Because J&J was a victim of a crime,
it was never blamed for complicity. The company shined because

it acted quickly to protect its market share. In doing so, J&J recaptured public trust. Today Tylenol has a higher market share of pain medications than it enjoyed before this crisis—a remarkable feat.

Virginia Tech

Although you probably already have read countless criticisms of Virginia Tech's (VT) tactical response to the horror on its campus on April 16, 2007, the press largely ignored one positive facet of VT's crisis response. While other campus leaders were managing the enormity of the massacre, a separate team orchestrated a massive public memorial service that would be held the day after the massacre at Cassell Coliseum on the VT campus. The sheer energy and logistical talent that came together to bring president George W. Bush, governor Tim Kaine (who flew immediately back to Virginia after having just arrived in Asia), various clergy, student speakers, and choirs was just extraordinary. Add to that mix all of the planning that went into the event's security logistics and speech writing, not to mention the effort that was surely involved in assembling psychological counselors to assist those coping with post-traumatic stress. Organizing all of this, with family members flying in from around the world, and at the same time coordinating with television networks, resulted in one of the most remarkably staged tributes to the victims of any crisis. I was overwhelmingly impressed.

Tommy Hilfiger Fights Back

In a wired world where facebook.com and millions of blogs and Web sites offer an opportunity to socially connect with others, companies are finding it increasingly difficult to monitor, let alone respond, to malicious rumors aimed at destroying brand equity.

A pioneer effort at rumor mitigation occurred in 1996 when Internet messages were flying out of control about fashion designer Tommy Hilfiger. Writing about the events of 1996, Timothy Coombs of Eastern Illinois University notes that online discussions at the time focused on an alleged heated interview between talk show host Oprah Winfrey and Hilfiger. In this interview, it was alleged that Winfrey asked Hilfiger if it was true that he was upset that African Americans, Asians, and Hispanics wore his clothes when they were intended for Caucasian clientele, and his answer was "yes," which led Winfrey to kick him off her studio set.

As Coombs points out, Hilfiger never appeared on Oprah, and his company enjoyed a track record of advertising that displayed a multicultural dimension. Hilfiger employed a research firm to detect the origin of the malicious rumor (both a newspaper in the Philippines and college bulletin boards were suspected) and then launched an aggressive counter-rumor campaign that included messages and postings on his company's Web sites; letters to retail outlets where local salespeople might be asked about the rumors; and information updates to operators at its company headquarters so receptionists would know what to say if customers called to ask about the rumor.

More than a decade later, on May 2, 2007, Hilfiger decided that enough time had lapsed to appear on Oprah's show and reaffirm his values. Hilfiger exemplified many of the qualities of a smart crisis leader. When his radar screen suggested that an "issue" was evolving into a "potential crisis," he acted swiftly and decisively and communicated facts through many channels. If Hilfiger had appeared on Oprah's show immediately after the rumors surfaced, he may have escalated calls for boycotts, because the controversy could have become a magnet for the mainstream media. Instead, Hilfiger focused on the Internet and discussion boards where false claims were escalating. As reported on Oprah.com, he didn't discuss the issue directly with Winfrey until the issue had evaporated, at which point Hilfiger was direct and emphatic:

OPRAH: Let's break this down. Tommy, in the 21 years that we've been on the air, have you ever been on the show before today?

TOMMY: Unfortunately, not.

OPRAH: And when you first heard it, Tommy, what did you think?

TOMMY: I didn't believe it . . . Friends of mine said they heard the rumor. I said, 'That's crazy. That can't be. I was never on

The Oprah Show. I would never say that.' And all my friends and family who know me and people who work with me and people who have grown up with me said that's crazy.

OPRAH: Well, did you ever say anything close to that? Where do you think this originated?

TOMMY: I have no idea. We hired FBI agents, I did an investigation, I paid investigators lots of money to go out and investigate, and they traced it back to a college campus but couldn't put their finger on it.

14
LESSONS FROM HISTORY

I'm often asked which of the various crises that have struck businesses worldwide are of great historical significance. Not surprisingly, there are literally thousands of them. Here are some of the more prominent disasters you may find worthy of additional study:

1906: San Francisco Earthquakes

On April 18, 1906, three monumental earthquakes, each of which measured an estimated 8.5 on the Richter scale, devastated most of San Francisco, California. Some 28,000 buildings were flattened or significantly damaged; the resulting fires lasted three days, leaving nearly 200,000 people homeless and 502 dead. Employees of the Bank of America literally carried cash out of the vaults of their company's various branches in the city to safe havens in nearby Oakland in wheelbarrows. Bank couriers covered the cash with clothes to prevent robbery amid widespread loitering.

1912: The *Titanic*

When the "unsinkable" *Titanic* sank on April 14, 1912, it was traveling at a velocity of 22 knots—well above the average speed of 10 knots that was common for ships of its size traversing iceberg-ridden waters in the early 1900s. By the time captain Edward J. Smith issued the order "Save Our Ship"—or SOS (the first time it was ever used in maritime history)—it was too late. Water had seriously compromised the vessel, and passengers had barely two hours to evacuate. Some 815 passengers and 688 crewmembers died. Several investigations found that Smith was disinterested in weather conditions. By not watching his "radar screen," Smith essentially allowed the *Titanic* to move at a reckless pace in the face of potential danger; historians have suggested that he may have been pressured by the ship's owners to accelerate his speed so they could publicize an early arrival in New York. Instead, funeral and memorial services were held around the world.

1917: Halifax Explosion

The French freighter *Mont Blanc* left New York on December 6, 1917, headed for a war-torn Europe and carrying TNT, gunpowder, and picric acid chemicals. These chemicals were vital weapons for the Allies who were mobilizing a coordinated war effort. Upon nearing the port of Halifax, Nova Scotia, the *Mont Blanc* collided with the *Imo*, a Belgium freighter, leading to what stunned observers called a floating barge of weapons. The ship simply could not be stopped as it sped closer and closer to port. When the *Mont Blanc* inevitably crashed into a pier, it literally flattened half of the city. About 3,000 perished from the immediate, extraordinary explosions and resulting fires, including 552 children, who could not escape from school buildings as they collapsed upon them.

1942: Cocoanut Grove Fire

When 100 people died at a Warwick, Rhode Island, nightclub in February 2003, after pyrotechnics were ignited on stage during a rock concert, historians of the hospitality industry only had to look backwards to find an incident involving similar devastation. On November 28, 1942, revolving doors stopped moving as hundreds of guests rushed to evacuate the smoke- and fire-filled Cocoanut Grove nightclub in Boston; the club was packed with several hundred partygoers after a Boston College/Holy Cross football game. It turns out that the exit doors to the club were intentionally locked because management feared that the nightclub's guests would depart without paying their tabs. The inferno started when cheap plastic upholstery near a paper palm tree was ignited by a lit match; an astounding 492 people died. Club owner Barney Welansky was sentenced

Remember that in any crisis, you may find that opportunists, thieves, and scoundrels may make a human catastrophe even worse.

to 12 years in prison for gross negligence. Remember that in any crisis, you may find that opportunists, thieves, and scoundrels may make a human catastrophe even worse. The crisis hit rock bottom when, as Paul Benzaquin notes in his account of that night, some of those who were dead or dying were robbed of their jewelry and wallets when en route to Massachusetts General Hospital. At least one critically wounded woman was sexually assaulted during triage.

1964/1989: Stadium Stampedes

Disasters at sporting events are particularly noteworthy because they often involve stadiums whose exits are limited or poorly marked. Add into this equation the fact that many fans often are excited by emotion and influenced by alcohol before they even become aware that a crisis is underway. On May 24, 1964, at least 300 spectators died at an Argentina vs. Peru soccer game in Lima, Peru, when police, interpreting fans' enthusiasm for the game as potential mass chaos, locked the stadium's doors. Ironically, the police created real chaos when spectators became aware that they were stuck inside the stadium. A mass stampede ensued.

Another catastrophe of mammoth proportions occurred on April 15, 1989, when some 54,000 people crowded into a Hillsborough, United Kingdom, stadium. Local roads leading to the stadium were extraordinarily crammed with game-day traffic due to ongoing construction, and many fans raced to the stadium gates when they finally arrived, fearing they might miss the start of the game. What followed was a combination of hysteria, anxiety, and a total lack of crowd control preparedness by stadium management when fans stampeded the stadium. There was just one police officer stationed at the extra gate that was hastily opened to accommodate the crowd overflow. A massive rush ensued; 95 people died, most of them crushed to death. Local medical facilities were initially unable to provide adequate triage to hundreds that were seriously wounded.

1980/2007: Casino Tragedies

When some 87 casino guests and employees died as a result of a fire-ball that erupted at Bally's Casino in Las Vegas on November 21, 1980, many guests refused to abandon their slot machines and poker tables, even as flames raced toward them. Some died in their sleep in hotel rooms. Deniability—the notion that "this can't possibly be happening"—was prevalent among many victims who escaped the Bally's fire just in time.

This same behavioral pattern repeated itself on July 6, 2007, at the New York-New York Casino in Las Vegas, when Steven Zegrean, an unemployed, clinically depressed, Hungarian refugee with a reported gambling addiction, shot and wounded four people from a balcony overlooking the casino. Three unarmed tourists—not security guards—subdued the perpetrator, preventing what could have been a massacre at a heavily populated resort. Two days after the shooting, Zegrean's family members acknowledged that they had alerted Las Vegas police a week *before* the shooting that the gunman was potentially violent and suicidal.

1983: Korean Air Flight 007

Korean Air Flight 007 allegedly violated Soviet air space when it in-advertently moved about 200 miles off-track during its transnational flight between New York and Seoul on August 31, 1983. The plane was intentionally shot down by Soviet military pilots, killing 269 civilians. The global community widely criticized the Russian government for knowingly destroying a civilian aircraft when it could have followed common aviation protocol and used its military jets to force the plane's landing. To this day, there are conspiracy theories that the Soviets' action was an intentional "hit," as one of the victims of the downed plane was Lawrence McDonald, a leading conservative member of the U.S. Congress.

1984: Union Carbide

A leak of 45 tons of highly toxic gas occurred at the Union Carbide plant in Bhopal, India, around 1 a.m., on December 3, 1984. An estimated 3,000 people died and another 200,000 were injured; mass graves were hastily dug to avoid further contamination and a potential outbreak of cholera. Union Carbide president Warren Anderson did the right thing and immediately flew to Bhopal to express his personal condolences, but he should have been better briefed regarding the legal and multicultural dimensions of the crisis. Upon arriving in India, Anderson was immediately arrested at the airport and charged with murder by negligence; he was released on bail and later exonerated of all charges. Union Carbide's lack of safety controls and warning systems, however, was widely criticized, as hundreds of local residents died in their sleep without being warned about the lethal leakage. An investigation conducted several years after the incident showed that the cause of one of the worst industrial accidents in history was likely employee sabotage.

1986: Chernobyl

A fast rise in temperature inside a nuclear complex can be devastating if carbon monoxide and hydrogen become ignited. Radioactive material is released, followed by rapid poisoning and massive fire. On April 26, 1986, that's precisely what happened at the Chernobyl nuclear plant in Kiev, Ukraine. The Ukrainian government, paranoid about negative publicity, neglected to inform much of the world for three days about the magnitude of this unprecedented release of nuclear toxins. Meanwhile, triage for the seriously ill failed miserably, as the doctors working in the limited medical facilities near the plant's surrounding areas had little to no experience in toxicology. To this day, no one knows how many died from radiation poisoning, but some environmental experts have estimated that the immediate and long-term death toll may have exceeded 100,000 people. Unfortunately, the Ukrainians have never taken disaster management very seriously. They still have yet to install advanced, instant notification systems in communities near nuclear power plants.

1988: Pan Am Flight 103

On December 21, 1988, Libyan terrorists planted a bomb on Pan Am Flight 103 and detonated it 54 minutes into a flight from London to New York; 260 people died in the air and on the ground when it crashed in Lockerbie, Scotland. Pan Am's global brand was ruined. Reservations tanked worldwide as travelers shunned the airline, and the company went bankrupt in 1992.

1989: *Exxon Valdez*

The captain of the oil tanker *Exxon Valdez,* Joseph Hazelwood, passed command of his vessel to a third mate late on the evening of March 24, 1989. Hazelwood was an experienced captain, but he could have benefited from a course in crisis management. After the third mate he had appointed had run the ship aground, Hazelwood severely underestimated the extent of the initial damage to the ship and advised the U.S. Coast Guard that "evidently we're losing some oil and we're going to be here a while." Well *that* was an understatement! Over 11 million gallons of oil were released into the pristine waters of Prince William Sound in Alaska. This catastrophe led to the death of nearly 35,000 birds and largely devastated the Alaskan fishing economy for several years. Exxon's CEO, Lawrence Rawl, hunkered down at company headquarters while consumers and elected officials screamed on talk shows for a faster response by Exxon. Many customers tore up their Exxon credit cards and refused to ever purchase the company's products again. Rawl's reputation as an oil executive had previously been favorable, but it would be permanently tainted by what many believed to be his corporation's insensitivity to the people of Alaska. Exxon went financially unscathed for many years after the spill, delaying penalties and court fines. But there's a lesson here: Exxon needed the sense of urgency exhibited by Anderson of Union Carbide; at least *he* recognized the magnitude of the scandal that could unfold if his company didn't act quickly. I'd rather see you arrested and released than accused of insensitivity to the public and the environment.

1995: Oklahoma City

Some 169 innocent people perished inside the Murrah Federal Office Building in Oklahoma City, Oklahoma, on April 19, 1995, after explosives planted by domestic terrorists inside a Ryder rental truck that was parked curbside to the building were detonated. Subsequent investigations concluded that a "progressive collapse" of the building occurred; shock waves rocked through columns of concrete in just 50 milliseconds, wiping out most of the third, fourth, and fifth floors of the building. The terrorists, Timothy McVeigh and Terry Nichols, reportedly chose to enact their plot on April 19 because of the date's correspondence to the historic battle between colonists and British troops at Lexington and Concord.

2007: *Sea Diamond*

Taking a vacation on a cruise ship is statistically one of the safest journeys you can enjoy. But accidents can impact even "safe" industries. The Greek cruise ship *Sea Diamond* sank when it hit a reef off the coast of Santorini in 2007, necessitating the evacuation of 1,600 passengers; two of the travelers were never found. Lawsuits over incidents at sea, whether caused by the Norwalk virus or navigational incompetence, can take years to settle.

> Accidents can impact even "safe" industries.

15

ASSESSING YOUR CRISIS RISK: OVERVIEW

Begin your evaluation of your organization's exposure to a potential crisis by completing this assessment of key categories of risk. This is often best accomplished by asking a team of your associates to work with you in a planning meeting. You can also use this assessment tool in your staff meeting to discuss ways that you can mitigate some risks, eliminate others, and adequately prepare for all that are relevant. Rank the following items on a scale from 1 to 10, with 10 representing the greatest damage a potential crisis could do to your people and enterprise, and 1 being the least. Use the space provided to include specific comments, past incidents, or industry trends that may be influencing your thoughts.

RANK
(1–10)

1. Threats against individuals (e.g., stalking and workplace violence)   _____

Comments:

2. Major fire or flood at key facilities   _____

Comments:

3. Power failure and sustained loss of utilities   _____

Comments:

4. Pandemic/flu sweeps across region of your enterprise
   (expected temporary loss of 30 percent or more of
   workers for more than three months)   _____

Comments:

5. Bomb and/or bomb threat at your facility   _____

Comments:

6. Terrorism specifically aimed at your company,
   people, facilities   _____

Comments:

7. Terrorism not aimed at your company in region that
   disrupts business travel, product shipment, port functions   _____

Comments:

8. Exposure to a costly product recall (includes harm to
   consumers/end users and damage to financial condition
   and brand)   _____

Comments:

9. Alleged compliance violation (e.g., European Union
   Act Tariffs, or allegation that one of your sales leaders
   violated the Foreign Corrupt Practices Act)   _____

Comments:

10. Geopolitical instability in core markets disrupts
supply chain   _____

Comments:

11. Sole source provider to your company is destroyed
or impaired   _____

Comments:

12. Major currency issue causes significant devaluation
(20 percent or more)   _____

Comments:

13. Community protests by local residents, union activists   _____

Comments:

14. Organized boycott of company   _____

Comments:

15. Competitive intelligence threat; theft of customer/
financial/design data   _____

Comments:

16. Widespread counterfeit product and/or adulteration   _____

Comments:

16

THE TWO-PHASE CRISIS COACH

P lace a bookmark on this page as an easy reference. When disaster strikes, these primary reminders can help you navigate the first hours of a disaster:

Phase I: Response

Respond First to Victims

- Identify incident commander who assesses needs of victims, assists in coordination with first responders, alerts senior management to nature/extent of crisis
- Crisis team gathers all facts, maps stakeholders and their anticipated needs
- Corporate Crisis Management Team (CCMT) to confirm facts, consider whether incident/scope could escalate
- Communications plan prepared with key messages to employees, customers, investors, others; phone operators alerted and Web site adjusted as needed
- Decide whether to activate the Emergency Operations Center (EOC)
- Track status of those impacted; consider psychological counseling needs
- Establish an hourly briefing schedule by conference call at 30 minutes past each hour

Respond Second to Organization

- Consider needs for 24/7 hour staffing at Emergency Operations Center (EOC)
- Ensure organization is speaking with "one voice" on key messages
- Ensure legal counsel, insurance company, and others are alerted to potential exposure
- Answer and log all incoming calls with pledge to return them promptly; delegate and allow teams to manage without being second-guessed
- Prepare CEO at rehearsal news conference with robust Q&A

Respond Third to Publics

- Launch news conference led by senior exec or CEO focusing on victims, prayers, and what company is doing to respond to needs of those impacted
- Provide employees updates, via e-mail or phone, on victims, witnesses, what you need and expect from them, and how you will help them, if needed
- Launch customer communications program to explain business recovery process
- Document key milestone decisions
- Swiftly move to recovery phase to protect your brand and reputation

Phase II: Mobilize and Restore

Respond to Recovery Needs

- Ensure Corporate Crisis Management Team (CCMT) is updated on all key decisions, milestones, and communications
- Determine if a new alignment of responsibilities is needed that differs from existing plans because of the nature or severity of the incident
- Conduct pulse-taking surveys using telephone- or Web-based tools to determine how customers, employees, and others feel about the organizational response
- Engage insurance brokers and underwriters to determine if the company should be documenting damage on the impact of

the catastrophe in a special format to accelerate the claims process

- Revisit the human impact of disaster to ensure that the human resources department and Employee Assistance Program (EAP) are actively meeting with those who need counseling as a result of what they experienced or witnessed

17

CRISIS RESPONSE AND RECOVERY: THE 40-PAGE PLAN

That dreaded phone call arrives, informing you that you're now managing, or expected to manage, a serious incident that is about to spiral into a crisis—or that you're already in it. Deep. Now what?

As a crisis leader, you must follow a comprehensive protocol that includes the implementation of teams, systems, and tools in order to respond to a crisis and recover from its impact. The two most important aspects of this protocol are the Corporate Crisis Management Team (CCMT), which represents your headquarters, and the Organizational Crisis Management Team (OCMT), which represents the individual locations or enterprises within your company.

Crisis management is uniquely focused on how to respond to victims, employees, and other stakeholders during those precious first eight hours of your situation. Business recovery continuity typically requires a separate set of demands, which generally will take longer than eight hours.

> Crisis management is uniquely focused on how to respond to victims, employees, and other stakeholders during those precious first eight hours of your situation.

If you hire an outside consultant, you could end up spending several thousand dollars on a Business Continuity Plan (BCP). But before you do that, here's a primer on all of the key terms and issues you need to be aware of before you get started.

Key Terms

Corporate Crisis Management Team (CCMT) Company officers reporting to the CEO who are responsible for coordinating with employees, guests, board of directors, investors, and other key stakeholders

Organizational Crisis Management Team (OCMT) Business unit-specific leaders under the supervision of the general manager who will coordinate all dimensions of business recovery

Business Recovery Team (BRT) Operational-focused leaders appointed by either the CCMT or OCMT who must ensure that you meet all objectives of returning the property to normalcy as quickly and efficiently as possible

Crisis Management Plan (CMP) Your company's stand-alone response document, which is intended as your "playbook" for the first eight hours following an incident; corporate generally has one plan, and your business units or locations typically will have another

Business Continuity Plan (BCP) The guide to your decisions *beyond* the first eight hours of a crisis

Incident Command System (ICS) The most common tool used in community disasters worldwide; local police and fire chiefs, for example, will quickly agree on a common incident commander and will want to work with the "one voice" leader at your organization who has the authority to make decisions, delegate others, and allocate resources

Emergency Operations Center (EOC) The predesignated conference room at your company where the CCMT will meet in the event of a crisis or disaster

Before the Crisis

Your crisis team will need to assess if it is prepared to handle the crisis at hand by considering if its leadership has the tenacity, as well as the physical and telecommunications resources, needed to sustain the company during a prolonged incident. Before disaster impacts your organization, the crisis management team should consider these "to-do" items:

- Provide instructions to the IT department to develop and maintain an IT Recovery Site Plan (IT-RSP) and secure an IT recovery site, as appropriate
- Meet twice annually to review the company's overall response plan and schedule tabletop or more detailed crisis prevention exercises
- Maintain an effective communications plan that includes FAQs and stand-by statements that can be customized for potentially major incidents
- Identify specific, qualified disaster response subcontractors (smoke/water mitigation services, construction services, etc.) that can be available on-site within two hours after a disaster
- Update your company's emergency hotline at 6 a.m. and 6 p.m., or as frequently as necessary
- Be prepared to advise employees regarding any evacuation, stay-in-place, or other similar orders

Timing, Planning, and Crisis Tools

Your crisis team should be able to understand all of the nuances of your company's CMP, because it is the ultimate playbook for leadership during the first eight hours of a critical incident. In general, after eight hours, you will need to move from managing the crisis' initial impact on your enterprise to the business continuity and recovery phase.

Phase I: Response (First Eight Hours)

Before we consider what your crisis and continuity plan should look like, clarify the roles and responsibilities of those who are vital to your crisis management program.

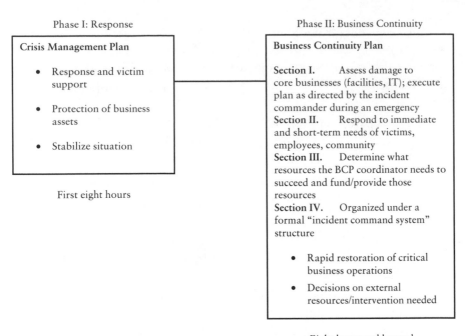

Phase I: Response

Crisis Management Plan

- Response and victim support

- Protection of business assets

- Stabilize situation

First eight hours

Phase II: Business Continuity

Business Continuity Plan

Section I.   Assess damage to core businesses (facilities, IT); execute plan as directed by the incident commander during an emergency
Section II.   Respond to immediate and short-term needs of victims, employees, community
Section III.   Determine what resources the BCP coordinator needs to succeed and fund/provide those resources
Section IV.   Organized under a formal "incident command system" structure

- Rapid restoration of critical business operations

- Decisions on external resources/intervention needed

Eight hours and beyond

Respond. Then Regain Momentum

KEY INDIVIDUALS
1. CEO
Your senior executive should be briefed on business continuity at least annually, as most milestone decisions of an enterprise generally rest on the shoulders of your CEO. In the event that a crisis strikes his or her organization, the CEO often will appoint an incident commander, who will act on his or her behalf after he or she is briefed on the nature of the incident.

2. Incident Commander
The incident commander is typically a senior or executive vice president and is responsible for leading the emergency response team. This individual makes decisions regarding how and where to allocate people and funds, as well as when and how to speak to the news media. He or she should brief the CEO on the fiduciary aspects of the crisis as it unfolds, typically on an

hourly basis. Because new information—such as victim counts, the extent of financial exposure, and potential lawsuits—continually emerges during the early hours of a crisis, the incident commander becomes the "air traffic controller" of your crisis.

3. **Vice President of Communications**

   During the first few hours following a crisis, your vice president of communications should serve as your company's primary communicator. He or she will be busy fielding phone calls from reporters, monitoring blogs, and making mental notes as to which community leaders should be informed of the details of the incident or crisis. As the hours unfold, the questions that your company's communicator must field may become more complex as more and more witnesses (and that may include your employees) begin sharing with reporters their version of what happened. Your vice president of communications must understand that any statement, no matter how innocent, has the potential to either harm or help your community.

4. **Legal Counsel**

   Business continuity can be an expensive proposition. Regardless of the cause of the crisis—whether it is a criminal, a storm, or something else entirely—your company will sometimes incur enormous costs. Your chief legal counsel may need to engage your insurance broker in early discussions to determine your company's fiduciary responsibility for the cost of crisis alleviation efforts. No matter whether you prefer adjusters, brokers, or others familiar with property casualty insurance, such individuals always should be included early in your management reviews of the crisis at hand.

   > Business continuity can be an expensive proposition. Regardless of the cause of the crisis—whether it is a criminal, a storm, or something else entirely—your company will sometimes incur enormous costs.

KEY TEAMS

1. Corporate Crisis Management Team (CCMT)

The CCMT assists in making emergency-related policy decisions. The responsibilities of this body include:

- Gathering and analyzing the conditions of the crisis
- Allocating and directing the distribution of company resources
- Requesting needed resources that are unavailable internally from available outside resources
- Approving final crisis plan and policy decisions
- Making strategic decisions during an emergency event

You'll want complete contact information from your CCMT members, including their names and all relevant telephone numbers (office, cell, home).

2. Organizational Crisis Management Team (OCMT)

Your OCMT is responsible for business resumption following a company emergency. The OCMT reports directly to the CCMT through the incident commander and is comprised of management personnel representing areas with critical plan execution responsibilities.

The OCMT is organized under the ICS and is led by an incident commander, who will be informed of updates on the severity of the incident; will determine the extent of the incident's impact on your people and operations; and then typically will deploy the necessary resources to help the enterprise recover. Gather the names and pertinent telephone numbers (office, cell, home) of the members of your OCMT.

MEASURING DISRUPTION

One of the first tasks of any response team is to identify the scope of the damage from whatever your company's calamity may be. The team should attend to the needs of all victims first and business obligations second. When it does start thinking about your company's operations, your crisis team should consider both short- and long-term needs. For instance, a construction accident could mean that you must make such necessary short-term arrangements as dispatching company personnel to area hospitals, notifying impacted families, and possibly arranging funerals, all of which are responsibilities that require your attention in the first eight hours following an incident. As for your company's long-term objectives, you will need to determine how long your customers' shipments could be delayed. Do you have alternative suppliers who can stand in for you in the meantime? Since you probably have signed contracts that promise the unconditional delivery of goods and services to customers, can you outsource some of your production burdens to your competition? Will existing customers be forgiving for a short period of time? How long? Minimizing disruption requires a strong understanding of logistics and business contracts and is only possible if your sales and marketing teams exercise great diplomacy. As such, they need to be updated on all key decisions made by your business continuity team.

WHEN CRISIS OCCURS

Here are some smart reminders for your response team during Phase I:

1. Because an emergency can occur at any time of the day or night, on weekends or on holidays, with little or no warning, your response team must be available 24/7 to respond to urgent needs. If your response team is not deployable at a minute's notice, it won't be until your CEO chooses the incident commander that your employees will be alerted to critical information, such as who speaks for your company, as well as who can make decisions, sign purchase orders, and accelerate the company's response to victims, witnesses, and others.

2. Remember that a crippling disaster could occur off-site and impact an entire community of people, especially in cases of flood, wildfire, and earthquake. As such, you must assume that it may be difficult—or even impossible—for your employees to physically reach your company. If you do not inform them in advance that they should touch base with you during an emergency to update you on the status of their well-being—or even how to contact you— your efforts to counter your crisis may become confusing or unmanageable.

3. If a major catastrophe requires you to close one of your locations for an extended period, your company's core leadership will need to report to predesignated locations that have adequate IT and telecommunications capacities to sustain your operations for days, and possibly even weeks, after the crisis.

> The executives that most skillfully can reassure a desperate public with the most empathy, sincerity, and breadth of knowledge should serve as your organization's "one voice" platform.

COMMUNICATIONS WITH THE MEDIA

The media can relay your key messages to those affected by your crisis, and the executives that most skillfully can reassure a desperate public with the most empathy, sincerity, and breadth of knowledge should serve as your organization's "one voice" platform. Here are several guidelines that I often share with spokespeople as they are preparing for a crisis news conference:

- We will answer questions honestly and in a timely manner and will minimize the use of technical terms and industry jargon.
- We will emphasize that we are cooperating with first responders and investigators and we will avoid speculation as to the cause of the emergency until government investigations are completed.
- We will *acknowledge* every question, but we also will recognize that we do not have to answer any question that requires speculation on the part of the company. We will avoid the phrase "no comment" and ask for the public's patience as we attempt to assess the complexity of our situation.
- We will provide our customers with realistic estimates as to what happened, but we will avoid speculative comments as to

why and how the crisis occurred until a complete investigation is performed.

- We will encourage our CEO to speak at a press conference or in a conference call only after we rehearse and refine our FAQs with draft answers that have been reviewed by legal counsel.

SAMPLE ANNOUNCEMENTS

What you say to your employees—and how you say it—in the midst of an incident at your organization could mean the difference between chaos and calm. In these types of situations, wording and a calm demeanor really are everything. Here are some company hotline samples you may wish to consider customizing to your unique situation:

- Tuesday, 3 p.m.: Due to the flooding earlier today, we are closing our corporate offices immediately and urge you to exercise restraint and care in your ride home. We expect to reopen tomorrow for normal business hours.
- Tuesday, 6 p.m.: Due to a fire at the rear of the facility, our factory will remain closed until Tuesday, August 1, at the earliest. You should not report to work until this message indicates as such, and you should check this message after 6 a.m., on August 1, to receive further information as to whether we will reopen on that date or not.
- Monday, 6 a.m.: The hurricane that struck Gainesville, Florida, has caused significant damage to our property. Only those employees that have been specifically instructed to do so should report to work today at our off-site EOC. All other employees should not report to work until further notice. This message will be updated at 6 a.m. and 6 p.m. daily. If you have access to wireless messaging, you can also check the company Web site for more information.
- Monday, 6 p.m.: Due to a serious construction incident in the new wing of the mall, only those personnel that have been instructed to do so should report for work tomorrow. We expect to reopen on Wednesday, October 19, and you should plan on reporting to work for your regular schedule on that day

and not earlier. You may check back for updates at 6 a.m. and 6 p.m. daily.

- Tuesday, 6 a.m.: Because an electricity outage continues to impact the greater Los Angeles area, only those employees that have been instructed to do so should report for work today. All other employees should not report to work today. Please check this message frequently, as we will update key information at 6 a.m. and 6 p.m. every day until the power issue has been resolved.

- Thursday, 3 a.m. (sent to employees' voice mailboxes and broadcast on companywide public address systems): There has been a spill of hazardous materials on a local road approximately one mile from our facility's headquarters in St. Louis, Missouri. We have been advised that everyone should remain inside, if possible. For your safety, we are closing all facility doors and shutting down our air filtration system to limit your exposure to any potentially harmful chemicals. Although we realize that such actions may cause some discomfort, based on the information we have acquired from local officials, we urge you to remain indoors. If you are pregnant or have a serious health condition, please contact 911 immediately.

- Friday, 6 a.m.: There was major explosion in the center of London, about six kilometers from our offices, at approximately 5:30 a.m.; the cause remains unknown. As a result, our company will not be open during normal business hours today; only those employees that have been instructed to do so should try to arrive at the property as soon as practical. All employees are to call in after 6 a.m. tomorrow for an update.

BUSINESS OPERATIONS

In the event of a business disruption, your BRT should review a checklist of responsibilities you customize in advance. Additional paper should be provided for group discussions and decisions when drafting key issues pertinent to your company. We will be asked a series of questions regarding such issues as:

Human Resources (includes payroll, benefits, and general workforce issues)

1. How long will I be out of work?
2. Will I be paid for the period during which our business operations are suspended?
3. Will benefits continue during the period in which our facilities are closed? If so, for how long will they continue?
4. I receive a paper check in person each pay period. How will I receive my paychecks now? Can you mail them to another state? Because of the tornado, I have moved to Arkansas.
5. How are you communicating with employees given the fact that the company's communications infrastructure has been so devastated by this incident? I don't have access to the Internet at home. How can I monitor schedules and the partial "report to work" schedule?
6. Will you take disciplinary action against employees who do not report to work because they are managing the impact of this disaster at home?
7. Will my job be jeopardized because I have lost my ability to travel to work (due to car damage, destroyed roads, the suspension of public transportation)?
8. I have a health condition (e.g., cardiac, pregnant) and have been told that the stress of coming to work during this period may compromise my health. What should I do now? I need this job.
9. Will you redeploy some long-serving employees from one company facility to another?

Facilities (includes the maintenance of physical buildings, environmental controls, and utility services)

1. How long will the facility be closed?
2. Have we confirmed that all customers, visitors, contractors, employees, and others related to the company are safe? Has this information been verified by at least three different groups on three separate occasions?
3. What core business operations that can no longer be conducted at this facility can be relocated elsewhere? How quickly, and in

what order, will those operations be relocated to this recovery location? Who will be responsible for each facet of that relocation plan?

4. Who has the authority to approve substantial budgeting for facilities, equipment, and core services that are necessary for business resumption? Has the list of projected expenses been circulated to key leaders?

5. Because looting is common after incidents such as this one, can an employee who does not typically serve in a security position be authorized to serve as a temporary security officer and secure the site? Can employees that volunteer to serve as temporary security officers be provided two-way radios that will help them stay in communication with core leaders?

6. Who will serve as the primary contact with our property and casualty insurer? Who will take photographs of the damage and have these digitally scanned and e-mailed to our insurer in Nashville, Tennessee? Who is authorized to speak with insurers, brokers, and adjusters?

7. Regulators likely will need a failure analysis so that they can better determine the actual cost of this accident. Who will hire a consultant to perform this analysis? Who will pay for this individual's services?

Finance and Accounting (includes accounting, financial reporting, risk management and insurance services, legal issues, and account management)

1. How much damage has this disaster wrought? What is your insurance coverage for such a loss?

2. Who is your insurer?

3. Do you accrue for business disasters such as this?

4. How much of an impact do you expect this disaster to have on quarterly earnings? Will the impact extend into the next quarter?

5. What kind of victim-specific—as opposed to construction- or engineering-related—financial liability do you have?

6. The CFO is on vacation/not available. Who, then, is in charge of finance during this disaster?

7. How much total revenue do you expect the company will lose as a result of this disaster?

8. How much do you expect to spend on contractors/restoration/reconstruction?

Information Technology (includes application of communications and support of information technology services, like data center operations, data center restoration, alternate site planning, critical data management of electronic information, and information security)

1. What is the current state of IT connectivity at each of our locations? Which sites are operating, and for those that aren't, when do you expect their systems to be fully operational?

2. Has there been a critical loss of data? If so, what is the nature of that information (e.g., financial, status reports, payroll)? What redundancy systems do you have in place? How confident are you in those systems?

3. Have you launched an off-site IT recovery hot site? If so, where is it? What do you expect the cost of IT recovery to be?

4. Has any guest's credit card data potentially been compromised because of this disaster? If so, what are you doing to notify those impacted?

5. Who is the "owner" of the IT disaster recovery process? Will he or she be primarily located at your EOC, or will he or she be working at the hot site?

Sales and Marketing (includes a seamless marketing communications effort)

1. When do you expect to reopen the factory for normal business?

2. When are you anticipating a partial or soft opening?

3. Will you provide a 100 percent refund to customers that were negatively impacted by this incident?

4. Will you cease all advertising and marketing out of respect for victims? If so, for how long?

5. In light of this disaster, what changes will you make to safety practices on-site? What specific procedural changes are you making?

6. Are you referring any of our customers to our competitors? If so, which customers are you referring to which competitors?
7. How will you keep key customers updated on your business recovery progress? Will you conduct Web-based seminars or conference calls, or will you use other methods of communication so they can visualize the progress that we are making without visiting the site?

Security (includes facility protection and threat monitoring)
1. Do you have surveillance cameras that captured the event or incident? If so, who has custody of those photographs and/or videotapes?
2. Were any of the perpetrators affiliated with or known by the company? Have you cross-referenced the perpetrators' cases/criminal histories with law enforcement officials?
3. How are you physically restricting access to the impacted property?
4. Are you hiring additional guards to protect your assets? How many, and for how long? How are they prequalified?
5. Had your security team ever discussed a similar scenario in its disaster planning? If so, did it ever implement any prevention efforts?
6. Did an employee or guest ever warn you of this risk in the past?

CRISIS PLAN ACTIVATION

When a community disaster strikes, your company's incident commander should rely on his or her crisis management team for updates. Remember also that the following sources will likely be reporting on updates as they become available via the news media and the Web:

- Department of Homeland Security (DHS)
- National Weather Service (NWS)
- Emergency Broadcast System (EBS)
- State police
- Local police and fire officials
- Emergency medical technicians

POST-CRISIS ACTIVITIES: PHASE I

Throughout Phase I, your team will want to review these checklists to ensure that you are meeting best practice standards:

Response (Hours 1–8)

- Address all life-threatening and dangerous situations first
- Contact all team members and open the EOC
- Assess workforce capabilities and damages to property
  - ○ Assess the number of employees that can be redeployed from their existing roles to temporary roles for disaster purposes—and make reassignments with their cooperation
- Conduct an initial damage assessment; communicate findings to the CEO and insurers
- Activate a communications plan
  - ○ Develop a consistent message to employees, guests, investors, community leaders, and other key stakeholders
  - ○ Contact the families of any injured employees and create a chart that documents any issues/needs/response and accountability
- Submit to requests made by first responders (police/fire/emergency) as necessary
- Conduct meetings of the OCMT at 5:30 a.m. and 5:30 p.m., or as frequently as necessary, prior to updating phone messages at 6 a.m. and 6 p.m.
- Contact critical suppliers and vendors; ask finance to keep ongoing account of expenses incurred and/or expected
- Arrange for psychological counseling for employees and communicate to them the availability of this service

Phase II: Business Continuity (Hour 8 and Beyond)

Now that you have an overview of the demands you will be expected to respond to during the first phase of a crisis, be ready to assume leadership during the more complicated effort of recovering from the incident and restoring normalcy to your enterprise as soon as possible. Here's a model:

CCMT
- Makes critical policy and strategic decisions affecting the business during an emergency
- Reviews key plans for checklist purposes
- Comprised of senior-level executives; led by CEO
- Immediate assignments in a "committee-style" format

BCP Coordinator
- Appointed by and consults with the incident commander
- Focuses on days/weeks ahead; planning/logistics of BCP documentation
- Responsible for organizing employees, deploying resources, and accelerating business resumption

Incident Commander
- A member of the CCMT
- Makes critical tactical and management decisions during the emergency
- Confers directly with the CEO and the OCMT during an emergency

OCMT
- Executes plan as directed by the incident commander during an emergency
- Responds to immediate and short-term needs of victims, employees, community
- Determines what resources the BCP coordinator needs to succeed and funds/provides those resources
- Organized under a formal "incident command system" structure

Contractors
- OCMT hires contractors required to launch business continuity needs (e.g., smoke/water removal, debris removal, facility and utility repairs, IT resumption, etc.)

Business Continuity Model

RESPONSE LEVELS

Your crisis team first calls senior leadership. You all should be on the same page and use the same language regarding the severity of the incident that has occurred. Here are three general descriptions shared by business recovery specialists worldwide:

Level 1—Minor Incident This would typically be a local event with limited impact that does not affect the overall functioning capacity of your company. Examples would be a contained, nontoxic hazardous material incident or a limited power outage that is expected to last less than one day. Local on-site or first responders typically will manage the situation without the intervention of your teams or any meaningful press coverage.

Level 2—Emergency An emergency is any incident, potential or actual, which seriously disrupts the overall operations of your enterprise. Examples would be a power outage that could compromise your operations for a day or longer. In a level 2 crisis, your incident commander should be notified, and such a crisis usually requires the activation of your hotlines, crisis communications plan, and BCP.

> An emergency is any incident, potential or actual, which seriously disrupts the overall operations of your enterprise.

Level 3—Disaster A level 3 incident seriously impairs or threatens your functionality as an enterprise. Examples might include a plane crash in which several of your executives are on board or a massive product recall that certainly will get the attention of consumers, as well as the news media and regulators. The event would likely disable business operations for at least two days.

EMERGENCY OPERATIONS CENTER (EOC)

The EOC is the location in which the company team will gather and execute both Phase I: Response and Phase II: Business Continuity. The primary EOC should be equipped with sufficient emergency supplies (food, water, tools, emergency equipment, etc.) and ideally should be supported by sufficient generator backup, media monitoring, and teleconferencing capabilities. Be specific as you build your template.

Following a disaster, the crisis management team will meet at our primary EOC location at:

_____

_____

Telephone: _____

Fax: _____

If the primary EOC is inaccessible, the backup EOC will be
located at:

_____

_____

Telephone: _____

Fax: _____

The Effective Emergency Operations Center

After 271 deaths were attributed to rollovers in Ford Explorers in
2000, Ford deployed its crisis management team, but no one ever expected that the team's EOC would be operating on a 24/7 basis for
over *six months*. That's the reality of a major incident that requires
you to communicate with customers on a global scale. Although your
resources or problems may differ from Ford's, here are some of the
basic needs of most EOCs:

✓ Conference tables and chairs
✓ White boards and markers
✓ Laptops with wireless capability, printers
✓ Uninterruptible power supply and electric surge protection
  devices
✓ Fax machines and speaker phones
✓ Two-way radios with rechargeable batteries
✓ Satellite phones
✓ Television/cable/radio to monitor multiple channels
✓ First-aid kits
✓ Safety glasses, work gloves, and hard hats
✓ Battery-operated and rechargeable flashlights
✓ One gallon of drinking water per person for two days
✓ Nonperishable foods stored in cabinet

When There's No EOC Available, Use the Phone!

Remember that your emergency leaders don't always need an EOC in order to assess the impact of a crisis, but it sure can help. In those situations in which it is not feasible to assemble the senior leaders of your company in your EOC, your Phase I team should conduct a conference call with as many company executives as possible to review key facts. Here is a list of smart questions for the team to review:

Conference Call Agenda

1. Do we have a strong sense of the number of injuries/victims, their names, and their next-of-kin?
2. Have we notified all law enforcement and first responder agencies?
3. Do we have senior managers on the scene or en route who can provide a proper assessment of the situation?
4. Can a videophone transmit photos or video footage to our incident commander so we can make a more accurate assessment of the disaster?
5. Does this event merit notification to our board of directors and/or to the investment community? Who will provide them updates as new, relevant data becomes available?
6. Have all OCMT members been notified?
7. Do those impacted by this incident know how to reach us?
8. Have we begun to draft an all-employee e-mail regarding our response to this incident?
9. Have we distributed a basic statement for phone operators who may receive outside inquiries?
10. Are we designing a communications strategy that includes a formal statement and draft Q&As for executive review?
11. Have we asked ourselves whether this incident could get worse; if new developments could fundamentally alter our response; and whether we may need additional support from administrative assistants and other teams if we are required to extend the EOC to a 24/7 basis for several days?

While conference calls can help your crisis management team's response effort, in most cases you will want to assemble your executive

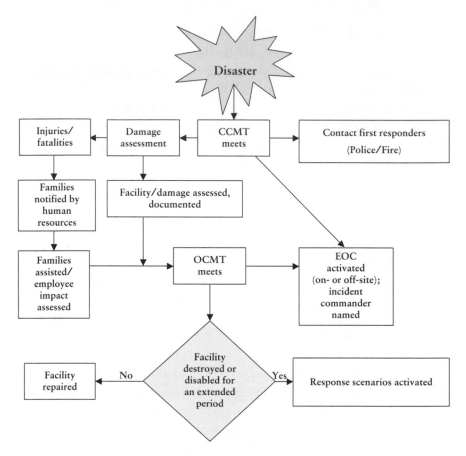

Incident Commander Response Steps

team in a convenient conference room, where leaders can review the scope and magnitude of the disaster. Here is a model that incorporates a company's immediate need to assess damage with the compelling issue of "could this get worse?"

POST-CRISIS ACTIVITIES: PHASE II

As you work your way through Phase II, the number of issues you are likely to confront will be significant.

Recovery (Hour 8 and Beyond)
- Determine timeline for facility repair and relocate business operations as needed

- Ensure that all interested parties (key investors, market analysts, victims' families) are fully informed of the disaster's status
- Ask your legal department to review inquiries and due diligence requirements
- Send a senior-level management representative to the OCMT meeting
- Shut down utility services as needed; remain in constant contact with appropriate utilities as needed
- Activate the EOC, as directed by the company's incident commander
- Assess building damage; send assessment reports to the OCMT
- Ensure that your security team is vigilant with investigative reporters and amateur photographers at the site of the incident
- Contact electric and perhaps other (water, sewer, gas) utility providers
- Contact appropriate suppliers, subcontractors, and vendors
- Account for and secure all hazardous materials; contact regulators as required and in concert with recommendations from your legal department
- Maintain an inventory of finance records, redundancy systems
- Develop and maintain disaster-related payroll policies and processing procedures
- Develop procedures to forward mail and financial accounting to a remote location
- Secure sufficient cash for business operations in an emergency situation (e.g., after a tornado, many local contractors may require cash payments)
- Secure and maintain proper levels of insurance
- Human resources will maintain the BCP for employees, and the EAP will review these plans with all new hires; ensure that all new hires know what to do in an emergency situation
- Consider a special compensation plan for employees required to work at recovery sites for prolonged periods, as this could constitute a significant disruption to family life
- Arrange travel and other logistics for employees who may need to be deployed temporarily to recovery sites

- Deploy human resources to assist employees as necessary; consider the following:
  - ° Psychological help
  - ° Day care center
  - ° Local transportation
  - ° Time off for personal needs
  - ° Temporary housing

INFORMATION TECHNOLOGY

Throughout both Phase I and Phase II, remember that the data needs of your stakeholders may be significant.

Continual

- Maintain a comprehensive IT Disaster Recovery Plan (IT-DRP) that includes
  - ° A Critical Data Management Plan for electronic information
  - ° Backing up critical data daily
  - ° Regularly securing this information off-site
- Implement a recovery plan for your data center
  - ° Document hardware and hardware configuration
  - ° Identify subcontractors that can assist you with hardware repair, replacement, and installation
- Develop and maintain an IT-RSP
  - ° Ensure that recovery site is impenetrable and meets industry standards
  - ° Update lists of IT vendors in the case that you require highly complex technological assistance
- Implement an Information Security Plan
  - ° Install antivirus software
  - ° Reset passwords and assess internal controls
  - ° Firewall your company's systems
- If you are in need of IT subcontractors or suppliers, insist that they either:
  - ° Have an effective Business Continuity Management Program that will enable them to provide services/supplies in the event of a concurrent disaster at their business, or
  - ° Identify backup subcontractors and suppliers

- Launch a shadow Web site to inform customers, corporate clients, investors, and others as to how your company is responding to this disaster
- Share damage assessment reports with your incident commander
- Estimate downtime (conservative vs. optimistic) and project a date of business resumption

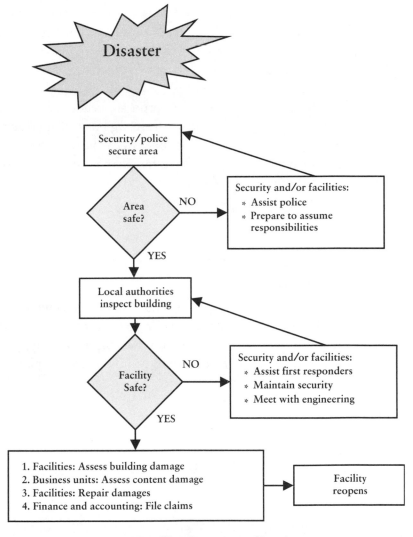

Facility Response Needs

- Consider if you need to hire a failure analysis expert; consult with legal counsel and insurers who will help you understand the engineering, structural, or mechanical failures that may have contributed to your incident

FACILITY RESPONSE NEEDS

Although your first concern should always be the victims of your crisis or disaster, in the event that one or more of your facilities is no longer usable, you eventually will need a physical space if you are to resume your business operations. After attending to injuries and deaths, most organizations will next assess what damage, if any, was done to their physical assets.

Your Phase I team will want to brief corporate headquarters and other business units or executives who are traveling but still are reachable about the magnitude of the catastrophe. Regardless of the kind of crisis your company experiences, use a template to share key updates with those who have a need to be informed.

Crisis Communication
Information Chaos

In any chaotic event, mixed signals, misinformation, and incorrect assumptions will abound. In light of this, if you want to create and maintain credibility with your stakeholders (which, assumedly, you do), you will want to be sure that your communications plan is staged, measured, and built on facts.

Message Plan

Your communications plan should ideally address these six elements:

1. Promise action
   This may include investigating, cooperating with agencies, laundering BCPs, communicating to key customers, and so on.

2. **Reinforce core values**

   Reiterate your company's core mission and values.

3. **Take control in press and other briefings**

   For example: "I have a brief statement and then you have just five minutes or so for questions. I will return later to update you when I have more facts." It is a universal standard for a company to provide an initial briefing before local police agencies and first responders present their reports to the press.

Communications Responsibilities

Responsibility	Primary Company Lead	Cell #	Alternate Company Lead	Cell #
Media Spokesperson				
Principal Liaison to Human Resources				
Employee Victims/ Relatives Liaison				
Customer Emergency Hotline Updater				
Investor Relations Lead				
Language Translators Contact				
Board of Directors Contact				
Insurers and Brokers Liaison				
Crisis Consultant Liaison				
Elected Officials and Regulatory Liaison				

4. **Correct inaccuracies**

Counter rumors and speculation with facts. Poor information is often the result of a gap in quality data. Communicate to alleviate anxiety among stakeholders craving constant updates during a catastrophe. You must strive for a proper balance.

5. **Defeat difficult questions**

You must address difficult questions in a manner that demonstrates poise and reflects sympathy. "Our thoughts and prayers are with those who have been affected." This is not a time to place blame when you do not have all the facts. "I cannot possibly answer all of your questions, but I promise to try to get to them as soon as possible."

> You must address difficult questions in a manner that demonstrates poise and reflects sympathy. This is not a time to place blame when you do not have all the facts.

6. **Bad news delivered at once**

You will strive to release as much bad news as possible *at one time*. This is better than releasing a stream of bad news over an extended period of time.

Employee Communication

As outlined in the Phase II continuity plan, in the event of a company crisis, your employees should be given directions to first call a predesignated company emergency hotline for emergency instructions. If this number is inoperative, you should consider rerouting calls to a remote provider. In most companies, human resources will be involved in creating the content of any emergency messages. Most companies that have faced a major calamity have found it necessary to update their messages at least twice a day, and good times to aim for are 6 a.m. and 6 p.m., or more frequently, as needed.

In the event of widespread telephony outage, your company's shadow Web site should be activated for redundancy purposes. It is very likely that many of your employees own Internet-accessible cell phones that will allow them to visit your company's shadow site and in doing so maintain some contact with you until phone service is completely restored.

Department-by-Department Guidelines

Here are some essential reminders for the key departments in your organization. You will want to customize this list to meet the unique needs of your industry.

Human Resources

You will want to acknowledge any heroes, those injured or killed, and especially the families and loved ones of victims. However, you must be mindful of privacy laws, such as the Health Insurance Portability and Accountability Act (HIPAA), and other expectations that are not regulatory in nature but are still reasonable. Human resources should identify:

1. How employees have been impacted, without naming them
2. How and when victims will be deployed to triage and/or asked to remain on-scene
3. Compensation and restitution issues that are unique to this crisis via consultation with legal counsel
4. An employee communications plan informing employees what your official response to the general public will be; when you communicate this information to your employees, you should ensure that they are aware of important company phone numbers that they can call for updates on the situation

THINGS TO CONSIDER
- Have you deployed a senior executive to respond to the needs of each impacted victim and his or her family members? What is that executive empowered to say and do?
- Do any victims have anyone else in their family that you employ? Can you cross-check through payroll? If you do employ a victim's family member, has someone tried to contact that person?

Legal

The legal department is one of the most vital participants in the response process. Most company lawyers will grasp the need for their organization to "get ahead" of the crisis by speaking before the company's critics and adversaries.

THINGS TO CONSIDER

- If the CEO is not available, whom can you dispatch that can effectively speak for senior management?
- Have all documents, reports, and written communications that may relate to the company's exposure been marked "company confidential"?
- If the crisis is outside your host country, have you properly briefed in-country senior executives, rehearsed draft Q&As with them, and informed them how to conduct employee briefings?
- Have you established credible contact with either the State Department or another governmental agency?
- Are there special legal requirements regarding corporate response and reporting that are unique to the country of jurisdiction of this incident?
- If the crisis is violence-inspired, do you have sufficient data to assess if you are adequately exercising your Duty to Care, Duty to Warn, and Duty to Act?

Strategic Planning

Your strategy team owns your roadmap to future business growth and should be intimately involved in crisis planning; it can anticipate how your banks, financing agents, and future business partners may react to news of this incident. Rely on its proactive thinking to help you characterize this crisis: Is it an incident? Are you a victim? Will events have "material" impact on your growth plans? During Phase II, your strategy team also can help you perform a comprehensive damage assessment, including an analysis that details the impact of the crisis on your company's human and physical assets. Updates should be provided on an hourly basis to the OCMT.

THINGS TO CONSIDER
- What is the likelihood that initial damage estimates could be wrong?
- If your disaster was an earthquake, are you prepared for aftershocks or a subsequent major disaster?
- Contractors will be in high demand; how can you be assured of priority status on disaster cleanup, restoration, and rebuilding?
- Have you notified your banks and insurers in a timely manner?
- Is there any way that this incident can be advantageous to your company if it is managed effectively and if you document small decisions and resume business quickly?

Finance

Based on available information, the OCMT will conduct a damage and recovery assessment during Phase II to include with insurance claims. If your claim is disputed, you will need to have detailed records of what was spent on clean-up and recovery, overtime for your employees and contractors, and necessary equipment or replacement materials and supplies. Most insurance policies also will cover the cost of hiring external consultants to travel to your facilities to assess the amount of fire, smoke, flood, and related damages incurred, but all claims may be dependent on the documentation you provide of the damages your enterprise suffered.

THINGS TO CONSIDER
- Is there any known damage to any buildings or structures?
- Have you experienced disruption to contractual customer commitments?
- What is the estimated recovery time?
- What might the direct, noninsurable costs of response and recovery be?
- How will business logistics (cash disbursements, salary and benefit continuation, currency issues, etc.) be managed in the event of a multi-country threat or major incident?

- If banking and stock systems are frozen for three or more days, what options exist for sufficient processing of the company's financial transactions?

International

If victims of this incident are residents of various countries, you may need to organize special meetings to assist them with their individualized needs. You will need accurate intelligence on the unique circumstances of those victims (e.g., religion, occupation, and next-of-kin). You may need to share a toll-free number for those residing in other countries to report missing loved ones. The OCMT should coordinate with human resources to publicize this number.

THINGS TO CONSIDER

- Which international agencies (e.g., Red Cross) and officials should be paramount in your outreach efforts?
- Should a scholarship fund be established in memory of the victims? Will you make the first contribution? How will donations be received and the funds publicized?
- In some cultures, loved ones are to be buried within one day. You will want to research this issue and work with a local mortuary to ensure that you are adhering to victims' cultural practices and helping families meet their desired objective if law enforcement agrees that such a step is acceptable.
- If a crime has been committed on your property by a foreign national and that person is an employee, his or her passport may need to be confiscated to prevent a flight from justice. Many executives keep their passports at work; your team should raise this issue with law enforcement officials.

Public Affairs

Your company may need to gather information from or relinquish some control to a number of government agencies, depending on the nature of the event.

THINGS TO CONSIDER

- Is the company capable of managing the complexities of these events?
- Should external support from a major public affairs or lobbying group be secured?
- Who will speak to various publics, including community leaders, regulators, and victims' families?
- Can your research department quickly ascertain organizational case histories of others who have faced similar incidents in the past so you can review their public affairs strategies, including what worked and what didn't?
- Do you have fiduciary obligations to review with investor relations? If this incident may impact quarterly earnings, for instance, your board may need to be notified.
- Will you have time to conduct a rehearsal news conference? Will you agree to specific and individual interviews with each of the local radio and TV stations, or will you communicate your messages to the entire press corps at one event?

Impacted Division
THINGS TO CONSIDER

- Has the leader of the impacted division been empowered to take all steps necessary to respond properly?
- Have you reminded employees that all news media inquiries must be referred to authorized spokespeople only?
- How long is the facility likely to be impacted? Will it be closed temporarily?
- How long can individuals reasonably remain inside and sheltered safely?
- What if a copycat incident occurs at another facility?
- What will your policy on compensation be if employees are told not to come to work and remain at home?
- What unique, logistical transportation needs may emerge as a result of this crisis?

Security
THINGS TO CONSIDER
- Assess the impact and effectiveness of on-scene response strategies and recommend whether evacuation, property closing, or other action should be taken.
- Recommend strategic solutions to the OCMT regarding restoration of operations to a state of normalcy.
- Ensure that all EOC systems, plans, and processes operate effectively. Delegate all additional support for logistics and response to field teams.
- Contact intelligence agencies regarding individual responsibilities and action plans needed for any specific executive.
- Who currently has access to surveillance tapes of the incident? Should these be turned over to legal counsel?
- Has security provided a script to telephone operators and receptionists that details what to say and how to manage inquiries from visitors and curiosity seekers?

Key Incidents

The following section offers specific, initial reminders that are germane to certain high-impact incidents. You should fill in details that are unique to your situation.

Aircraft Crash/Commercial
- Dispatch a human resources representative to the scene.
- Establish a staging area for the media within reasonable distance from the scene; the best protocol will be a joint news conference with the National Transportation Safety Board (NTSB), the Federal Aviation Agency (FAA), or other agencies.
- There will be questions as to whether the company has a policy limiting the number of executives on a single plane; was that policy followed?

- If there are multiple victims, the OCMT should conduct a conference call with the hospital spokesperson and discuss key details.
- Refrain from offering names/personal information about victims until family members have been contacted by law enforcement officials.
- Confirm the general information (i.e., "A plane crash has occurred near Paris, France. We believe that four of our employees were on the plane.").
- Request a media embargo until the task of communicating with families is accomplished.
- Immediately but discretely suspend any paid broadcast/print advertisement featuring any impacted employees.
- Similarly, any pending news releases mentioning impacted executives should be suspended, along with any product launches quoting them.
- Request a "no-fly zone" over the crash site from the police and aviation authorities.
- "Our first concern is for the well-being of those who were impacted by this terrible event. We are working with the rescue team and providing our complete support to help in any way possible."
- Since employees and family members may be calling for information, publicize a hotline or a Web site where they can access more information. Phone operators should refer callers to that number only.

Biohazard

Because at least one of your facilities probably is adjacent to a major highway on which a variety of hazardous materials are transported, such as petroleum products, industrial wastes, and biotoxic wastes, you will want to be sure that your team is well rehearsed in the proper evacuation techniques in the event of a biohazard. If hazardous materials spill near one of your facilities, you should:

- Define the scope of the situation and prevent exaggeration of the circumstances by maintaining close communications with state and national health officials; consider if one of your teams should engage an independent biohazard expert from a local research university.

- If needed, determine an appropriate location to stage regulators, scientists, and technical personnel who will be needed to review the incident; provide timely updates on pertinent information.
- Issue cautiously worded customer and employee messages regularly as the situation evolves. Many related symptoms do not evolve for hours, even days, after exposure to biohazardous materials.
- Refrain from offering names or personal information about victims until family members have been contacted.
- "We are working with the appropriate authorities to determine the overall impact of this incident, and we will provide regular updates as information becomes available."
- Assume the situation may get worse (e.g., the deadly sarin gas in Tokyo evolved over a three-hour period before the full scope of deaths and injuries could be calculated).

Bomb or Bomb Threat

- Ensure in advance that phone operators have a bomb threat form so they can document what a caller says, the time of day he or she calls, his or her wording about a specific time and location of a potential detonation, and any background noise, accent, or other pertinent details.
- Work with law enforcement officials to ensure that the scope of the threat or incident is defined in order to help prevent media exaggeration.
- Communicate frequently with customers and employees on pertinent details. Encourage those who may have witnessed anything unusual to contact the Federal Bureau of Investigation (FBI) or local police.

Work with law enforcement officials to ensure that the scope of the threat or incident is defined in order to help prevent media exaggeration.

- If a device is found, confirm facts and refer detailed questions to law enforcement officials (i.e., "An object that may be an explosive device has been found at _____. We have evacuated the area and are working closely with law enforcement officials. We have no further information at this time.").
- "The safety of our customers and employees is our highest priority, and we are taking all necessary steps to promote the well-being of those on our property."
- "We do not detail our security measures because to do so would compromise their effect."

Employee Incident/Violence

One of the most disturbing acts that could be committed against your company is an incident of violence. The imagery of such an incident and the media's awareness of it will be substantial. Thus, you must be ready with a compassionate message program.

- What was the employment history of the employee? Was the team aware of any past incidents, threats, or charges against the individual?
- Had the employee been referred to EAP in recent months, and under what circumstances? Are there any privacy or Family Medical Leave Act (FMLA) issues or pending requests?
- Is or was the individual dating another employee? Are there any friendship or relationship issues that could foreshadow a broader and widening story?
- Your company will want to place this issue in a historical context, such as, "We consider this an extremely rare and sad occurrence. Although every reasonable step is taken to ensure the well-being of those at our facilities, we understand that circumstances—on very rare and very isolated occasions—may prevent even the best organization from being able to predict when someone will act in a manner it does not understand. We are heartbroken over today's incident."
- Immediate coworkers of a perpetrator may need special counseling based on the nature of the incident.

- If there is any possibility that the company may be found culpable of complicity in the crime, an independent investigator may be needed to assist your company with interviews, record retention, and other details.

Earthquake/Tornado

- Coordinate your EOC's response with federal and state authorities to ascertain the extent of the quake and to determine the number of casualties/injuries and the scope of physical damage.
- Whether in Tokyo, St. Louis, or elsewhere, aftershocks are common. A tsunami could occur in several parts of the world. Prepare for a second crisis, including a lengthy loss of any existing communication and power sources.
- Additional security may need to be contracted to supplement existing resources. Assume that local police will be deployed to civilian needs and largely unavailable for all of your company's needs for at least 72 hours, based on past history of catastrophic earthquakes.
- IT and telephony systems will likely be compromised and could be out of commission for several days to several weeks. Redundant systems will need to be activated immediately to ensure minimal disruption to customers.
- Looting after earthquakes and tornados is common. Additional contracted security teams may be needed to ensure that your facilities and assets are secure.
- Tornado warning systems in adjacent communities should be activated after the first warning signs, but a loss of power often makes this difficult. The use of cell phones can be invaluable in alerting other segments of your company.

Hostage Situation/Kidnapping

- Refer all questions regarding the crime to law enforcement officials until the senior legal counsel believes that a statement is prudent. In most cases the company will make no comment until a due diligence review is completed by police officials.

- Public relations will coordinate draft message points with law enforcement officials.
- Refrain from offering names/personal information about perpetrators and victims.
- Since a hostage situation could be perceived as potentially related to terrorism, the spokesperson should seek clarity from police on the perpetrator's motive.
- Determine if the ethnic origin of the perpetrators and victims could escalate public interest in the story.
- Customer and employee messages should be issued regularly. "Our thoughts and prayers are with everyone who is impacted."
- Security should contact specialists as needed, especially if you are facing a kidnap situation overseas. Firms such as Kroll Associates specialize in helping corporations through complex hostage and kidnap situations outside the United States.
- Since the media may try to interview customers and employees about the situation, remind all employees that only authorized spokespeople may speak to the news media. Speculation can aggravate a perpetrator.
- It is paramount to accurately determine whether the abduction is a random act or not. If it is a domestic dispute that spilled onto your company's property, this should be emphasized to the media and reinforced by law enforcement officials.

Major Fire/Hazardous Materials

- Communicate that you are working with the fire department (and/or emergency rescue teams) and will provide timely updates on pertinent information.
- The media will likely ask about victim compensation quickly; answers should be prepared.
- Refrain from offering names/personal information about victims until family members have been contacted by authorities.
- Local communities have HAZMAT teams that are uniquely trained to manage many complex issues related to biohazards. If these teams are not capable of assisting you because you are

located in a remote area, consider hiring a biochemist or other specialist from an area college or university.

- Ensure that employees who may have health issues that could be compromised by this incident, such as those with cardiac or pregnancy issues, receive special and priority attention throughout the incident, including follow-up care, as is appropriate.
- Contact neighborhood and community organization leaders to keep them informed on what you are doing.

Mass Fatalities

In the event of a community catastrophe, the coroner may not be able to provide meaningful assistance for 72 hours or longer. Therefore, your company must take action to ensure the safe handling and storage of the deceased until the coroner or other-designated personnel can respond.

- The coroner is responsible for the collection, identification, and disposition of the deceased during conditions of disaster or extreme peril.
- You will need to thoughtfully decide on and set aside a secure area that can be used as a temporary morgue.
- Witness statements are essential in these cases. If you are located in a small or rural community, local law enforcement officials may be overwhelmed. You may want to ask permission from law enforcement agencies to authorize or deputize your security and/or legal teams to capture key witness statements that are most valuable in the hours immediately after the incident.
- Press and litigation interest in a situation involving mass casualities is typically extraordinary. Added security may be needed to supplement existing resources.

Sex Crimes

- Refer all questions to and coordinate messages regarding the crime with law enforcement officials.
- Refrain from offering names/personal information about perpetrators and victims.
- Be alert to the possibility of media coming onto the property. Establish criteria for access to the area or building immediately.
- Define the scope of the incident and characterize the situation in context.
- Emphasize that you are cooperating fully with law enforcement officials in this matter.
- Remind employees of your policy that only authorized spokespeople may speak to the media.
- Verify your human resources process to determine if this employee was hired under a process in which a comprehensive background check was conducted. Also check the area sex offender list to determine if he or she appears on that list.

Shooting or Violence On-Site

- Send a leader to the scene immediately and refer all questions regarding the crime scene to law enforcement officials; co-ordinate message points with their public information officer (PIO).
- Refrain from offering names/personal information about victims until family members have been contacted by police.
- Since a shooting could be perceived by some as related to terrorism, it is important to ascertain the facts rapidly.
- Communicate with employees and customers quickly. Contact your EAP provider and offer comprehensive counseling services to victims, witnesses, and others impacted.
- Emphasize that the safety of your employees is your highest priority and you do not detail your security measures because to do so would compromise their effect.
- Remind the media that you conduct a comprehensive criminal background check on all new employees.

- Dispatch EAP immediately to support victims and their families, as well as witnesses. If EAP is not available (e.g., in Russia or Mexico), ask the responsible on-site leader if counselors should be hired and dispatched by a local hospital or university.
- Copycat incidents are increasingly common in high-profile murders involving automatic weapons. Consider accelerated security at all locations.

Terrorist Threat/Incident

- Refer all calls regarding the threat to law enforcement officials and emphasize in all public and private communications that you will cooperate in every regard. Seek guidance from your security team and legal department.
- Work with law enforcement officials to ensure that the scope of the situation is clearly defined in order to help prevent media exaggeration.
- Do not stage or host media on property; the use of non-company properties, such as a hotel, may be more appropriate.
- Issue updates regularly and encourage employees to listen to taped updates as the situation evolves.
- In the event of a national emergency in which the company is not an immediate target, you may want to refer to procedures used by companies on September 11, 2001. Consider whether your offices/locations should be closed, if evacuations should be ordered, or if additional contracted security should be secured for all, or specific, sites.

Special thanks to rothstein.com for assistance with this chapter.

18

TEN PILLARS OF BUSINESS CONTINUITY

I'm often asked, "After we have begun to manage a crisis, how do we transition to the phase where business continuity, as opposed to incident response, begins?" The simple answer is that you will sense a diminishment in the pulse of questions and demands for resources and decisions. But to properly launch a post-crisis stability program, take note of the following best practice standards of business continuity.

	Ten Pillars of Business Continuity
1.	Respond to customers/victims personally and rapidly. You can never overcommunicate with those who have been injured or impacted by a serious incident.
2.	Inform your employees, contractors, and vendors what is expected of them. Tell them via 24/7 messaging on your voicemail and Web platforms what you expect of them and when you expect them to return to work. Encourage them to report extraordinary hardships to your emergency phone line.
3.	Launch your off-site IT recovery before system failures force you to do so. Back up critical data. Launch your Emergency Operations Center (EOC) and prepare to evacuate key personnel to an alternative off-site location, if appropriate.

(continued)

4.	Authorize your finance department to continue salary and benefits throughout the disaster as approved by senior management. Consider union issues as appropriate. Authorize your incident commander to purchase equipment, hotel rooms, and consulting services necessary to accelerate business resumption. Inform your insurer of initial damage estimates, and document damage to facilitate you while you monitor casualty, repair, and recovery costs.
5.	Ensure that contradictions to policies and rumors are kept to a minimum. Appoint one spokesperson who will articulate when you will resume operations. Remind all personnel that no one should speak to the news media except authorized spokespeople.
6.	Engage a qualified psychological counselor or Employee Assistance Program (EAP) to offer on-site groups and individual counseling to those impacted by any notable tragedy.
7.	Offer updates to key organizational leaders, investors, and regulators three times a day about progress made, pending issues, and timetables for next milestones. Be honest, realistic, and confident in the accuracy of your assessment.
8.	Validate that your vendors and key suppliers will deliver what they have promised to accelerate your timely recovery. Be emphatic with critical third parties who violate service contracts that you expect them to comply with actual needs.
9.	Conduct scenario testing before you declare the disaster over and you "resume" business. To avoid further embarrassment and opportunity costs, implement a multi-tiered return to normalcy to avoid a "big bang" that could fail.
10.	Conduct a detailed post-crisis assessment of recovery, success, system failures, and opportunities to improve. Be specific about accountabilities and reward the heroes who exceed your expectations.

19

CLOSING THOUGHTS

Sometimes when I give seminars, I'll be asked: "So, how did you ever get interested in all of this?" It's not an easily answered question, but here's a quick story that may serve as an explanation. When I was 12 years old, I was attending a Boston Red Sox game with my friends Roberta and Stephen, and as we left Fenway Park, I heard screams—the type that only a mother can create when she realizes in horror that her child has been harmed. Brakes. Slam. Crowds. People running. I was 12 years old, but I got it.

Turning the corner, I witnessed a young girl, about my age, lying in between the street and the sidewalk. A utility truck had made a fast turn on a crowded street, trying to avoid the onslaught of fans departing the game that would block his lane; while he was turning, he accidentally struck a cement light pole that fell and crushed the girl to death. Nurses ran from inside Fenway Park with towels and first-aid kits. Ambulances raced. Unfortunately, CPR was not well understood or administered at the time, and it probably would have been futile, given what I witnessed. What impressed me was the speed, the degree of care, the attentiveness given to a horrible situation by ordinary citizens and medical personnel. I have remembered the importance of the role of first responders ever since, whether they are police officers, fire fighters, or company safety leaders.

Today there are millions of other first responders embedded in companies, only now they are called risk managers, directors of public relations, vice presidents of security, or chief information officers. All of them can play a critical role in protecting our people and our organizations.

So walk away and plan as an optimist, for there's something wonderful happening when people anticipate disasters, and here's one of the best examples with which I can leave you.

When a moderate earthquake of 7.0 hit Gujarat, India, on January 26, 2001, nearly 20,000 people perished and an astounding 600,000 were instantly homeless. But when an earthquake of the same magnitude struck Seattle, Washington, just 33 days later, on February 28, 2001, only one person died, and that was from a heart attack. Many experts believe that the differential is very clear: Preparedness, strong building codes, community notification, and pre-disaster planning and response save lives. Each of them makes a difference.

> Preparedness, strong building codes, community notification, and pre-disaster planning and response save lives. Each of them makes a difference.

Don't run and hide under your covers. There's hope. Your organization has you, which is a great place to begin. You can also groom and hire great talent that has experience in risk and crisis management. There are tons of government resources available if you know how to source them, and the public's general awareness of crisis leadership has never been higher. You're in a sweet spot.

Chances are that you'll remember some of the war stories in this book. Although I was a bit sarcastic at times, the bottom line is that I have tremendous admiration for the security teams, human resources departments, risk managers, and first responders that are embedded into so many organizations. They are the best defense we have against the thugs, terrorists, and assorted con artists who want to create havoc in our lives. And as for Mother Nature, well, you can't prevent a hurricane or an earthquake, but you can certainly be ready for one.

Now it's your turn to think about preparedness. If you have comments or suggestions, or need help, you can e-mail me at: larry@larrybarton.com.

And finally, remember . . . it's a jungle out there!

REFERENCES

Abadie, Alberto, and Javier Gardeazabal. "Terrorism and the World Economy." Study prepared for Harvard University/NBER and the University of the Basque Country, October 2005.

Alexander, Dean, and Yonah Alexander. *Terrorism and Business*. Ardsley, NY: Transnational Publishers, 2002.

"Alive." *Time*, May 2, 2005.

Allison, Graham, and Zelikow, Philip, *Essence of Decision*. New York: Little, Brown and Co., 1971.

"An American Tragedy." *Time*, September 12, 2005.

Arnst, Catherine, et al. "A Hot Zone In The Heartland." *BusinessWeek*, September 19, 2005.

Babiak, Paul, and Robert Hare. *Snakes In Suits*. New York: Regan Books, 2006.

Barton, Laurence. "Why Businesses Must Prepare A Strategic Response to Corporate Sabotage." *Industrial Management*, March 1993.

Barton, Laurence. *Crisis In Organizations II*. Cincinnati: Southwestern Books, 2001.

Barton, Laurence. "Workplace Violence: Signal Detection Within Business and Industry." Presentation to FBI Academy, September 11, 2007.

Barton, Laurence, and Bill Turner. "It Can't Happen Here . . . Can It?" *Loss Prevention*, July–August 2006.

"Battling Employee Sabotage In The Wired Workplace." *ARA Content*, November 16, 2001.

Benjamin, Daniel, and Steven Simon. *The Next Attack*. New York: Owl Books, 2006.

Bennett, Brian. "How Did This Happen?" *Time*, September 12, 2005.

Benzaquin, Paul. *Fire In Boston's Cocoanut Grove*. Boston: Branden Press, 1967.

BillMalter.com

"BP Faces Expanding Criminal Investigation Of Refinery Blast." *The Boston Globe*, January 30, 2007.

Brady, Diane. "Pepsi: Repairing A Poisoned Reputation in India." *Business Week*, June 11, 2007.

Brilliant, Larry. "The Spreading Epidemic." *Forbes*, May 7, 2007.

"British Petroleum in Their Own Words." *The Economist,* March 24, 2007.

Buffa, Denise, Jennifer Fermino, and Dan Mangan. "500G Thief Bookkeeper Busted at Ritzy Riverdale." *New York Post*, May 25, 2007.

Calhouhn, Frederick S., and Stephen W Weston. *Contemporary Threat Management*. San Diego: Specialized Training Services, 2003.

Cauchon, Dennis. "The Little Company That Could." *USA Today*, October 10, 2005.

Cavuto, Neil. "Why Taco Bell Is Botching E. coli Crisis." Fox News Transcript, December 16, 2006.

Chu, Kathy. "Katrina Keeps Closed Signs Up." *USA Today*, March 13, 2007.

"Coca-Cola Sues Over Dasani Smear Effort." *USA Today*, July 13, 2007.

"Coming Home To Roost." *The Economist*, January 25, 2007.

"Comment: Shootings." *The New Yorker*, April 30, 2007.

Conant, Eve, and Pat Wingent. "A Long, Strange TB Trip." *Newsweek*, June 11, 2007.

Coombs, W. Timothy. *Code Red in the Boardroom*. Westport CT: Praeger Books, 2006.

Cooper, Anderson. "Is Nation's Food Supply Safe?" 360 Degrees Transcript. December 6, 2004.

de Becker, Gavin. *The Gift of Fear*. New York: Bantam Books, 1997.

DHS Natural Disaster Proposal, University of California at Irvine for Study of Coastal Infrastructure.

Doods, Paisley. "British Slowly Trade Privacy for Security." *Las Vegas Review-Journal*, June 3, 2007.

Dossier 2: Terrorism, Intelligence and Law Enforcement—Canada's Response to Sikh Terrorism, Commission of Inquiry Into the Investigation of the Bombing of Air India Flight 182, February 19, 2007.

Dubash, Manek. "Study Notes Link Between IT Sabotage, Work Behavior." *TechWorld.com,* February 2, 2007.

Dunn, Marcia. "Shuttle Equipment Sabotaged." *Associated Press*, July 26, 2007.

Dwyer, Jim. "911 Tapes Echo Grim Struggle in Towers." *New York Times*, April 1, 2006.

Dychtwald, Ken. *Age Wave*. New York: Bantam Books, 1990.

DzaKovic, Bogdan, Statement to the National Commission on Terrorist Attacks upon the United States, May 22, 2003.

"An F For Integrity." *Time*, May 28, 2007.

Fein, R. A., and Vossekuil, B., "A Guide for the State and Local Law Enforcement Officials." U.S. Department of Justice, 1998.

Fleckenstein, Bill. "Warning: This Mess Will Only Get Worse." MSN Money, March 19, 2007.

"Former Enron Exec Dies in Apparent Suicide." CNN.com, January 26, 2002.

Forrester's Enterprise and SMB Hardware Survey, North America and Europe, Q3 2007.

Fox, Justin. "A Meditation On Risk." *Fortune*, October 3, 2005.

Frank, Thomas. "Campus Killers' Warnings Ignored." *USA Today*, June 13, 2007.

Friedman, Alan F. "Mental Health and Workplace Violence: Insights on Psychological Assessment," in *Workplace Violence Prevention*. American Bar Association, forthcoming.

Garin, Kristoffer A. *Devils on The Deep Blue Sea*. New York: Viking, 2005.

Gibbs, Nancy. "An American Tragedy." *Time*, September 12, 2005.

Golaszewski, T. "Shining Lights: Studies That Have Most Influenced the Understanding of Health Promotion's Financial Impact." *American Journal of Health Promotion* 15 (May/June 2001), quoted in Kimberley Bachmann, "Health Promotion Programs at Work: A Frivolous Cost or a Sound Investment?" Conference Board of Canada, Ottawa, 2002.

Hanson, Neil. *The Great Fire of London In That Apocalyptic Year, 1666*. Hoboken, NJ: John Wiley & Sons, 2002.

Hare, Robert D. *The Psychopathy Checklist-Revised*. 2nd ed. Toronto: Multi-Health Systems, 2003.

Harvey, Thomas J. "Battling Employee Sabotage in the Wired Workplace." ARA Content, November 2001.

Hathaway, Starke R., and McKinley, J. C., eds.

Helm, Burt, and Paula Lehman. "Buying Clicks To A Tragedy." *BusinessWeek*, May 7, 2007.

Hertsgaard, Mark. "Nuclear Insecurity." *Vanity Fair*, November 2003.

Hoopes, Townsend, and Brinkley, Douglas. *Driven Patriot*, Annapolis MD: Naval Institute Press. 1992.

"Japanese Massage." *The Economist*, March 24, 2007.

Javers, Eamon. "I Spy For Capitalism." *BusinessWeek*, August 13, 2007.

Kalinich, Kevin P. "Network Risk Insurance: A Layman's Overview." Presentation to Risk and Insurance Management Society. Honolulu, April 24, 2006.

Kaplan, David. "Suspicions and Spies in Silicon Valley." *Newsweek*, September 18, 2006.

Karlgaard, Rich. "Strike One, You're Out." Forbes.com, May 10, 2007.

"Kmart Employee Sabotage." Posted on www.libcom.com, December 29, 2005.

Larry King Live, CNN (March 13, 2005).

Lewis, Jessica. "Their Only Lifeline Was Wal-Mart." *Fortune*, October 3, 2005.

Lindeman, John. "The Next Level of Disaster Recovery." *Disaster Recovery Journal*, Summer 2007.

Lipka, Sara. "A University Accused of Hushing Up A Murder." *Chronicle of Higher Education*, March 23, 2007.

Litke, Jim. "The Thin Blue Line Ruptured." *Concord Monitor* (NH), September 5, 2005.

Lubrano, Alfred. "Terrorist Hunter." *Philadelphia Inquirer*, July 22, 2007.

Marriott, Edward. *Plague*. New York: Metropolitan Books, 2002.

"Mattel CEO: 'Rigorous Standards' After Massive Toy Recall." CNN.com, August 15, 2007.

McCabe, Francis. "New York-New York: Tourists Take Down Shooter." *Las Vegas Review Journal*, July 7, 2007.

McIntosh, John L. "Rate, Number and Ranking of Suicide for Each USA State." *Journal of the American Academy of Suicidology*, 2004.

Minnesota Multiphasic Personality Inventory 2 (MMPI-2). University of Minnesota, 1989.

"MIT Dean Resigns Over Misrepresented Credentials." Associated Press, April 27, 2007.

Mizoguchi, Kozo. "Nine Die In Group Suicides." Associated Press, March 10, 2006.

Monahan, John. "A Jurisprudence of Risk Assessment: Forecasting Harm among Prisoners, Predators, and Patients." (92 *Va. L. Rev.* 391, 2006).

Montaldo, Charles. "Atlanta Courthouse Shooting Trial To Be Moved?" CNN .com.

Montgomery, Christina. "Airport Takes Diagrams Off Its Web site." *The Province* (Canada), June 17, 2007.

"More Outside Directors Taking Lead in Crises." *Wall Street Journal*, March 19, 2007.

Mueller, Robert. Testimony, National Commission or Terrorist Attacks on The United States.

Myers, Amanda Lee. "US Airways CEO Arrested On DUI Charge." Associated Press, February 10, 2007.

Nicols, Bill, and Mimi Hall. "Mayor Issues a Desperate SOS." *USA Today*, September 2–5, 2005.

Nussbaum, Bruce. "The Next Big One." *Business Week,* September 19, 2005.

O'Toole, Mary Ellen, "The School Shooter: A Threat Assessment Perspective," Critical Incident Response Group. FBI Academy, 2000.

Ozminkowski, O.J., et al. "A Return on Investment Evaluation of the Citibank, N.A., Health Management Program." *American Journal of Health Promotion* 14 (September/October 1999), quoted in Kimberley Bachmann's "Health Promotion Programs at Work: A Frivolous Cost or a Sound Investment?" Conference Board of Canada, Ottawa, 2002.

The Procter & Gamble Company v. Randy L. Haugen and Freedom Associates, Inc. and Freedom Tools Incorporated and John Does 1–10, 1:95CV 0094W in the United States District Court of Utah Central Division.

"Protecting Global Trade Against Terrorism." Paper presented by The Japan Society, September 24, 2002.

Ramstad, Evan. "Karaoke Bar Fight Has Hanwha Chief Singing the Blues." *Wall Street Journal*, May 18, 2007.

Reed, Dan. "jetBlue Tries to Bounce Back from Storm of Trouble." *USA Today*, June 7, 2007.

Rhoads, Christopher. "At Center of Crisis, City Officials Faced Struggle to Keep in Touch." *Wall Street Journal*, September 9, 2005.

Rugala, Eugene A., and James R Fitzgerald. "Workplace Violence: From Threat to Intervention," in *Clinics in Occupational and Environmental Medicine*. Philadelphia: W.B. Saunders, 2003.

Rutledge, Anne. "Protecting Global Trade Against Terrorism." Paper presented for The Japan Society, September 24, 2002.

Satter, Marlene Y. "Inside Job." *Investment Advisor*, August 2007.

Schweitzer, Glenn E., and Carole C Dorsch. *Super-Terrorism*. New York: Plenum Books, 1998.

"September 11 Aftermath: Ten Things Your Organization Can Do Now." *John Liner Review* 15, no. 4 (Winter 2002).

Service, Robert. *Lenin: A Biography*. Cambridge: Harvard University Press, 2000.

Shutske, John. "Protecting Our Food System from Intentional Attack." 2003 Annual Report to Biosystems and Agricultural Engineering Department, University of Minnesota.

Sikich, Geary. *Integrated Business Continuity: Maintaining Resilience in Uncertain Times*. Tulsa: Pennwell Corporation, 2003.

Skipp, Catherine, and Arian Campo-Flores. "A Bad Buzz at NASA." *Newsweek*, August 6, 2007.

Smith, Roger. *Catastrophes and Disasters*. Edinburgh: Chambers, 1992.

Sonnenfeld, Jeffrey. *Firing Back*. Cambridge: Harvard Business School Press, 2007.

Sonnenfeld, Jeffrey. "The Real Scandal at BP." *BusinessWeek*, May 14, 2007.

Sowers, Carol. "Scottsdale Schools Worker Accused of Embezzlement." *Arizona Republic*, June 1, 2007.

Spector, Ronald H. *Eagle Against The Sun*. New York: The Free Press, 1985.

"Spores Wars." *Forbes*, June 6, 2005.

Staff Report to The National Commission on Terrorist Attacks (Monograph on Terrorist Financing, undated).

Stancill, Jane. "Duke Post Seeks to Defuse '88' Ad." *The News and Observer*, January 17, 2007.

Stern, Gary M. "Brrr! How jetBlue Shook off PR Crisis." *Investors Business Daily*, July 2, 2007.

"System Failure." *Time*, September 19, 2005.

Taggart, Jacqueline, and Jamie Farrell. "Where Wellness Shows Up on the Bottom Line." *Canadian HR Reporter* 16, no. 18 (October 20, 2003).

"Ten Things Your Organization Can Do Now!" 9th Annual Conference Proceedings for The International Emergency Management Society, May 2002.

"Text Messaging Pushed for Use as Disaster Warning Systems." *New York Times*, December 31, 2004.

"A Therapy Revolution." *Forbes*, April 9, 2007.

Thomas, Evan, and Mark Hosenball. "Doctor of Death." *Newsweek*, July 16, 2007.

"A Threat Assessment Perspective," Critical Incident Response Group (CIRG), National Center for the Analysis of Violent Crime (NCAVC), and the FBI Academy at Quantico, Virginia.

"The Top 100 Brands." *BusinessWeek*, August 6, 2007.

Tumulty, Karen. "Four Places Where the System Broke Down." *Time*, September 19, 2005.

Tzu, Sun. *The Art of War*. El Paso, TX: El Paso Norte Press, 2005.

Vijayan, Jaikumar. "Fidelity National Data Theft Affects 8.5 Million Customers." *Computerworld*, July 27, 2007.

Wearne, Phillip. *Collapse: When Buildings Fall Down*. New York: TV Books, 2000.

Every effort has been made to list all works that meaningfully contributed to my analysis. Any omissions will be rectified in the next edition. If you have comments or suggestions, please feel free to write the author at larry@larrybarton.com.

RESOURCES

As you continue on your journey to a safer workplace, here are several resources that you may find helpful.

Over the years I have found that rothstein.com offers a robust library of tools and books that will help most professionals interested in risk and crisis management.

Another Web site, ready.gov, is managed by the U.S. Department of Homeland Security and provides a wide array of sample plans and documents to get you started.

When you hear that a crisis has occurred, you most likely will turn to television news channels for more information. But if you want to know what assignment editors and producers are thinking about that crisis, check out tvnewser.com. This is the definitive blog that will tell you what broadcast insiders think about you and your organization.

Several organizations can provide cost-effective and sound solutions. You may want to investigate the resources of the Risk and Insurance Management Society at rims.org and European-based resources at gla.ac.uk.

For issues related to forensic accounting and internal fraud, my highly reputable resource is Frederick H. Graessle, CPA; this former FBI agent can be reached at integrityassurancellc.com.

Charles Chamberlin impressed me as director of security for Motorola and he fundamentally changed how the company viewed threats in Asia when he was based in Hong Kong. His company is Management Consulting Services and is located in Elmhurst, Illinois.

My friend and colleague, Dr. Alan Friedman of Northwestern University Feinberg School of Medicine, is an expert in psychological assessments and has conducted definitive work on the Minnesota

Multiphasic Personality Inventory (MMPI-2) evaluative tool. He can be reached at draf48@aol.com.

Geary Sikich is well versed in military and community exercises that test preparedness. He can be reached at gsikich@aol.com.

Professor Stephen Sloan is arguably the world's most objective expert on terrorism and its impact at work; he lived 11 blocks from the Murrah Federal Building in Oklahoma City, Oklahoma, when it was the target of a domestic terrorist attack. Steve is a senior faculty member at the University of Central Florida in Orlando.

INDEX

ABOUT THE AUTHOR

Laurence Barton, Ph.D., is a leading consultant and speaker on crisis prevention and threat management who has led the response to over 1,400 serious incidents worldwide, including workplace violence and threats, product recalls, executive malfeasance, and industrial accidents.

Dr. Barton has designed vulnerability audits, crisis plans, simulations, and executive presentations for a client list that includes The Walt Disney Company, Nike, Emerson, The Gap, British Petroleum, American Family Insurance, Honda, Gaylord Entertainment, Exxon-Mobil, ESPN, and many of the world's leading casinos and resorts. He provides strategic counsel to companies worldwide during critical incidents.

A three-time college president, he has led DeVry University/Phoenix, Heald College, and The American College in Bryn Mawr, Pennsylvania, where he is serves as the O. Alfred Granum professor of management. He is a former faculty member at Harvard Business School; Penn State University Graduate Center; University of Nevada, Las Vegas; and Boston College. Dr. Barton served as vice president of crisis management at Motorola for five years, where he led crisis communications teams in Chicago, Hong Kong, Tokyo, and Geneva. As the first Fulbright Fellow in crisis management, he extensively analyzed crime and terror threats in Japan. Dr. Barton has served on the faculty of the University of Nevada at Reno Institute on gaming for more than 15 years.

His articles have appeared in more than 40 scholarly journals worldwide, and he is the author of three previous books on crisis strategies. Dr. Barton has been interviewed by major television and radio networks regarding trends in disaster preparedness. He wrote a definitive study on workplace violence for Columbia University that led to major changes in threat evaluation practices at the U.S. Postal Service, and he has taught at The FBI Academy, U.S. Army War College, and other government agencies on issues related to violence in the workplace.

A native of Arlington, Massachusetts, he received an A.B., magna cum laude, from Boston College, an M.A.L.D. from The Fletcher School of Law and Diplomacy at Tufts University, and a Ph.D. from Boston University. Dr. Barton is married to Eliza Alden, and they have two sons, Matthew and Mark. Dr. Barton may be contacted through his Web site, larrybarton.com.